"It is possible that you will be surprised and educated by what you find in this book. Determination, kinship, wisdom (and some heartbreak) walk hand in hand through its pages with a rousing breadth, unlikely to be available at a single institute. The writers of the letters have been generous with their experience. Agreements emerge: the profound value of personal analysis, free from artificial institutional requirements, and the necessity of steeping oneself in the literature. Another voice is also audible. Readers of Dante will hear: 'Retain all hope, ye who enter here'—much hardship awaits you, as do human splendors."

Charles Baekeland, I.P.S.O. President-elect

"As I have done, I strongly encourage you to immerse yourself in the pages of this book. The words—I mean the thoughts, the feelings, tales and experiences—here come as in a dream dreamt at night; once afar, now close. We want to hear what they want to say. More than that, deep inside some place of ours, we need to. Our psychoanalytic/symbolic fathers, mothers, those who walked the path a little ahead, before us, turn back and tell us a bit of what they saw. So here they come.

As the I.P.S.O. current editor, I could not have hoped for more, than to tell you now: let's go there together. I invite you, my colleague, to this chorus: Dear analyst, 'Talk to me like the rain, I will lie here and listen,' as the man in the play by Tennessee Williams would say."

Cláudia Antonelli, GEP Campinas, Brazil

"*Dear Candidate* is a truly moving book which brings to life the real and personal aspects of analytic training and life beyond training. Like a good analysis, the journey of reading through the letters stirs one up while at the same time provides encouragement and curiosity for the many conflicting emotions encountered during candidacy. Unlike any work thus far in analytic literature, this book is a guide on how to have compassion for one's internal and external world as a candidate and future analyst. A powerfully rich book that every candidate should read at the beginning and end of candidacy. *Dear Candidate* will surely prove to be a comforting companion to candidates around the globe during psychoanalytic training for years to come."

     Angela Vuotto, Secretary of the American Psychoanalytic Association
                                     Candidate Council

"I enthusiastically read this compendium of analyst letters to candidates, hailing from the three I.P.A. regions (Latin America, North America and Europe), assimilating the work not as institutional missives but rather as personal communiques with building thematic overlays. I was impressed by their overarching tone of compassion and generosity of spirit. The letters are instructive to the current generation of candidates, emphasizing the evolution of analytic teaching and thinking. Many letters highlight the vital need for candidates to gain analytic exposure and training outside their institutes or societies, as being foundational and invaluable to their growth as analysts, with some letters emphasizing the crucial role of active involvement with the I.P.A.'s candidate organization, I.P.S.O. (International Psychoanalytical Society Organization, www.ipso.world)."

                        Kathryn McCormick, I.P.S.O. President.

Dear Candidate: Analysts from around the World Offer Personal Reflections on Psychoanalytic Training, Education, and the Profession

In this first-of-kind book, senior psychoanalysts from around the world offer personal reflections on their own training, what it was like to become a psychoanalyst, and what they would like most to convey to the candidate of today.

With forty-two personal letters to candidates, this edited collection helps analysts in training and those recently entering the profession to reflect upon what it means to be a psychoanalytic candidate and enter the profession. Letters tackle the anxieties, ambiguities, complications, and pleasures faced in these tasks. From these reflections, the book serves as a guide through this highly personal, complex, and meaningful experience and helps readers consider the many different meanings of being a candidate in a psychoanalytic institute.

Perfect for candidates and psychoanalytic educators, this book inspires analysts at all levels to think, once again, about this impossible but fascinating profession and to consider their own psychoanalytic development.

Fred Busch, Ph.D., is a Training and Supervising Analyst at the Boston Psychoanalytic Institute, and on the Faculty of the Los Angeles Institute and Society for Psychoanalytic Studies. He has published over 70 articles in the psychoanalytic literature and has been invited to present his thinking about clinical technique throughout the world. He's published four books on the psychoanalytic method, the last two with Routledge, *Creating a Psychoanalytic Mind* (2013) and *The Analyst's Reveries: Explorations in Bion's Enigmatic Concept* (2019).

Dear Candidate: Analysts from around the World Offer Personal Reflections on Psychoanalytic Training, Education, and the Profession

Edited by Fred Busch

LONDON AND NEW YORK

First published 2021
by Routledge
2 Park Square, Milton Park, Abingdon, Oxon OX14 4RN

and by Routledge
52 Vanderbilt Avenue, New York, NY 10017

Routledge is an imprint of the Taylor & Francis Group, an informa business

© 2021 selection and editorial matter, Fred Busch; individual chapters, the contributors

The right of Fred Busch to be identified as the author of the editorial material, and of the authors for their individual chapters, has been asserted in accordance with sections 77 and 78 of the Copyright, Designs and Patents Act 1988.

All rights reserved. No part of this book may be reprinted or reproduced or utilised in any form or by any electronic, mechanical, or other means, now known or hereafter invented, including photocopying and recording, or in any information storage or retrieval system, without permission in writing from the publishers.

Trademark notice: Product or corporate names may be trademarks or registered trademarks, and are used only for identification and explanation without intent to infringe.

British Library Cataloguing-in-Publication Data
A catalogue record for this book is available from the British Library

Library of Congress Cataloging-in-Publication Data
Names: Busch, Fred, 1939- editor.
Title: Dear candidate : analysts from around the world offer personal reflections on psychoanalytic training, education, and the profession / edited by Fred Busch.
Description: 1 Edition. | New York : Routledge, 2020. | Includes bibliographical references and index. |
Identifiers: LCCN 2020025938 (print) | LCCN 2020025939 (ebook) | ISBN 9780367617639 (hardback) | ISBN 9780367617622 (paperback) | ISBN 9781003106487 (ebook)
Subjects: LCSH: Psychoanalysts--Psychology--Case studies.
Classification: LCC BF109.A1 D445 2020 (print) | LCC BF109.A1 (ebook) | DDC 150.19/5023--dc23
LC record available at https://lccn.loc.gov/2020025938
LC ebook record available at https://lccn.loc.gov/2020025939

ISBN: 978-0-367-61763-9 (hbk)
ISBN: 978-0-367-61762-2 (pbk)
ISBN: 978-1-003-10648-7 (ebk)

Typeset in Goudy
by MPS Limited, Dehradun

My thanks to the many candidates I've had discussion with who unintentionally planted the seed for this book. Also, my appreciation to Cordelia Schmidt-Hellerau who reacted with such immediate pleasure and enthusiasm when I first mused on the idea of this book. Finally, my gratitude to the contributors who responded so positively when I invited them to participate in this project.

When Anna Freud was asked by Heinz Kohut to say what she thought was essential to becoming a psychoanalyst, she responded that what she thought essential to becoming a psychoanalyst was to have a great appreciation for truth, i.e. personal truth and scientific truth. She felt the appreciation for truth must be held higher than any distress over learning disquieting facts about one's inner world, or the world outside oneself.[1]

Note
1 My thanks to Harriet Wolfe, who alerted me to this letter uncovered by Robert Galatzer-Levy.

Contents

Contributors		xii
Introduction by Fred Busch (U.S.A.)		xxii
1	Arthur Leonoff (Canada)	1
2	Michael Diamond (U.S.A.)	6
3	Roosevelt Cassorla (Brazil)	11
4	Eric Marcus (U.S.A.)	15
5	Cláudio Laks Eizirik (Brazil)	19
6	Theodore Jacobs (U.S.A.)	23
7	Paola Marion (Italy)	27
8	Otto F. Kernberg (U.S.A.)	32
9	Stefano Bolognini (Italy)	35
10	Cordelia Schmidt-Hellerau (U.S.A.)	38
11	Abel Mario Fainstein (Argentina)	43
12	Jay Greenberg (U.S.A.)	46
13	Heribert Blass, (Germany)	50

14	Elias and Elizabeth da Rocha Barros (Brazil)	54
15	Daniel Jacobs (U.S.A.)	58
16	Eike Hinze (Germany)	63
17	Alan Sugarman (U.S.A.)	66
18	Paola Golinelli (Italy)	70
19	Allannah Furlong (Canada)	73
20	Barbara Stimmel (U.S.A.)	76
21	Abbot Bronstein (U.S.A.)	80
22	Cecilio Paniagua (Spain)	84
23	Ellen Sparer (France)	88
24	Harriet Wolfe (U.S.A.)	91
25	Maj-Britt Winberg (Sweden)	95
26	Arlene Kramer Richardson (U.S.A.)	99
27	Gohar Homayounpour (Iran)	101
28	Ines Bayona (Colombia)	104
29	Donald Moss (U.S.A.)	108
30	Virginia Ungar (Argentina)	111
31	Arnold Richards (U.S.A.)	115
32	Ellen Pinsky (U.S.A.)	117
33	H. Shmuel Erlich (Israel)	121
34	Bent Rosenbaum (Denmark)	126

35	Fredric Perlman (U.S.A.)	130
36	Claudia Lucia Borensztejn (Argentina)	134
37	Jane Kite (U.S.A.)	138
38	Gabriela Goldstein (Argentina)	143
39	Eva Schmid-Gloor (Switzerland)	146
40	Adriana Prengler (U.S.A.)	150
41	Rachel Blass (Israel)	154
42	Donald Campbell (England)	158
43	P.S. (Fred Busch)	162
	References	163
	Index	165

Contributors

Ines Bayona – Psychoanalyst, Colombian Society of Psychoanalysis. Dedicated to her private practice and seminars for candidates at the Colombian Psychoanalytic Institute. Latin American Co-Chair for the I.P.A. Interregional Encyclopedia-Dictionary of Psychoanalysis. Latin American Co-Chair for the I.P.A. Working Parties Committee. Participation in many International Congresses. International and Local publications. Author of two books, *From Tradition to Creation: Conceptual Investigation in Psychoanalysis* (2012) and *Clinical Investigation* (2014). She was the winner of the F.E.P.A.L.-O.C.A.L. prize when she was a Candidate and authored "Influence of Freud´s Biography on my Psychoanalytical Training."

Heribert Blass, Dr. med. – Training and Supervising Analyst, also Child and Adolescent Analyst, Köln-Düsseldorf Psychoanalytic Institute of the German Psychoanalytic Association (D.P.V.), President of the European Psychoanalytic Federation (E.P.F.). Has published several articles on male identity and sexuality, the image of the father in human mental life and on supervision in psychoanalytic education. Latest publication: *Nimm dir das Leben und gib es nie/auch wieder her-das narzisstisch-depressive Dilemma und seine Bedeutung für die gegenwärtige und nächste Generation* (In press, 2020) (English translation: Take your life and never/also give it back: the narcissistic-depressive dilemma and its meaning for the present and next generation.)

Rachel Blass Ph.D. – Training and Supervising Analyst at the Israel Psychoanalytic Society, a member of the British Psychoanalytical Society, formerly a professor of psychoanalysis in leading universities both in the U.K. and in Israel. She is a representative on the Board of the International Psychoanalytic Association and is on the Board of the *International Journal of Psychoanalysis* where she is the editor of the Controversies section. She has published a book and over 80 articles that elucidate the foundations of analytic thinking and practice, with a special focus on Kleinian psychoanalysis and its Freudian roots. She lectures, teaches, supervises, and offers clinical seminars in many countries and her writings have been translated into 15 languages. She is in private practice in Jerusalem.

Stefano Bolognini – A Psychiatrist, Training and Supervising Psychoanalyst and former President of the Italian Psychoanalytic Society. He has been President of the International Psychoanalytical Association and is the founder and current Chair of the I.P.A. *Inter-Regional Encyclopedic Dictionary of Psychoanalysis*. He published 240 articles in psychoanalytic journals, and his books have been translated into several languages.

Claudia Lucia Borensztejn, M.D. – Psychoanalyst trained in Argentine Psychoanalytic Association (A.P.A.). Child and adolescent psychoanalyst. President of A.P.A. for period 2016–2020. Former director of Revista de Psicoanálisis de A.P.A. period 2008–2012. Editor of *Diccionario de Psicoanálisis Argentino*. Editor, *Argentine Psychoanalytic Association Revista*.

Abbot Bronstein – A Psychoanalyst in San Francisco, he attended The Johns Hopkins University, Hebrew University and Ferkauf Graduate School of Yeshiva University (Ph.D., Clinical Psychology). He was the Chief Psychologist at San Francisco Children's hospital. He graduated from the San Francisco Psychoanalytic Institute (S.F.C.P.) and continued two supervisions there and with Betty Joseph, Elizabeth Spillius, and others in the British Contemporary Klein group for 25 years. He is a Training and Supervising Analyst in the I.P.A. and San Francisco Center for Psychoanalysis. He is an associate editor of the *International Journal of Psychoanalysis* (IJP) and Editor of the Analyst at Work Section, North American Representative to the I.P.A., and Co-Chair of the Comparative Clinical Methods Working party group. He has written and published over 20 papers.

Fred Busch, Ph.D. – Training and Supervising Analyst, Boston Psychoanalytic Society and Institute. Dr. Busch has published over 70 articles in the psychoanalytic literature, numerous book chapters, and four books, primarily on the method and theory of treatment. His third book was *Creating a Psychoanalytic Mind: A Method and Theory of Psychoanalysis*. His last book was published in March 2019, *The Analyst's Reveries: Explorations in Bion's Enigmatic Concept*. He has been on several editorial boards, and served on numerous committees of the International Psychoanalytic Association and the American Psychoanalytic Association.

Donald Campbell, M.S.W. – Training Analyst, Distinguished Fellow, Past-President of the British Psychoanalytical Society, and former Secretary General of the International Psychoanalytic Association. He also served as Chair of the Portman Clinic in London, where he worked in outpatient psychoanalytic psychotherapy as a child, adolescent, and adult analyst for 30 years with violent and delinquent individuals and patients suffering from a perversion. He has published papers and chapters on such subjects as adolescence, doubt, shame, metaphor, violence, perversion, child sexual abuse, self-analysis, and horror film monsters. Most recently he co-authored a book with Rob Hale, *Working in the Dark: Understanding the pre-suicide state of mind*, which was published by Routledge.

Roosevelt Cassorla, M.D., Ph.D. – Training Analyst of the Brazilian Psychoanalytic Society of São Paulo and the Campinas Study Group. He is Full Professor of Psychological Medicine at the State University of Campinas, member of the editorial board of *The International Journal of Psychoanalysis*, and collaborator on the I.P.A. *Encyclopedia Dictionary*. He is author of a number of papers and book chapters on psychoanalysis and medical psychology. His last books are *Advances in Contemporary Psychoanalytic Field Theory* (co-editor, with Katz and Civitarese), London: Routledge, *The Psychoanalyst, The Theater of Dreams and the Clinic of Enactment*, London: Routledge, 2018, and *Suicide: Unconscious Factors and Sociocultural Aspects* (*Portuguese*), S. Paulo: Blucher, 2017. He received the Mary S. Sigourney Award for outstanding achievement in psychoanalysis.

Michael Diamond, Ph.D., F.I.P.A. – Training and Supervising Analyst, Los Angeles Institute and Society for Psychoanalytic Studies. His major publications are on psychoanalytic technique and the analytic mind, trauma and dissociation, masculinity and gender, as well as fathering and the paternal function. He has written and edited three books including *The Second Century of Psychoanalysis: Evolving Perspectives on Therapeutic Action* as well as *My Father Before Me: How Fathers and Sons Influence Each Other Throughout Their Lives*. His latest book is scheduled to appear in the next year and is entitled *Masculinity and Its Discontents: The Male Psyche and the Inherent Tensions of Maturing Manhood*. He has a private practice in Los Angeles, California.

Elias da Rocha Barros, M.D. – Supervisor and Training Analyst at the Brazilian Association of Psychoanalysis of São Paulo; Fellow of the British Psychoanalytical Society and Institute; Past Editor for Latin America of the *International Journal of Psychoanalysis*, Cochair for Latin America of the I.P.A. *Encyclopedic Dictionary of Psychoanalysis*. He has published widely in the psychoanalytic literature and received the Sigourney Award.

Elizabeth da Rocha Barros, M.D. – Supervisor and Training Analyst at the Brazilian Association of Psychoanalysis of São Paulo; Fellow of the British Psychoanalytical Society and Institute; D.E.A. in Psychopathology, Sorbonne University Paris, France; Child Analyst Tavistock Clinic; author of several papers on Symbolism and Representation.

Cláudio Laks Eizirik, M.D., Ph.D. – Training and Supervising Analyst, Porto Alegre Psychoanalytic Society. Professor Emeritus of Psychiatry, Federal University of Rio Grande do Sul. Former President of the I.P.A. Chair of the I.P.A. Committee on International New Groups. His last book, with Giovanni Foresti, *Psychoanalysis and Psychiatry: Partners and Competitors in the Mental Health Field*, was published in 2019. Published papers, chapters, and books on analytic training and practice, the human life cycle, mainly aging and the relation of psychoanalysis and culture. Received the Sigourney Award in 2011.

H. Shmuel Erlich, Ph.D. – Former President and Chair of the Training Committee of the Israel Psychoanalytic Society, and a Training and Supervising Analyst and Faculty of the Israel Psychoanalytic Institute. He was Sigmund Freud Professor of Psychoanalysis (Emeritus) and Director of the Sigmund Freud Center at The Hebrew University of Jerusalem. He chaired the I.P.A. Education Committee, served four terms as European Representative on the I.P.A. Board, is currently Chair of the I.P.A. Institutional Issues Committee, and has received the Sigourney Award. His publications span adolescent development and psychopathology, experiential dimensions of object relations, group and organizational processes, as well as two books: *The Couch in the Marketplace* and *Fed with Tears, Poisoned with Milk*. He is in private practice in Tel Aviv.

Abel Mario Fainstein, M.D. – Master in Psychoanalysis. Training Analyst and former President of the Argentine Psychoanalytical Association (A.P.A.). Former President of the Latin American Psychoanalytical Federation (E.P.A.L.). I.P.A. Board and Executive Committee Representative. Founder of Otra Mirada, A.P.A. cultural journal. Founder of the A.P.A. new editorial board. Professor at the Angel Garma Institute of the A.P.A. Organizer and member of the Board of the Master's and Ph.D. Programs in Psychoanalysis, Universidad del Salvador, and A.P.A. Chapters in different books and co-editor of *On Training Analysis*, A.P.A. Editorial Board. Clinical supervisor at different hospitals.

Allannah Furlong, Ph.D. – Psychologist, full time private practice, member of the Société psychanalytique de Montréal; former president of the Société psychanalytique de Montréal; and former member of the North American Editorial Board of the *International Journal of Psychoanalysis*. Has written about different aspects of the frame (missed sessions, symbolic payments in state covered health care, informed consent, confidentiality, the issue of patient consent for the use of clinical material in publications and clinical presentations). Co-editor in 2003 of two inter-disciplinary collections on confidentiality. North American member on the I.P.A. Confidentiality Committee. Most recent work on trauma and temporality in lovesickness, dehumanization as a shield against our helpless openness to the other, and informed consent in psychoanalysis.

Gabriela Goldstein, Ph.D. – Training, Supervising Analyst and professor of the Institute in Argentina Psychoanalytical Association A.P.A. Member of the I.P.A. Culture Committee since 2007. Member of the Community and Culture Committee F.E.P.A.L. in 2014. Board member of A.P.A. 2009–2013. She has won the Mom-Baranger prize in Psychoanalysis with *The Aesthetics of memory*, *Freud at the Acropolis* and the Storni prize for conceptual contributions in Psychoanalysis with *Transcience, or the time of beauty*. Published her book *The Aesthetic Experience: writings on Art and Psychoanalysis* in 2005, with Editorial Del Estante, in Buenos Aires. In 2013, she published and edited *Art in Psychoanalysis* by I.P.A.-Karnac. She is both an Architect and a painter.

Paola Golinelli – Training and Supervising Analyst of the Italian Psychoanalytic Society. Chair of the I.P.A. Liaison Committee of the Croatian Provisional Society till 2017. Consultant of the "European Film Festival of Psychoanalysis" (epff), from 2000 to 2014. She is Member of the I.P.A. "Psychoanalysis in Culture Committee." She has been Chair of the Annuals of the Annata Psicoanalitica Internazionale of the Int. J. of Psychoanal. Editor together with Andrea Sabbadini and Ilany Kogan of the book *Psychoanalytic Perspectives on Virtual Intimacy and Communication in Films* (Routledge, 2019). Author of the book *Psychoanalytic Reflections on Writing, Cinema and the Art: Facing Beauty and Loss*, which will be published in March 2020 by Routledge.

Jay Greenberg, Ph.D. – Training and Supervising Analyst, William Alanson White Institute; Editor, *The Psychoanalytic Quarterly*; former Editor for North America, *International Journal of Psychoanalysis*; former Editor, *Contemporary Psychoanalysis*; co-author, *Object Relations in Psychoanalytic Theory*; author *Oedipus and Beyond: A Clinical Theory*; Recipient, 2015 Mary S. Sigourney Award for Outstanding Achievement in Psychoanalysis.

Eike Hinze – Training and Supervising Analyst, Karl-Abraham-Institut Berlin, German Psychoanalytic Association (D.P.V.). Chair of the I.P.A. Task Force on Collegial Enhancement of Training (C.Q.E.T.), Member of the Comparative Clinical Methods (C.C.M.) Association. Has published many papers on Psychoanalytic Training, Psychoanalytic Practice and Psychoanalytic Therapy of Elderly Patients.

Gohar Homayounpour – Author and psychoanalyst and member of the International Psychoanalytic Association, American Psychoanalytic Association, the Italian Psychoanalytic Association, and the National Association for the Advancement of Psychoanalysis. She is the Training and Supervising psychoanalyst of the Freudian Group of Tehran, where she is also founder and former director. Dr. Homayounpour has published various psychoanalytic articles, including in the International and Canadian Journals of Psychoanalysis. Her book, *Doing Psychoanalysis in Tehran*, published by MIT Press in August 2012, won the Gradiva award and has been translated into many languages. Dr. Homayounpour is a member of the scientific board at the Freud Museum in Vienna and a board member of the IPA group *Geographies of Psychoanalysis*.

Daniel Jacobs, M.D. – Training and Supervising Analyst at the Boston Psychoanalytic Society and Institute and Director of the Hans Sachs Library there. He is also Director of the Center for Advanced Psychoanalytic Studies (C.A.P.S.) in Princeton and Aspen. Among his publications are *The Supervisory Encounter* (Yale University Press) and *Grete Bibring: A Culinary Biography* (Boston Psychoanalytic). He has also co-edited *Psychoanalysis and the Nuclear Threat* (Analytic Press) and *The Photographs of Edward Bibring* (Psychosocial Verlag). His novel *The Distance from Home* (IP Books) was published in 2018. He has over 35 publications to his name.

Theodore Jacobs, M.D. – Clinical Professor of Psychiatry (Emeritus), Albert Einstein College of Medicine. Training and Supervising Analyst, New York and P.A.N.Y. Psychoanalytic Institutes. He has published over 80 articles in the psychoanalytic literature, mostly on psychoanalytic technique, and the analyst's use of his countertransference thoughts and feelings. He has also published three books, *The Use of The Self: Countertransference and Communication in the Analytic Situation*, *The Possible Profession: The Analytic Process of Change*, and *On Beginning an Analysis* (co-edited with A. Rothstein). He has also published a novel, *The Year of Durocher*. He is a recent winner of the Sigourney Award.

Otto F. Kernberg, M.D., F.A.P.A. – Director of the Personality Disorders Institute at The New York Presbyterian Hospital, Westchester Division, and Professor of Psychiatry at the Weill Medical College of Cornell University. Dr. Kernberg is a Past-President of the International Psychoanalytic Association. He is also Training and Supervising Analyst of the Columbia University Center for Psychoanalytic Training and Research. He is the author of 13 books and co-author of 12 others, including: *Borderline Conditions and Pathological Narcissism*; *Severe Personality Disorders: Psychotherapeutic Strategies*; *Contemporary Controversies in Psychoanalytic Theory, Techniques and their Applications*; *The Inseparable Nature of Love and Aggression*; *Psychoanalytic Education at the Crossroads*; and, most recently, *Resolution of Aggression and Recovery of Eroticism*.

Jane Kite, Ph.D. – Training and Supervising Analyst at the Boston Society and Institute and a member of the San Francisco Center for Psychoanalysis, where she completed her psychoanalytic training in 1993. She is an active participant in the American Psychoanalytic Association (Program Committee) and the International Psychoanalytic Association (North American Co-Chair, 2019 meeting on Femininity), and an Associate Editor of *J.A.P.A.* She has an abiding interest in the concept of character in psychoanalysis, and more recently what we actually mean by "ethics" in psychoanalysis. In addition to several reviews and commentaries, her most recent article is "The Fundamental Ethical Ambiguity of the Analyst as Person" (J.A.P.A., 2016).

Arthur Leonoff, Ph.D., C. Psych. – Supervising and Training Analyst with the Canadian Psychoanalytic Society (C.P.S.). He is a Past-President of the C.P.S. as well as a former Board Representative of the International Psychoanalytic Association. He is an Honorary Member of the American Psychoanalytic Association and recipient of the C.P.S.'s Citation of Merit. Dr. Leonoff remains an active contributor to the I.P.A.'s institutional life. He has written and presented extensively in psychoanalysis as well as in its applications to family law.

Eric Marcus, M.D. – Professor of Clinical Psychiatry, Columbia University College of Physicians and Surgeons, Supervising and Training Analyst, Columbia University Center for Psychoanalytic Training and Research. His latest book is *Psychosis and Near Psychosis: Ego Function, Symbol Structure, Treatment*, revised third edition, 2017, Routledge. The first edition won The Hartmann Prize of The New York Psychoanalytic Institute.

Paola Marion, M.D. – Training and Supervising Analyst for the Italian Psychoanalytic Society and a Child and Adolescent Psychoanalyst. She is past Chair of the IPA Outreach Committee for Europe and presently Editor of the Rivista Italiana di Psicoanalisi. She has published papers in the I.J.P., other reviews and collections. Her most recent book, *Il disagio del desiderio. Sessualità e fecondazione al tempo delle biotecnologi* (*The discomfort of desire. Sexuality and procreation in the time of biotechnology*), was published in 2017.

Donald Moss – Founding member of Green Gang, a group of psychoanalysts and scientists working on the climate catastrophe. Author of 60 articles and four books, most recent: *At War with the Obvious* and *I and You*. Chair, Program Committee American Psychoanalytic Association, he was awarded the Elizabeth Young-Bruehl prize from International Psychoanalytic Association for anti-prejudice work. Private practice in New York, 40 years.

Cecilio Paniagua, M.D., Sc.D. – He resides in his native Madrid (Spain) where he obtained his medical and doctoral degrees. Trained in Psychiatry (T. Jefferson College of Philadelphia) with a Fulbright scholarship. American Board-Certified Psychiatrist. Psychoanalytic training at the Baltimore-Washington Institute. Fellow of the American College of Psychoanalysts. Member of the London Freudian Study Group. Honorary Professor of Universidad Autónoma (Madrid). He has published over one hundred articles in the national and international psychoanalytic literature. Translator of four psychoanalytic textbooks. Author of the books, *Técnica Psicoanalítica: Aportaciones de la Psicología del Yo* and *Visiones de España: Reflexiones de un Psicoanalista*.

Fredric Perlman, Ph.D., F.A.B.P. – Graduate of the Postgraduate Center for Mental Health and the Institute for Psychoanalytic Training and Research (I.P.T.A.R.). He is on the institute faculty of the Psychoanalytic Association of New York (affiliated with N.Y.U. Medical School), where he teaches foundation courses on the writings of Sigmund Freud. He previously taught psychoanalytic theory at the Postgraduate Center and at I.P.T.A.R., where he was a Training and Supervising Analyst. He is a Past President of I.P.T.A.R., served two terms as President of the Confederation of Psychoanalytic Societies (C.I.P.S.), and has served on the executive bodies of the I.P.A., A.Psa.A., and the North American Psychoanalytic Confederation (N.A.Psa.C.). He is the Series Editor for the C.I.P.S. Book Series on the *Boundaries of Psychoanalysis*.

Ellen Pinsky – Comes to psychoanalysis as a second profession following 25 years as a middle school English teacher. She says her experience in the classroom with 12- and 13-year-olds taught her most of what she needed to become a creditable clinician. About her book, *Death and Fallibility in the Psychoanalytic Encounter: Mortal Gifts* (Routledge, 2017), Thomas Ogden writes: "*Mortal Gifts* is a necessary book—necessary for analysts and necessary for the analyses they conduct. In it Ellen Pinsky addresses a long-neglected issue in the practice of psychoanalysis: the analyst's failure to include in the very fiber of the analysis the fact of his or her mortality." A 2006 graduate of B.P.S.I., she was awarded B.P.S.I.'s Deutsch Prize for her essay "The Olympian Delusion" (J.A.P.A., 2011).

Adriana Prengler, F.I.P.A. – Trained in clinical psychology and psychoanalysis in Caracas, Venezuela, before emigrating to the United States in 2010. She is a Training and Supervising Analyst at the Caracas Psychoanalytic Society and the Northwestern Psychoanalytic Society and Institute in Seattle, Washington. She teaches there and also in Wuhan, China. She has presented her work at national and international congresses and writes articles on clinical matters and applied psychoanalysis. She is the founding Chair of the I.P.A. Psychoanalysts' Emigration and Relocation Committee (P.E.R.C.) and the Candidates Loan Panel of the I.P.A. She has worked on a number of administrative committees over the years in both F.E.P.A.L. and the I.P.A. and is Vice President Elect of the International Psychoanalytical Association. She has a private practice in Sammamish, near Seattle, Washington.

Arnold Richards, M.D. – Training and Supervising Analyst and Faculty member at multiple psychoanalytic institutes. Editor of *The Journal of The American Psychoanalytic Association* (J.A.P.A., 1994–2003) and Editor of The American Psychoanalyst (T.A.P., newsletter of The American Psychoanalytic Association), for three years prior to that. He is the Editor of internationalpsychoanalysis.net and the Publisher of ipbooks.net. Dr. Richards was a winner of the Mary S. Sigourney Award (2000) and the Hans Loewald Awarde of the I.F.P.E. (2013). Recipient of the Distinguished Contributor Award, American Psychoanalytic Association. He is the author of *Controversial Conversations: Selected papers of Arnold Richards, Volume 1*, published by ipbooks, *Perspectives on Thought Collectives, Selected papers of Arnold Richards, Volume 2*, and a multitude of other books and papers.

Arlene Kramer Richardson – Mother of three middle aged children. Training and Supervising Analyst, Contemporary Freudian Society, American Institute of Psychoanalysis, Fellow Institute for Psychoanalytic Training and Research, Board Member American Psychoanalytic Association, former Board Member International Psychoanalytical Association, former North American Chair of Committee on Women in Psychoanalysis of I.P.A., present Member China Committee of I.P.A., author of *Listening to Understand*, translated into Chinese.

Bent Rosenbaum, MDSci – Specialist in Psychiatry Training and Supervising Analyst, and chair of the Scientific Committee, Danish Psychoanalytic Society (D.P.S.). President of the D.P.S. (2003–2011), European co-chair of I.P.A. Committee for New Groups (2009–2013), Member of I.P.A. Board (2013–2015). His main areas of publication have been psychoanalysis and psychoanalytic psychotherapy for people with psychosis, severe trauma, and suicide risk. He is adjunct professor at the University of Copenhagen, Department of Psychology, and senior researcher at the Clinic for Psychotherapy, Psychiatric Centre of Copenhagen.

Eva Schmid-Gloor – Psychoanalyst in private practice in Zürich (Switzerland). Member and Training Analyst of the Swiss Psychoanalytic Society. Held various positions in the Swiss Psychoanalytic Society (S.G.Psa.), the European Psychoanalytical Federation (E.P.F.) and in the International Psychoanalytic Association (I.P.A.). Former Co-President of the Freud Institute in Zürich, former Vice President of the Swiss Psychoanalytic Society, former Co-President of the Training Committee in the Swiss Psychoanalytic Society, 2012–2020. Vice President of the European Psychoanalytical Federation. Since 1996 teaches regularly at the Freud Institute in Zürich and offers clinical seminars in Germany: in Berlin, Hamburg, and Hannover.

Cordelia Schmidt-Hellerau, Ph.D. – Training and Supervising Analyst, Boston Psychoanalytic Institute and Society and Swiss Psychoanalytic Society. Chair, I.P.A. culture committee. Has published over forty articles in the psychoanalytic literature. Her latest book, *Driven to Survive*, published in 2018, is a finalist for the American Board and Academy of Psychoanalysis Book Prize. Her first literary book, the novel *Rousseaus Traum*, was published in German in 2019.

Ellen Sparer, Ph.D. – Supervising and Teaching Analyst, Paris Psychoanalytical Society. Director, Paris Psychoanalytical Institute.

Barbara Stimmel, Ph.D. – Faculty: Mt. Sinai School of Medicine (M.S.S.M.), Contemporary Freudian Society (C.F.S.); Training Analyst: International Psychoanalytic Association (I.P.A.), C.F.S.; Past-President: C.F.S.; Associate Secretary: I.P.A.; North American Chair, I.P.A. Berlin Congress Program Committee; Chair/member of various C.F.S./I.P.A./A.PSa.A./M.S.S.M.

committees; among the founders of N.A.P.S.A.C. (currently C.I.P.S.) as well as C.F.S. representative. Published, presented in major journals, symposia, national and international congresses; "From Nothing to Everything" (J.A.P.A., 1996) nominated for journal prize; Editor, *Consciousness Redux: Waking, Sleeping, Dreaming, and States In-Between*; *Collected Papers of Martin H. Stein*.

Alan Sugarman, Ph.D. – Training and Supervising Child, Adolescent, and Adult Psychoanalyst at the San Diego Psychoanalytic Center and a Clinical Professor of Psychiatry, University of California, San Diego. He is the Head of the American Psychoanalytic Association Department of Psychoanalytic Education and on the editorial boards of the *Journal of the American Psychoanalytic Association*, *Psychoanalytic Quarterly*, and *Psychoanalytic Psychology*. He has published over forty articles in the psychoanalytic literature.

Virginia Ungar M.D. – Training Analyst at the Buenos Aires Psychoanalytic Association (A.Pde.B.A.). She lives and practices in Buenos Aires, Argentina. She specializes in child and adolescent analysis, was the former Chair of the I.P.A.'s Child and Adolescent Psychoanalysis Committee (C.O.C.A.P.) and of the I.P.A. Integrated Training Committee. She was given the Platinum Konex Award for Psychoanalysis in 2016. She is currently the President of the International Psychoanalytic Association.

Maj-Britt Winberg – Training and Supervising Analyst in the Danish Psychoanalytic Society. Belongs to the Expert Council of the Wennborg Foundation, which supports psychoanalytic research and publishing for dissemination of knowledge. Editor-in-Chief of *Scandinavian Psychoanalytic Review*.

Harriet Wolfe, M.D. – President-elect of the I.P.A., Clinical Professor of Psychiatry at the University of California San Francisco School of Medicine, and Training and Supervising Analyst at the San Francisco Center for Psychoanalysis. Her scholarly interests include organizational processes, clinical application of neuroscientific research, female development, and therapeutic action. She teaches analysts-in-training, psychiatric residents, and junior faculty psychodynamic understandings of severely ill patients and the value of listening in the clinical setting. She has a private practice of psychoanalysis, psychoanalytic psychotherapy, and couples and family therapy in San Francisco.

Introduction

Dear Candidate,

As a first-year candidate, I remember attending the initial meeting of what was to become our local candidate organization. We met at another candidate's home, and I wondered why we were getting together there and not at the Institute where all other meetings were held. As we began, I sensed, though it was not said directly, that this gathering was not one that some senior members of the Institute would approve of. Nobody was hiding the fact that it was taking place, but no one was suggesting we shout out that it occurred either. Thankfully, things have changed a lot since then.

It was at this first meeting I realized the importance of candidates getting together to talk about their training. My belief was further strengthened by attending my first meeting of our nascent national candidates' group, where it was eye opening to hear about variations in training and the candidates experience of their institutes. *A theme you will read in many of the letters is that without the opportunity to hear about different models of training, along with how to think about one's path to becoming a psychoanalyst, one's view can become parochial, thus limiting the capacity to reflect on these important issues.* In this context it gives me great pleasure to bring these letters from a distinguished group of senior analysts who will share with you their personal experiences. Hopefully, it will contribute to the way you think of your own education and maybe broaden the conversation among your fellow analysts in training. The capacity to *reflect* upon one's training from a wide-ranging perspective will be crucial when thinking about how to refine the training of future candidates, which ultimately many of you will be responsible for. Thus, I was motivated to bring you these letters, which I hope you find inspiring and thought provoking and help you think about your own training and entrance into this intriguing profession.

Writers of these letters are from the three regions of the International Psychoanalytic Association: Latin America, Europe, and North America. They greeted my invitation to participate in this project with great enthusiasm. It seemed I had touched on an important issue, and people felt strongly they wanted to share their experiences, memories, and reflections with you. Many contributors told me how much they enjoyed writing these letters. I think it was a chance for them to reflect on issues that weren't in the forefront of their thinking, but once activated, there came a trove of rich ideas that may have even surprised them. You will see in these letters the enthusiasm these analysts have for their work, their commitment to the profession, while not shying away from the complications of becoming a psychoanalyst. I'm sure I could have doubled or tripled the number of analysts willing to write letters, and it was only the limitations of space that prevented me from doing so.

In reading these letters you will find much wisdom about psychoanalytic training and the psychoanalytic profession. They helped me reflect, once again, on my own experience of training. I realized some time ago that, as a candidate, I felt seminars were often taught indifferently. In retrospect it seemed the theoretical seminars didn't fully mine the depth of meaning of what we read. Also, clinical thinking was not integrated with clinical theory so that we ended up with a lot of clinical folklore taught as clinical fact. I always knew these experiences played a significant role in what kind of teacher and supervisor I became, emphasizing what I felt was missing in my own training. As such, *it is an example of what is experienced as a deficit in training can spur one to think through what was missing and try to influence how training can be better*. Conversely, I've seen candidates unconsciously identifying with looseness in thinking, and not developing further, which is a loss for them and the Institute.

For my part, I believe when I entered analytic training, I over-valued my experience as a psychotherapist, and it wasn't so easy for me to distinguish between doing psychotherapy and psychoanalysis. I later wrote about this (Busch, 2010). When I started psychoanalytic training, I was a University Professor who taught psychoanalytic thinking to residents in psychiatry and graduate students in psychology, and thought I knew more about psychoanalysis than, in retrospect, I did. Looking back, I believe it was only many years after graduating that I had an inkling of what it meant to be a Psychoanalyst. It was still some years later before I *became* a Psychoanalyst, and the journey continues. For some this statement will be freeing; for others it could be discouraging. I found it exhilarating to realize that one is always in the process of *becoming* a psychoanalyst. To do so means to be open to a life-long process of learning and to testing one's ideas in discussions with colleagues, publishing, and attending national and international meetings. Many colleagues in this volume reiterate this idea.

As Editor of this book, I felt it wise to not put the letters in any categories or order, and therefore the letters are presented pretty much as I received them. I can assure you there is wisdom throughout all these "letters." I think various letters will appeal differently to each of you, as they did to me. I did, however, believe it was important to intermingle letters from different geographical regions, to see if differences in psychoanalytic cultures could be observed.

Finally, let me warmly welcome you to this incredibly interesting, but complicated profession. At times it will amaze you, and other times it will befuddle you. If you can keep yourself open to the wide range of experiences you'll have, our profession will reward you.

Let me end with the best advice I can give you during your training and life as a psychoanalyst, which comes as a quote attributed to Isaac Babel, "He who thirsts for knowledge must stock up with patience."

Fred Busch (Chestnut Hill, Massachusetts, USA)

P.S. Any profits made from this book will be used to help candidates in their training.

1 Arthur Leonoff
Ottawa, Canada

Dear Candidate,

It is an honor to share this moment of retrospection on my psychoanalytic training. This task provides a valuable nudge in the direction of après coup, re-imagining the past or at least how I might experience this past, in expectation of what comes next. Indeed, there is always a "next." I use the word "imagining," to highlight the *creative and dynamic aspect of remembering*. What I remember seems alive with the present. Much as metaphor captures the known to anticipate the unknown, the past opens doors to what is the current challenge.

In any case, my recall is a distillate of what I experienced during my Institute years, as compared to anything empirical or encyclopedic. As I share this with you, it will do "double duty," communicating something of what constituted psychoanalytic formation in my case and, secondly, what this means to me now in terms of identity and even ambition. Perhaps this might help you imagine your own unfolding career.

As much as I have felt the need at various points to reflect on my analytic training, to revisit its valuable teachings, I have also had to work through experiences of disillusionment. There is always something to mourn, a loss of innocence, a family dysfunction that threatens to undermine what is most precious. This could describe psychoanalytic training, but it also depicts life as it is lived – the precious and profane less in combative tension than having to work out an inevitable compromise.

I entered psychoanalytic training as a 38-year-old psychologist who had begun reading Freud in my undergraduate years but found real, exciting application in the analytically inspired works of David Rappaport and Roy Shafer on metapsychology and projective testing. When I trained as a psychologist at a psychiatric hospital, I was amazed that clinical case conferences would be postponed if I had not yet completed the dynamic formulation the clinical team was eager to hear and on which they depended. Understanding the patient as a person was never something to be taken for granted, I learned. It whetted my appetite.

It would never have been enough for me simply to enjoy the intellectual pursuit of psychoanalysis. It had to make me a better clinician with wider scope and expertise. This is why I applied to become a psychoanalyst.

It was unclear to me then, and likely even now, what would be the fate of my identity as a psychologist, even if professional psychology was the gateway and legal structure in which I could practice and earn a living. In the end, it has been an ambivalent relation, more necessity than choice. I would have given it up entirely if I could. Psychoanalysis has been my métier, perspective, and working identity. My colleagues and friends include the psychoanalysts that I have met worldwide. What were breaches to this foundation, the disappointments encountered along the way, were assuaged by the caring, thoughtful colleagues that populate our profession wherever in the world they practice. These can be your mainstay when the winds of disillusionment blow, as they inevitably will. *Look beyond your own locale.*

Thus, psychoanalysis was less the identity that formed in my case than a re-finding of something that already inherently defined me. The training was presented by the Institute at the very moment that I imagined it through my own aspirations and self-expression. In this regard, psychoanalysis has always served as a subjective object that is both me and not-me. It is very personal, which makes it special.

If becoming an analyst is a transformative process, as it would seem to be, then the Institute as well as the candidate must play its part. This has to do with the centripetal action of analytic training that creates the ferment from which psychoanalytic identity can evolve. Although rarely discussed, the makeup of the class is important. I joined a class of ten. My fellow candidates were bright, creative, and accomplished in their own right. It was exciting and dynamic and, for me personally, a relief. The Institute proved to be precisely the fertile ground that I was seeking.

In reminiscence, when I revisit the curriculum and those analysts who taught us, it reinforces how much their devotion to psychoanalytic teaching amplified their very real contributions. Teachers travelled from near and far to supplement the heavy load born by local faculty at my small Institute. Robert Langs and the controversial Freud scholar, Peter Swales, came from New York. We had students of Kohut to teach us Self-Psychology, a British trained child analyst for a year-long exposure to infant observation, and a historian of medicine to introduce us to the Viennese and French origins that gave rise to psychoanalysis itself. In retrospect, all of this mattered. It was the education that I had always wanted, and I treasured it then as now. It was both foundational and aspirational, which covers a lot of ground.

Psychoanalysis enters through the intellectual and emotional pores where it mixes with other influences to create a unique amalgam. I had begun a personal analysis four years before entering the Institute and continued during the next four years of training. What remained unsolved from the first analysis was remedied in a second treatment of three years. If I had not done the second treatment, I might have had difficulty believing in analysis. I needed it to work for me where it most counted. My impression is that analytic careers must be built on a foundation of a solid personal analysis. As such, it should be good and not simply good enough. There is simply too much riding on it.

Disillusionments have been harder to work through, but there is important benefit to this work. It is part of wisdom. The inspiration behind the Institute was a disruptive chairman of the university's psychiatry department, who, in his munificence, imported talent from all over the analytic world, only to alienate many in hostile disputes fairly quickly. The fact that this analyst was the "father" of the Institute was troublesome at best. He had almost nothing to do with my training directly, but his presence was disconcerting, a source of splitting and rancor that roiled under the surface for years and impacted on the Institute. The Training Analysts who were instrumental in implementing the training had to make some sort of peace with him, which placed them inevitably on his side in the fragmenting conflicts that undermined the cohesion of the small analytic community.

Notwithstanding the turbulence that swirled around our training, there was a protective bubble that allowed the class to learn together relatively unimpeded. There was even a formal complaint to the International Psychoanalytic Association (I.P.A.) that was investigated and found to be without merit. The truth was that we were receiving an excellent psychoanalytic education no matter how faulty the container was. This was due to the high quality of the teaching, careful management by the Training Committee, and the quality of the candidates.

The second source of disillusionment, and one that will now somewhat contradict what I said above, was the revelation that none other than the Director of the Institute had been having sex with a disadvantaged young woman he saw as a patient. For the candidates for whom he was their personal analyst, not me, this must have been a disaster. He supervised my first case, however, and, I must admit, I learned a great deal from him. He also personally attended every seminar over the four years, a practice that I have never seen duplicated. My recollection is that this sullying disaster came to the surface after the seminars were completed. I felt terrible for the patient and the confusion and pain she must have experienced.

It would be ameliorative if I could say that the entire local analytic community and what remained of the Training Committee rallied around the besieged candidates. Sadly, this did not occur. There was only a deafening silence and a sealing over that occurred almost immediately. This included a foreclosure on his name and, to some extent, his existence. As I reflect on this handling of the situation, I realize that this had much to do with helplessness and shutting off of the destructiveness that was unleashed. It amounted to a profound attack on his profession; his wish to smash it to pieces and escape whatever prison in which he perceived himself living. It was less a lesson in the potential destructiveness of sexuality than in how destructiveness can use sexuality to vent its nihilistic fury.

These assaults on patients, colleagues, the Society and Institute, and ultimately, psychoanalysis itself, are particularly hard on candidates. The destructivity ricochets through the ranks and threatens to poison the well from which candidates are eagerly drinking. Yet, and this might surprise, what affected me most was the passivity of my own Institute. The unmistakable message was that personal analysis is the all-purpose tool for dealing with any adversity. In other words, talk about it with your analyst. This missed the point entirely. It was a self-protective and defensive response that was inadequate. If anything, however, it propelled me to be more activist in my life and career. Although psychoanalysts are not a school of fish swimming in collective rhythm, our ethics of responsibility have to go beyond the consulting room. I think that this has spurred my extensive and meaningful involvement in the IPA, to which I am hugely grateful.

Thus, this adverse event did not destroy the "good" or deprive me of the opportunity to be an analyst. There is something about the *élan vital* of psychoanalysis, the intellectual fervor and clinical aspiration to help people, that it creates its own exciting and forward-facing momentum. It was not the case of time healing as much as investing in a psychoanalytic way of working and thinking that was preservative and fostering even in the midst of disillusionment. This has only deepened and widened with experience, teaching, and study.

Psychoanalysis can certainly be nostalgic, but if it delves into the past, it does so with a temporality that bridges past, present, and future. I cannot say that what this errant mentor did was unthinkable. In fact, it was the opposite—too thinkable, which is what made it particularly scary. It was a story that has dogged psychoanalysis from its outset, although often disavowed as the perverse idiosyncrasy of a few. If this incident was a further expression of a collective trauma, the thinkable sliding too easily into the doable, then the risk to identity is a type of defensive nostalgia, idealizing and laundering a past that perhaps never was. Psychoanalysis has its external detractors for sure, but its real enemies have been from within its own membership. This was not something I was prepared to know at the time but could be summarized as: "psychoanalysis can never escape the human condition of which it can only be a reflection."

I am thankful that I had a very good father in my life. We were close friends until his death when I was 60 and he was 92 years of age. If I am nostalgic, it is for this man and this lived childhood experience. It would never be Freud or his namesake, the deviant Director of Training. Moreover, the "good" was firmly represented in my working and learning ego, and even this toppling disillusionment did not destroy a foundation that had begun forming even before I entered the Institute.

Further. I will never have the space in my life or time to address or mourn all the disillusionments accumulated along the way, including the times I have failed to live up to my own standards and expectations. In the end, I chose to embrace psychoanalysis with all its frailties as a very human enterprise that does far more good in the world than bad. One can certainly go down the rabbit hole of collective trauma, which is deep and cross-generational, but there is also a collective dream, and this is extremely vibrant and resilient. There is a vein of destructiveness in every aspect of human life. Psychoanalysis does not get a pass.

I understand better now why analysts work well into their old age and sometimes through it. There is certainly often a monetary issue, we are "piece workers" limited by hours in the day and energy, but this is not the main reason. There is the excitement in being an analyst—the capacity to help people deeply, to inch them towards deeper change, to learn what has been previously unknowable, all the while further refining one's analytic capacity that continues to grow. It is hard for me to imagine giving this up as long as there are patients willing and eager to work with me and profit from what we as a group of committed clinicians have to offer.

I remember as a young analyst being at a conference, the annual meeting of the Canadian Psychoanalytic Society. The late Dr. Henry Kravitz, a senior Montreal Training Analyst and one of my supervisors, was discussing a case. He had asked the presenter to pause after hearing the beginning of the presentation, which he was hearing for the first time. What followed was an amazing unpackaging of the dynamics, an eloquent clinical portrayal offered as a series of hypotheses. When the presenter continued, it was clearly evident to the audience that what Dr. Kravitz predicted was totally confirmed by the clinical material that followed. I thought at the time—"I want to be able to do that one day."

2   Michael Diamond
Los Angeles, U.S.A.

Dear Candidate,

I wish to share some musings that might help you get the most out of your psychoanalytic training. Memories from my own candidacy in progressing from being a psychotherapist to becoming a psychoanalyst, as well as continuing experiences as an analyst, teacher, supervisor, writer, and active member of a vibrant analytic community play a major role in shaping my contribution to this unique and broadly needed book.

Now that you've opened yourself to a completely unique way of life as a psychoanalyst, it helps to remember that being an analyst not only commands hard work and considerable responsibility, it also embodies perhaps the most *personal* of careers—namely, a livelihood that Freud regarded as an "impossible" profession that seemed to be marked by "unsatisfying results" (given its unrealizable ideals). Moreover, as a candidate, the temporal, financial, and personal/familial demands are extensive, and subsequently, *patience*—with oneself, one's patients, and the analytic learning process—is everything! I hope to clarify how the challenges of candidacy will set the course for a uniquely rich and lifelong, albeit often tension-filled journey that will change your life's direction while providing enormous opportunities for steady learning and personal growth. You may be surprised to discover when traveling in the domain of the psyche that there might be major changes to the kinds of relationships you have and perhaps the kinds of people you choose to spend time with. For many reasons, then, the role of your personal psychoanalysis—in addition to your readings, course work, and supervised clinical experience—becomes pivotal in navigating the pathways ahead.

Because candidacy itself accesses conflicts and unexpected regressions, the choice of a personal psychoanalyst becomes vital. So, it is wise to interview several potential analysts before choosing one you can trust with your most primitive parts—one who, as one candidate noted, "can hold your *crazy*." Still, given the inherent limitations of training analyses, you may even wish to undertake a second, post-training analysis (often with an analyst not connected to your training institute).

What begins in candidacy will hopefully grow into a career-long project to develop your capacity to work with unconscious material and appreciate the life of the psyche. Yet, this will invariably test your ability to tolerate uncertainty, confusion, insecurity, and intense feelings, often in ways that entail considerable *vulnerability*. Additionally, particularly through helpful supervisory experiences and your personal analysis, you must reckon with your ability to tolerate disappointment, responsibility, and manage narcissistic investment in your work, often in great inner *solitude*. Despite the intimacy within analytic space, we are unutterably alone in the deepest and most important aspects of our work. Your solitude as an analyst must become an anchor where you can eventually find your way, often amid turbulent and unfamiliar conditions that candidacy can help you learn to accept and even bear with curiosity.

Freud made it very clear (in his *An Outline of Psychoanalysis*, published posthumously in 1940) that his life's work in addressing the "psyche" had been devoted to understanding as fully as possible the world of man's *soul*. He was convinced that, despite the language of metapsychology, the soul must be thought of (and I would add, *related to*) in order to comprehend his system. Because you might often feel besieged with complex psychoanalytic terms and concepts as well as experiential overload, it helps to consider that clinical work fundamentally involves the *soul*, which in line with Freud's thinking (emerging from John Stuart Mill's perspective) entails "that which *feels*."

From this nexus of soulful, experientially alive analytic work, psychoanalysis requires attempting to make contact with what might be occurring in the patient's largely unconscious inner world to provide what has been referred to as "*the experience of being understood*." This stands in contrast to *getting understanding* through the analyst's theoretically based, clever, yet inert interpretive activity removed from meaningful emotional engagement. It demands far more than simply attempting to make patients feel better or rid them of unwanted feelings, symptoms, or parts of the self. In short, there's no escaping the *personal nature* of successful psychoanalytic work that brings about psychological development through direct emotional contact by creating a *new way of relating* both to one's own and our patient's mind.

As a more seasoned and hardier guide and explorer of psychic life, the analyst's humanity, integrity, compassion, and courageous commitment to understanding unconscious mental functioning brings psychoanalysis to life. As you find your way as a candidate, the focus must be on becoming immersed in *listening to* the patient rather than *listening for* confirmation of theoretical ideas or appeasing one's supervisor or teacher. This is easier said than done and is particularly challenging given the evaluative aspects of candidacy. Persistence and faith in one's development is necessary despite experiencing frequent moments of "not knowing," of endless repetition, repeated disappointments, perturbing limitations, and intense countertransference experiences. *Shame*—both among candidates and even among the most experienced of analysts—often occurs when exposing our work and limitations to colleagues and supervisors. Nonetheless, know that a certain level of courage, stamina, discipline, and persistent determination, as well as an eventual, well-earned faith in psychoanalysis, will help you to maintain an open, reflective space with most every patient (and yourself).

So, I return to the fundamental idea of developing *patience*, which when young to the craft, is vitally important. Though as analysts we trade in words and language, many events that occur in the complex, structured intimacy of the psychoanalytic space are initially inexpressible, taking place in a realm in which no word has ever entered. As an interpreter of another's unconscious, you must learn to allow your own interpretive opinions (that is, hypotheses) to ripen and develop, which, as I have learned, *cannot* be pressured or hurried. There is a kind of motherhood or fatherly procreating that is much like giving birth; hence, the *art* of the day-to-day work of analyzing that goes well beyond technique is akin to *gestation* that allows for the ripening and bringing forth of deep understanding.

As a beginning psychoanalyst, it is incumbent to create the requisite *inner reflective space* that makes use of what has been stimulated inside you in order to understand your patients. This requires cultivating an openness to surprise as well as receptivity to *not* comprehending. Hopefully, you will be supported throughout much of your training to develop and maintain your *curiosity*, *ability to observe* (without necessarily understanding), and *acceptance* of human experience. As you learn to believe more skeptically and doubt empathically, your success as an analytic candidate and future analyst will rest partly on your sense of restraint, narcissistic balance, and integrity.

One challenge is that you will be conducting control analysis while still undergoing your own personal psychoanalysis. Being part of an institute "family" with highly charged personal and group dynamics releases negative transferences and powerful regressions that require considerable time for working over. You may experience periods of extensive doubt as to the value of psychoanalysis (or one's personal analyst), just as your control case patients question your work, often well before you've acquired a hard-won trust in the analytic process itself. Believing in psychoanalysis amidst societal and personal resistances may require a "blind faith" while you endure considerable tension in solitude. Though you may even feel "different" from some of your enthusiastic cohort, it is helpful to know that most experienced analysts have weathered bearing similar tensions during their formative analytic years.

A particular issue when beginning analytic work pertains to the role played by the inevitable *idealizations* and *identifications*. It is necessary to internalize analytic ideals and aspirations to support clinical work and reinforce analytic functions during the learning process, which itself involves identifying with admired teachers and analysts. Training involves exposure to brilliant intellectual thinking and concepts as well as a tendency to idealize ideas and charismatic purveyors of psychoanalytic thinking. In fact, before achieving our own unique view of analytic work through experience, we need to rely on authority figures while identifying with the analytic ideals of theories we are exposed to and value. In this context, intellectual ambitions and clinical aspirations often produce feelings of inadequacy as well as competitive and envious feelings, particularly among one's cohort and toward teachers, supervisors, and training analysts.

Given the proliferation of theoretical systems, and the development of psychoanalytic ideas across different cultural communities, candidates are continually challenged to interrogate new ways of thinking that compete to shape theory and practice. While some candidates are more theoretically inclined, others may not be and yet are equally or more clinically skillful (perhaps working more intuitively). If at all possible, try not to be hard on yourself when confused by the multiplicity (of names) and complexity (of cases and concepts) as you learn to respect your own, analytic mindedness and ways of being analytic. I believe it is useful to realize that concepts and theories learned throughout the course of training (and post-training life), which when subsequently integrated into your analytic technique, need only to be *held lightly* (rather than rigidly) in the clinical context where the soul-to-soul connection is paramount. Achieving your unique view of analytic work requires considerable time and experience in order to differentiate sufficiently from authority figures and assuage the hold of internalized ideals that in the beginning were necessary to cling to for support.

I find it beneficial to remain aware of the inherent *tension* in being a psychoanalyst that must be borne and managed. Arguably, a persistent strain is created, particularly for beginning analysts about whether or not their work is genuinely "psychoanalytic." In fact, an ongoing debate has been present since its inception about what psychoanalysis is. It is necessary to learn to accept experiencing the tension required to tolerate paradox and living in a transitional zone between historical reality and psychic truth. It takes substantial time that will test your ability to tolerate uncertainty, ambiguity, and insecurity in order to learn to sustain and utilize this tension *creatively* (and with sufficient humility and psychic freedom).

Therefore, I hope that you can be gentle with yourself in order to nurture a steady patience, resilience, and persistent fortitude when facing the limits of your understanding and skills—perhaps, what Samuel Beckett described as the ability to *fail better*. Ideally, both your didactic training and personal psychoanalysis will further your *capacity to recognize and relate to your own narcissism* without too easily resorting to grandiosity, retaliation, overzealous and premature action, and/or defensively withdrawn inactivity. Achieving a healthier relationship to your narcissism will remain crucial both to your analyzing ability and capability of living satisfactorily within wider psychoanalytic communities.

Indeed, your classmates, colleagues, and larger psychoanalytic community are usually quite vital to success as an analyst. Developing mastery typically requires a team of colleagues—a band of analytic brothers and sisters—to contain, support, and challenge us throughout the work's inescapable pressures and profound, yet often mysterious, benefits. Most successful analysts need to work with committed colleagues with their unique perspectives and psychodynamics. Still, as Freud and Bion remind us, the analytic collective, particularly within institute life with its regressive systems, is comprised of complicated group processes and dynamics that typically remain quite unconscious; thus, the support of trusted colleagues and mentors can be decisive.

Finally, it is *not* uncommon during candidacy to experience painful, narcissistic wounding's and unsettling disappointments—often through interactions with teachers, supervisors, peers, and occasionally even one's own analyst. Trusted colleagues and experienced mentors as well as friends and partners become all the more important when navigating the complex dynamics of the analytic pathway. Remaining inquisitive and resonant with the world around, while opening yourself to an ever-deepening interior life, occasions the consummate opportunity and privilege to become more receptive to human suffering, yet more alive to tenderness, both in our work and in the ineffable preciousness of life itself.

In closing, I fervently wish you a robust as well as sufficiently benign and long enduring voyage!

3 Roosevelt Cassorla
Sao Paulo, Brazil

Dear Candidate,

The other day, you told me euphorically that one of the assessors of your clinical report said: "Your text is perfect. I have no questions to ask and nothing to add." You were proud, and I know that you wanted to share your happiness with me. You found it strange that I didn't seem pleased, and because we have a close relationship you asked me what was the matter. I am initiating this dialogue in writing, but I am sure that we will address this in greater depth when we meet.

Your perception was correct. I felt affected and ill at ease and was unable, at that point in time, to put my thoughts into words. I shall explain: a "perfect" work of psychoanalysis, one which doesn't raise any questions or problems, cannot be good work. Flawless analytical sessions and texts do not exist. I have encountered situations before when I have thought that the presenter has glossed over his or her own interventions. This gloss conceals, yet it also reveals. The psychoanalytically trained listener doubts the truthfulness of the account.

From what I know of you, I am sure that you presented yourself in a genuine manner. We have no way of knowing the motives that led to your assessor's inability to "dream" your material and broaden its meanings. It is interesting to note that you omitted the name of your admirer. You must have had reasons for this.

I remember a situation during my own training when a fellow trainee's piece of work was failed. The assessor in charge claimed he was unable to read the work all the way to the end because it was sending him to sleep. He added that the correlation with the theory was poor and that the work would have to be redone. I don't want to bore you with the details, but the institution acknowledged that it was unfair that the work had been failed and that this reflected personal and political disputes. The candidates banded together, and we contributed towards changing the regulation at the Institute in such a way as to prevent similarly negative situations. This episode, in addition to various others, gradually led to the democratization of the institution. We candidates felt proud to have contributed towards this transition.

I imagine you are curious to know how we managed to do this. I do not know exactly, but we were fortunate enough to have formed a united group, and we knew how to present our arguments in a powerful way, controlling the aggressive outbursts of youth. As you know, in any human group it is the younger generation that identifies and reveals collusions that are repeated in a rigid form, without the older generation realizing what is happening.

It is not easy to evaluate what is going on around us, especially when we are part of what we are experiencing. The psychoanalyst is both observer and participant in the analytic field. He tries to objectivize his subjectivity. In the clinic as much as in institutional groups, the candidate participates in a tangle of crossed projective identifications that influence the perception of events. This is why it is important for groups to think through what is happening.

I notice that in the previous paragraphs I have been trying to encourage your involvement with the psychoanalytic Institution. There is ample space for this, and if this did not exist, then it should be fought for. I believe that the candidate can and should be political, in the sense of acting on behalf of the well-being of the group. Experiencing these things while you are in personal analysis can help with personal development, both for the institutions and for psychoanalysis itself. Furthermore, I propose that you go beyond the institution and get involved in society to seek ways to make psychoanalysis useful for greater numbers of people.

You may disagree. You may tell me that real psychoanalysis can only take place in consulting rooms, with high-frequency analysis involving the attendance of financially privileged people, at least in our milieu. I am certain that psychoanalytic knowledge is useful when it comes to working with the community, in healthcare and educational institutions, and with vulnerable and violated people, etc. Our challenge is to broaden the use of psychoanalysis. I am not concerned with what is "true" or "false" when this dichotomy approaches fanatical thinking.

I don't know whether what you're reading now is of any interest. This is one of the problems with one-way communication, and with psychoanalytic writing in general. I have noted the difficulty some candidates have with writing their reports and their first scientific texts. One obvious factor is the action of a strict superego that prevents them from writing anything that is not "perfect." Another factor, related to the first, is the difficulty in developing mourning. The author wants to write down "everything" and has difficulty choosing what aspects are important. Creative writing, like life, depends upon the capacity to develop mourning.

It is not easy to gain awareness of our limitations. We will never be the psychoanalysts who, in an ideal world, we would like to be. Our analyses will never be "complete" because our minds are infinite and in a permanent state of transformation. It will not be possible to know all the theories and follow their developments. And we have to remind ourselves that there is more to life than just psychoanalysis. If there wasn't, something would be wrong.

This leads me to your discomfort with the word "Candidate." You tell me, jokingly, about a patient who told you that you had been demoted from "Ph.D. in Psychology," to a simple Candidate. You and your fellow trainees are concerned about the possibility that potential patients may doubt the capacity and professional experience of "Candidate." I recall that this word comes from the Latin "Candidus," which means white and, by extension, purity and innocence. It was the color of the togas worn by postulants at public functions. I imagine that, in Rome, they hoped that the candidates, once they were selected, would work honestly for the State. As you can see, the idealization of candidates and institutions goes way back. I know of a situation where candidates have successfully argued for their denomination to be "Affiliated" Member (Membro Filiado in Portuguese).

The institution, at times, does not trust the candidates' claims and starts to "analyze them." I think that this is an abuse of psychoanalytic knowledge. The analysis of the candidate should take place in a suitable setting, with the candidate's analyst.

Remember that being a candidate at the International Psychoanalytic Association (I.P.A.) is a privilege. Beyond the known tripartite—training analysis, supervised clinical work, and in-depth study of the theory—I value the fourth axis: being part of the institution. I realize that you are not sufficiently informed of the various activities that the I.P.A., I.P.S.O. (International Psychoanalytic Studies Organization), and the Regional Federations are offering for Candidates. Exchanges, supervisions, and discussion groups with analysts from different societies, financial aid bursaries, and Working Parties, etc. Many of these activities take place online. The I.P.A. is, without doubt, one of the global institutions that most creatively takes advantage of this.

Psychoanalytic institutions have been showing themselves to be more generous, transparent, and creative. Beyond the sociocultural factors, I think that these changes also reflect developments in psychoanalytic knowledge. There is value placed on what occurs in the analytic field, between the members of the dyad, what each member "provokes" in the other. The meticulously studied movements whereby the members of the dyad meet or fail to meet one another. These movements reveal/conceal the ways in which the mind constitutes itself and also its deficits. This technical and theoretical emphasis has led to the reconsideration of analysts as people, with their intuitive and imaginative abilities. Their internal setting. Analysts, confronted by difficult situations, are stimulated to conduct experiments while carefully observing their consequences. I notice that analysts have more freedom to observe and to think, abandoning rigid ideas. This freedom means that the candidate can benefit even more from personal analysis.

In this way, we observe the reduction of dogmatic thinking and of uncritical adherence to a specific psychoanalytic theory, sometimes considered to be the only one that is true. We must remember that theories are hypothetical constructs designed to give meaning to the clinical experience. These theories can and should be altered or substituted for constructs that make better sense. Fortunately, the religious aspect of psychoanalysis is disappearing. The psychoanalyst's identity no longer receives the adjective of a classic author (Klein, Kohut, Bion, etc.). They are who they are; they have their own identity in which, without being too eclectic, they take advantage of what makes sense to them, relentlessly developing their creative capacity. What a great time to be a candidate at this point in the development of psychoanalysis!

We must still be wary of the strains of populism and fanaticism that have been infiltrating current democracies. We know how authoritarian governments hinder the development of psychoanalysis. This runs the risk of the psychoanalytic institutions themselves becoming repressive, although some of the analysts resists. I remember a Czech colleague telling us about the secret use of psychoanalysis during the communist regime. The most highly regarded Professor of Psychiatry in the country stated that psychoanalysis was a good form of treatment. But with one caveat: as long as they got rid of everything Freud had written! Unfortunately, mass exoduses of psychoanalysts have been common. Membership of the I.P.A. has made the insertion of colleagues in other countries less difficult.

You have not experienced these situations, and perhaps you cannot imagine them. I sense, however, that you and your fellow trainees will have to contend with them. As you know, Eros and Thanatos are in constant struggle, and this will never end.

So, let's embrace what is different and welcome foreigners who knock on our door, accepting them as they are. Psychoanalysis helps us to develop Hospitality, as much for the other as for parts of our own minds. Hospitality and ethics are intermingled, and without them we would not be psychoanalysts (or decent human beings). Psychoanalytic work with the initially undesirable guest helps us to develop loving creativity between the guest and host. This is not always possible, and we must be on our guard against fantasies of paralyzing omnipotence.

The elderly tend to say that they do not regret what they did with their life. This remark, which seems like wisdom, often sounds to me like defeated resignation. This is not the case for me: I feel like I have allowed myself to be contaminated by the psychoanalytic "plague" (in Freud's words) in such a way that I have risked sacrificing other aspects of my life. From what I know about you, you are running a similar risk, are you not? I was able to observe what was happening to me using psychoanalysis. The "plague" was transformed into remedy.

Being a psychoanalyst is fascinating. We have the privilege of being challenged all the time and of giving meaning to so many lives (as well as our own). And this never stops. May you be able to benefit from everything that the analytic training has to offer you.

4 Eric Marcus
New York, U.S.A.

Dear Candidate,

I welcome this opportunity to tell you about the profession I love and to which I have devoted my career, one that has taken many forms, illustrating the varied uses of psychoanalytic knowledge.

I waited a long time to do psychoanalytic training. I wanted to experience medicine and psychological social science and psychiatric work with very ill patients as well as neurotics. I was interested in how the mind works in individuals and groups. I wanted to see the relationships in the bio-psychosocial model and use it to do what I love most—individual responsibility for patient care. My most moving professional experiences are in patient care. So I practiced medicine for ten years part time while going to graduate school in theoretical ethnology doing research on comparative hospital culture, then doing a psychiatry residency, and then running an in-patient neuropsychiatric diagnostic unit focusing on treatment failures, one group of which are patients with serious ax 1 and ax 2 illnesses, mainly mood and character disorders. Then, I did psychoanalytic training that deepened my work in all these areas and allowed for the deepening of the journey to a depth not attainable in any other way. And every year it gets better and better. I see more and more clearly the processes that organize mental life in all its marvelous forms. My ability to help gets better and better. The satisfaction is ever more fulfilling. Psychoanalytic training is a gift that keeps on giving.

That said, the training is not easy. It is time intensive. It is financially difficult. It is emotionally demanding. It is self-confronting. It helps if you want it very badly, if your interest is compelling, if you love patient care, if you need to think deeply about the mind. In training you learn difficult theory, treat challenging patients, are supervised in uncomfortably personal ways, and read an exciting but seemingly endless and dense literature. Because the study is personally so demanding, you meet many puffed up egos, one adaptation to the humbling of grandiosity. *Ignore the ego aggrandizement.* The field is riven theoretically, as all growing fields tend to be, and you see many heated arguments. Enjoy the show, and don't confuse truth with the theoretical sturm und drang. Do not click on the emotional click bait of pedagogy. Focus on your learning. Learn from all.

Integrating theory and developing your clinical working style are lifelong developments.

Keep your good sense and values. Keep your individuality. The treatment is a human to human, a human with human, treatment. It is done differently by each analyst and each analytic pair. This is a major appeal to us caregiver types. You will want to develop yourself and your sensitivity into what is called your analytic instrument, your emotional ability to help the patient. It requires a trained ability to tolerate intensity; of affect, of images, of desires, of envies, of hatreds, of dreams and fantasies, in ourselves and in our patients.

The most crucial of the tripartite elements of learning—personal analysis, supervision, class, and reading—the most crucial and catalytic is personal analysis. The more the better. The deeper the better. It takes time. *Don't end it too early. Ten years is a minimum!* When you have a supervisor you admire or a teacher you respect, ask them how long their analysis was. I had two; a treatment analysis of ten years before training and a training analysis of eight years during and after training. The teachers and analytic practitioners who I felt had the best and deepest grasp and who I most admired usually had long analyses.

Supervision. Ah, supervision. The only way to learn to do something. What did I learn? And how did I learn it? And at what price? Let's do the price first. The price is humbling. No matter how smart you are, no matter how much you read, doing something is very different. *It requires a long period of learning until you accept that this will be infinite, and that is a good thing. The best attitude you can bring to supervision is an attitude of wanting to learn, not of wanting to demonstrate how smart you are and what you know.* This is no different than any complex learning or any learning at all. But there are particular challenges in our work. Learning psychoanalysis requires years. It requires an openness to learning about yourself as well as others. It requires the capacity to tolerate not knowing. But it is also challenging because of the commitment we make to it and the strong wish to help others and the anxious need to know while doing. It is supervision that can get you through. In the best supervisions you feel you are in it together. It broadens into a mentorship bond that can be sustaining and lifelong.

So, what did I learn? I learned the ability to empathically enter the emotional experience of another human being in ever increasing depths of the unconscious. I learned to use this information to help patients resume their normal growth and development. I learned to be a very active listener and to experience that as a doing. How did I learn this? I had the opportunity to be supervised by a classical analyst who had the prejudicial view that because I had been in practice before psychoanalytic training, surely, I must be contaminated in my technique by the more active psychotherapy a general psychiatrist practiced. On our first meeting, therefore, he forbade me to speak to the patient for the first two years! I asked if perhaps two years was an exaggerated way of making a point. He repeated, two years. Now was my chance to leave. I would never do such a thing, nor did I need to. My consolidated identity as a physician and as a general psychiatrist did not require acquiescing to such a bizarre idea. But then I thought perhaps there was a way to experience the learning of the discipline he was requiring while helping the patient. So, I asked, "Can I say, 'Hi, come on in'?" He said, "I don't care about that." I said, "Can I say, 'Ah, and oh, and hmmmmmm, and hah'?" He said, "I don't care about that." I said, "Can I say, 'sorry time is up'?" He said, "Don't say sorry." Because my patient was a young woman, voluble and talkative, who had repeated traumas in her development and badly needed to share them with someone, I thought that with the holding environment expressed by my empathic utterances, the frame might hold and actually benefit her from the simple retelling of her life story. And so that is what I did. And it went very well. At the end of only one year, my supervisor said, "Now you can talk." I said, "What do I say?" He pointed out that I was now so saturated with her story and her attitude and reactions that when I had something to say I would probably be in the ballpark and he would point out in what ways I was wrong. I translated that to myself as he would point out in what ways I could've said it better. And thus, progressed a long analysis, past my graduation. It was very helpful to my patient's growth and to my growth as an analyst and as a person. Since then, I have no trouble with attentively listening in empathically communicated silence for the minutes or sessions in which that is necessary to allow patients to unfold their story and deepen their emotional connection with it. To allow patients to connect with and formulate what it is they need to express. And I am much better at understanding not only what is said but knowing when and how to formulate what will help patients understand even better and catalyze the uncovering of the next layer. My relationship with my supervisor grew into a warm friendship that lasted many years. I think the turning point for him came when upon my graduation, after only 4-1/2 years, he assumed I would drop the patient who was low fee and needed a long analysis. I was shocked and offended by his assumption and told him that I was a doctor and would consider dropping her an abandonment and a violation of my deepest professional identity and that the patient and I had a mutual commitment to the treatment. He said, "Other candidates do this." I said, "I don't." This touched him, although I didn't know why because for me it was the expectable. I later found out from him about his own maternal abandonment. This mirrored the patient's repeated traumas that were a type of maternal abandonment trauma. On reflection in my own analysis, there is some of that in my history as well. This illustrated for me, early on, the syncretic and deeply moving emotional resonances and rhymes that occur when humans connect their emotional life each to each.

So how did I apply psychoanalysis? In many ways: to theory of mind, to neurophysiology of representation, to narrative medicine, and to social science research in medical education. Scattershot? No; all around the idea of symbolic alterations of reality. The most fun was social science research of medical education where I studied the capacity for the development of medical empathy by collecting medical student dreams about medical school and residency training. I then got the opportunity to be in charge of all the human science courses at the medical school where I teach. I weaved them into an integrated sequence using the dreams to identify progressive developmental traumatic teaching experiences and the underlying psychological need so that the curriculum could be less traumatic to the empathic capacity.

One piece of advice about professional limits—never interpret your significant others: wives, husbands, partners, children. To do so is an intrusion that is aggressive and may provoke intense negative transference and deformation of your relationship. If you use your analytic training in ordinary human relationships, do so with your increased empathic understanding not with interpretations that outside of the analytic situation tend to be based on reductionistic manifest content. To desist from interpreting our relationships is a form of love and concern in human relations even as love and concern in analysis requires interpretation but with the long opportunity of preparing the patient and being able to handle the complications of your method.

Devote time to your relationships, your life partner, your friends, your children, your pets. I have done many things none more satisfying than raising children. From them I learned human development. From them I learned about myself and my own developmental history. And I learned how intense a love devotion can be. Psychoanalytic careers should not be used to avoid the connections of social relationships. Avoid becoming one of those who teach what they can't do. Your work with patients and your ability to help them comes out of who you are, not merely what you know. It is the analysis of that human emotional connection that is the healing power Freud discovered.

5 Cláudio Laks Eizirik
PorteAlegre, Brazil

Dear Candidate,

When I think of you, several faces come to my mind: my students at the medical school; the residents of psychiatry and psychologists I supervised or mentored in their MsC and PhD studies; the many candidates who were or are my patients; supervisees or students at seminars; my own daughter, who is concluding her analytic training; and myself as a young candidate full of enthusiasm, anxieties, dreams, hopes, and an almost blind faith in psychoanalysis.

Of all these people, the one I imagine I know best is me, so I will talk with you looking at my past, at the present we share, and at the future, in which you will live.

When I look back to when I did my analytic training, in the mid-seventies and early eighties, what I see is a very different world. What I mean is that the world seemed bigger then, communications were more difficult (for instance, we had to read Freud in Spanish or English, unlike today when we have excellent Portuguese translations), travels were more expensive, and in Brazil we were living under a military dictatorship, against which many of us took different kinds of attitude. Some of my colleagues were tortured and killed. Others expressed their opposition in a more cautious way, but there was always a price to pay.

Let me give an example. When I was approved in a public contest to become a teacher at the Medical School, one of the many agents of the intelligence service that were spread in all institutions told the Rector of the University that I (and several others) could not be hired because we were subversive people. The Rector did not accept it and risked his job to hire us all. I was only aware of this situation many years later, but this courageous professor remained as a good example of integrity and the paramount importance of democracy. This is my first remark to you: we are first of all citizens, and all other things, including being analysts, only come after that. History tells us that psychoanalysis can only exist in democratic regimes, will suffer in authoritarian ones, and was prohibited during Nazism and Stalinism. That's why I was always very concerned with the world and the country we live in, as I am today, and many analysts share the same concerns and clear political views on the need to preserve and fight for democracy, in a moment when we have so many corrupt and dangerous leaders and groups in the government of several countries.

I think that the social and political atmosphere has a direct influence on our institutions, among them the psychoanalytic ones. When I trained, there were few training analysts, and the prevailing theoretical content was stricter than the pluralistic scenario of today, and the paranoid feelings among candidates were stronger than the current ones, as far as I can see. For instance, candidates very seldom offered comments at meetings of the Society, and some remained as silent participants for many years. Of course, some people feel more at ease to participate than others, but the prevailing atmosphere was not so inviting as today. An important development was the constitution of candidates' associations, at each Institute and at each country, and the establishment of the IPSO.

Here goes my second suggestion to you: try to participate in the meetings of your Institute and Society, dare to ask questions and make comments at the seminars, and don't accept anything without raising your doubts, when it's the case. If you think a concept is strange, unjustifiable, or even ridiculous, share your ideas and ask for clarification. One of my colleagues recently told me that when a paper fails to portray extensively Freud's main concepts, there are always colleagues who consider themselves the guardians of the cathedral, and sometimes react as inquisitors. Do not feel intimidated. Freud was not like that; he was always able to question, change, and discuss. The wish to change from one analyst or supervisor to another was something unthinkable, when I was candidate. In fact, I do not remember a single situation of this kind. I do not think it is an easy process, but it is seen as a possible thing today, and a necessary one, when the analytic couple does not work well together.

Something that possibly remains similar to those days, and I doubt that this will ever change, is the extraordinary experience of personal analysis, and when it works well, the almost unending possibilities and avenues for feeling, thinking, and transforming mind and soul. It is a very moving experience, too, when I can witness and share the blossoming of new candidates' analytic function; it is as if I live jointly with him or her what happened to me so many years ago. Supervision is another fascinating opportunity for both candidate and supervisor to rediscover, in each case, the analytic method and jointly build ways of understanding and giving meaning to each narrative that is constructed in the analytic field.

Like the changes in the world, psychoanalysis has also changed internationally, and its main institution, the IPA, has been in the last years an open, pluralistic, welcoming one that has been able to acknowledge that we have at least three training models; that the oldest of them, the Eitingon model, could become more flexible; that our training remains a solid one; that our congresses are great opportunities to get in touch with many creative colleagues; and that we are growingly active in the community through several different committees, all of which have candidates actively involved.

Since I was a candidate, I tried to include myself in the psychoanalytic community. When someone visited our Society, and there was a request to present clinical material, I was always available. You may think this was an expression of my greed. Instead of answering to you that yours is a wild interpretation, I will agree with you. Yes, I was (and so I remain) always eager to learn more, not only through reading but also through living clinical and institutional experiences. Believe me, this was a rewarding attitude, and I learned a lot. I treasure those moments as inspirational ones until today, and I often use them to teach about analytic practice.

Since that time, there have been many theoretical and clinical developments, for instance, the growing inclusion of the analyst's mind in the analytic field and the importance of countertransference, reverie, enactments, transformations, and so on. I told you before that at the beginning I had an almost blind faith in psychoanalysis. Several decades of continuous work and dozens of analytic cases later, I can tell you that today I have a more realistic view of the possibilities and limitations of our method.

Nowadays, we see more regressive patients; we sometimes work with patients who also see psychiatrists and are under medication; and in my view, we dare to explore deeper levels of the mind and to see, for instance, elderly patients analytically. As I wrote some years ago, for me psychoanalysis is a work in progress; it is not and never will be ready; and today we are better analysts than were Freud, Abraham, Ferenczi, Klein, Winnicott, Bion, Lacan, Green, Mahler, Erikson, the Barangers, Racker and so many others. How is this possible? Because we have all of them with us, in our mind and in the analytic room, as well as our analysts, supervisors, teachers, and a lot of current analytic thinkers who do not stop stimulating us with their ideas and creative minds. And you, my dear candidate, and your colleagues will be better analysts than we are today, because you will have all those masters plus the ones of today.

Sometimes we may become so involved in our analytic career, and its many dimensions, for instance the institutional ones, that we may neglect some fundamental areas of our lives. Previously I told you that we all are first citizens, and then other things, but maybe I should correct myself now and tell you that, in fact, we are first human beings and then all other things, including being citizens. Human beings need to have love relationships, and the first ones are found in our family, and after them in the people we love and who will be our partners, our children, grandchildren, and friends. In my view these relations are also indispensable for someone to be a good psychoanalyst. There are also other sorts of relationships, those with literature, poetry, music, the movies, and so on. Not infrequently, what comes to my mind in order to understand something during a session, is a line of a poem, or from a novel, or from a song.

So, allow me to remind you that, despite the fascination so often found in our method and its great possibilities, do not forget to live your own life, with your family and your friends, and to follow your own interests, the cultural or artistic ones, as well as do not forget that you have not only a mind, but also a body, that needs to be cared for and exercised.

Finally, if I look forward, trying to imagine the future in which you and your analytic colleagues will live, I cannot let aside a question often raised, sometimes with great concern, about the future of psychoanalysis. Considering so many challenges of the present, so many competing treatments, so many difficult situations in many places concerning health systems, some people think that psychoanalysis will not survive.

Remember that this dark prediction was made many times, even at Freud's time, and here we are, alive and full of development, activity, meetings, publications, and analytic work where there are analytic institutions, or practicing analysts, but also new analytic groups being established throughout the world. So, do not feel afraid of the future and the many challenges you will have to face, as we and our predecessors did and are doing now. Work hard, read a lot, enjoy your life, try to feel pleasure in what you do, do not forget that you are also a citizen of your country and the world, and I am confident that you will have the same rewards and feeling of fulfillment that I and so many of my colleagues are happy to share today.

I wish you a happy journey through the future, full of good, bad, but always inspiring moments in our shared work in progress, psychoanalysis.

6 Theodore Jacobs
New York, U.S.A.

Dear Candidate,

I have been puzzling over what I might say to you that will be of value, both during your candidacy and in the years beyond that. Not surprisingly, what I have come up with is what I have found personally helpful over the years that I have been in practice. Some of what I have to say consists of words of guidance and advice passed on to me by teachers and admired authorities in our field; some are simply thoughts of mine drawn from my experience as a student and teacher.

In the former category, I think of the statements made to me and others by the late Charles Brenner with whom I worked closely for more than four decades. Brenner was a person of strong convictions about psychoanalytic theory and practice, which he conveyed clearly in his teaching and extensive writings. I did not subscribe to everything Brenner taught—I thought he underplayed the importance of the analyst's psychology on the process, for instance—but what he had to say about managing the troublesome countertransference feelings that we all have to contend with from time to time has stayed in my mind and is something I have turned to many times when negative feelings about a patient threaten to break out and do damage to the treatment.

Brenner said, "Always remember that patients can only bring themselves to our offices, that is all they can do. No matter how angry or hostile or provocative patients may be, no matter how recalcitrant to our best efforts, this is who they are at this moment and they cannot be otherwise. It is our job to understand what has caused them to be the people they are and to help them understand and better resolve the maladaptive solutions to their conflicts that underlie the unhappiness that has brought them to us."

All true, you may say in reply, but a lot easier said than done. And I would agree with that. This attitude towards our patients represents an ideal that we fail to live up to many times over, but I have found that just keeping Brenner's words in mind at times of stress has helped me avoid acting on negative countertransference feelings. Recalling Brenner's words has also, in general, helped me attain a more positive and helpful stance when working with the more difficult and emotionally challenging patient.

Another comment of Brenner's has stayed with me over the years. This concerns the number of theories, many conflicting, with which students are presented these days. This is a confusing situation for seasoned practitioners and immeasurably more so for candidates who are seeking to learn the basic principles of analytic theory and practice. How are students to know which theories are valid and can serve as a guide in their clinical work and which do not hold up in practice?

On this issue Brenner's words were clear and, I find, practically useful. He said,

"Let your patients be your teachers. The analytic material that comes directly from the couch provides the best means of assessing which theories are valid and reliable and which fail that test. Theories that are based on, and can be confirmed by clinical evidence, are likely to be sound and useful. Those that are intellectually appealing but do not correspond to what patients actually bring to us in analytic sessions are purely speculative and tend not to be reliable guides in analytic work."

Although perhaps oversimplified in some respects—Brenner's idea does not speak to the question of unconscious thoughts and fantasies—I have nevertheless found it to be a good way to begin to sort through the maze of conflicting views and theoretical positions with which we are assaulted in today's psychoanalytic world.

Over the years I have also kept in mind and tried to apply in my own work a way of thinking about patients that was articulated by one of the great contributors to our field: the late Hans Loewald.

Think of your patients not only as they are now, but as they may yet become, Loewald counseled. To my mind, this is a profound statement because it contains within it two centrally important ideas: (1) The analyst serves as the bearer of hope for his patients, and (2) his view of them and their prospects for growth and change, although not verbalized, are inevitably conveyed to patients and have an important, if not always recognized, impact in the course and outcome of treatment.

Loewald understood that our patients read us just as we read them, and they respond to our unspoken attitudes towards them in ways not dissimilar to the way that a child is affected by her parents unspoken thoughts and fantasies about her.

In the same vein, words I have also tried to hold in my mind, is Freud's dictum that we should always treat our patients like honored guests in our homes.

This, again, is an ideal not easily realized. We cannot sustain this attitude at all times with our patients. It is true, though, that it expresses an important idea; that the courtesy and respect with which we treat our patients operates, along with insight, interpretation, and the working through of conflict, as an essential ingredient in the therapeutic action of psychoanalysis.

At this point you may wonder when—and if—I am going to step down from the preacher's podium. I don't blame you for your impatience, but if you will bear with me, I have just a couple of more school-marmish bits of advice to offer.

The first concerns what and how you learn during your candidate years. Today there is a trend towards slighting the classical literature in psychoanalysis.

I am speaking of Freud and his contemporaries who wrote in the early to middle part of the last century.

This I believe is a mistake and one that I hope that you will not make. Taking the opportunity to immerse yourself in the writing and thinking of those remarkable figures who were our forebears will provide you with a foundation for your work as analysts that is irreplaceable. You will learn how our field developed; which ideas, theories, and clinical approaches proved valuable and which had to be discarded; and how we got to where we are today. This may seem unimportant and irrelevant to your interest in learning to do analysis, but this kind of classical education will enrich your understanding, not only of the field of depth psychology, but of the approaches that seasoned clinicians have taken in working with patients not unlike those who will appear in your offices today. An obvious corollary to this old goatish advice is the importance of reading. I mention this because as a teacher I have noticed an increasing trend among students to skim the assigned readings or not to do them at all.

I understand the burdens that you are under in being a candidate as well as trying to earn a living and meet your responsibilities to your families and how difficult it is to find the time to do the course readings, but I urge you, nonetheless, to read as much as you can. There is no substitute for immersing yourself in our literature and learning from the greatest minds in our field. Courses on technique and supervision are valuable, but without reading widely and learning the principles on which analytic technique is based, they tend to become simply utilitarian lessons that lead to mechanical ways of practicing. You do not want to find yourself practicing in that manner.

Just one more thing. There is a tendency among analysts and analytic institutes not only to favor a particular point of view; Freudian, Kleinian, Relational, etc., but to disparage others with which they disagree. This attitude was prevalent in my own training years, along with an unspoken injunction against candidates taking an interest in perspectives other than that of their institute. Things are more open today. Candidates are exposed to a number of theories, which are taught respectfully. Nonetheless, more than a little of the older attitude remains in a number of institutes and among quite a few teachers. This involves more than their favoring a particular perspective. It communicates a negative, and often dismissive, attitude toward rival theories. This message has a powerful effect on students who identify with their teachers and the position of their training center. The result is to cut down the student's receptivity to new and different ideas and to induce a kind of conformity of thinking that is anti-creative and ultimately deadening.

Much better and far more enlightening is to approach the rich array of ideas and theories in our field today with the attitude taken by the conductors of world-class orchestras. The best of them have a broad appreciation of a wide variety of musical styles and approaches. And it is with equal enthusiasm that they conduct composers as varied and different as Handel and Mozart and Beethoven and Stravinsky and Philip Glass. No doubt they have their favorites and know that some composers are far more accomplished than others. But they seek out and appreciate what is unique and valuable in each work that they conduct.

Such an open and appreciative attitude will serve you well. I will allow you to seek out and find what is unique and valuable in the ideas and theories to which you are exposed rather than shutting your mind to them and missing out on ways of thinking that could broaden and enhance your understanding of your patients and provide more tools to work with them.

In short, try not to fall into the biased and chauvinistic attitudes still operating in our field. Instead strive to open your mind, learn all you can, and then test what you have learned against your own clinical experience.

And trust your intuition, the workings of your own unconscious. Analysis is an art as well as a science, and as an analyst you need to respect the artist at work in yourself. True understanding does not come from the application of theories or correct analytic technique. These help set your mind to the right wave lengths, but it is your trust in, and openness to your own mind, silently at work, reaching out to and making contact with the mind of another, that produces the flash of understanding, the compelling insights that bring light to a person who has been dwelling in darkness and who has lost his way. And it is that understanding, that resonance with the deepest fears and yearnings of our patients, that causes them to feel known, that conveys the analyst's empathy, that sparks hope, and that helps our patients gain the courage to confront the demons within that have been the source of so much pain in their lives.

Wishing you every success in your future career.

7 Paola Marion
Rome, Italy

Dear Candidate,

Thinking about the journey you are beginning, when I compare it to my own, the first thing that comes to my mind is how brave you are being. Nearly 30 years have passed since I did my training. If your passion and that of all those who are setting out on this path are the same as ours back then—and I see it in the seminars we do together, in the supervisions, in your involvement along with other young colleagues—the only thing that has changed then is the world around us and the conditions in which you will begin practicing your profession. These are profound changes, and I only note them in passing. A sense of continuity seems to have been broken. There may be multiple reasons and external causes for this: there has been the phenomenon of globalization; the arrival of the internet; the use of social media and virtual reality, which profoundly alters the dimensions of space and time and allows a magical extension of boundaries; the achievements of biotechnology; not to mention other moments that have deeply marked us all, such as September 11 or the economic crisis of 2008. All of these and more were still far off when I began my training, and back then we could look to the future with a greater sense of the continuity of tradition.

It is natural that generational leaps bring radical changes with them, but the ones we are talking about and living in seem to be marking the anthropological landscape. Bollas calls the present epoch "the age of bewilderment" to indicate that what has happened has occurred at a deep level and affected Western consciousness: something that had accompanied us over time and seemed very familiar to my generation, and to the generations before me, seems to be in danger. Bollas offers us a way of looking at this and of reflecting on how the digital world, the world of virtual reality, which emphasizes the means of communication more than its content, discourages the desire for contact with the internal world, the urge to investigate it, to explore it and look for its meanings.

This is a profound change in which you too are immersed, as are the patients who will come to see you, a change that is connected to the clinical situations we encounter and that you encounter now and will encounter in your work. Indeed, we find ourselves more and more faced with requests for help and treatment from extremely anxious people terrified by contact with themselves and with the other, terrified by dependency and intimacy; individuals in whom *action* predominates over thought. Or else we find ourselves in the presence of people who have great difficulty respecting the classical analytic setting, who because of their work, among other reasons, have to be constantly or frequently on the move, but who are also used to considering it a fact of life that one no longer stops for a while to reflect on oneself, to take or give oneself time for that. I am talking about a large number of patients who put us in a paradoxical situation. Their apparently adequate functioning on the social level hides a psychic void, the absence of an internal reality with which to measure themselves, an inability to make a deep relationship with themselves or with others.

It is no coincidence that we more and more often find ourselves faced with the task of "constructing the analytic patient," as the scientific literature has for some time been calling this phenomenon. It is a phenomenon that was completely absent when I was training, and there was certainly no reflecting about the problems that this creates at the start of the analysis for training. These conditions, which indicate an external climate less inclined to reflection and internal investigation and more focused on functionality and practical results, make the conditions in which we work more delicate and complex and make more subtle and pervasive the defenses we may develop to challenge the feeling of insecurity and difficulty this causes us. As Freud wrote, "What is new has always aroused bewilderment and resistance."

The subject is all the more delicate for those like you who, besides setting out to learn and practice the profession, and therefore are all the more concerned with matching up to the training criteria, are at the same time engaged in constructing your own analytic identity. What kind of impact do the present-day transformations have on this process? The reality outside us, but within which our profession moves, and the kinds of patient I mentioned earlier put us in direct contact with the conflict between an analytic ideal, an ideal to which I and the colleagues of my generation refer almost naturally and with which we naturally tended to identify when we were young analysts, and the present demands for treatment which in the first instance seem to be in direct conflict with these principles, or to push towards an expansion and extension of the rules and conditions that characterize the setting. All in all, the young candidate like you must take account of today's changed panorama and learn more quickly to tolerate the instability and uncertainty stirred up by the difficulty of finding patients with the right analytic characteristics. I think our role, in seminars as well as in supervisions, should be directed to helping you bear the emotional burden that this brings with it, to help you learn to respond to the demands of potential patients with a flexibility that does not alter the specific character of the psychoanalytic experience and to learn to look with curiosity at new scenarios, to the extending of the method that they require and the challenges they pose.

I would like the teaching we offer you and your young colleagues not to foster a split between an ideal psychoanalysis and what actually happens, what we actually do in the session. The promulgation of psychoanalytic principles, the unconscious and the analytic devices for gaining access to it, the transference and countertransference, and the free association method must be accompanied by the promulgation of a psychoanalysis in the service of the patient, and not the other way around, as we sometimes still find. This means taking care to receive patients on their own terms, in the way they relate to their objects, to the affective quality of their exchanges, and to the construction of the relationship. This part of the work concerns a process in which there are fewer certainties, one that more involves the analyst's sensitivity and ability to work with what is closest to the patient, as our colleagues Busch and Bolognini maintain. This is not an easy situation for those who are still inside the training process and feel the urgent need to recognize themselves and be recognized by the institution that also guarantees their identity. You and your colleagues are looking for answers, and the attempt to bear the weight of uncertainty can make you feel discouraged and frightened.

The rapport with an ideal dimension is part of formative growth. The conflict created between adherence to a psychoanalytic ideal and the rugged terrain of clinical practice can give rise to defenses that are also difficult to get into focus and may compromise candidates' growth. One of these concerns what Rangell in 1982 and more recently Bolognini have called transference onto theories. This is a valuable reflection that I have not come across in my analytic journey, and it concerns the quality of the transference relationship that the psychoanalyst entertains with his or her preselected psychoanalytic theory or with one author in particular, and with the group that forms around that thinking. Bolognini has told us about the dangers that arise from too strong and exclusive identification with one author or one school, helping us to understand how this kind of transference may act as a defense. But a defense against whom or what? The exclusive identification with an "immeasurable single parent" (Bolognini)—whether this refers to an Author, a theory, or a group—may create the illusion of living in a secure fortress protecting us against the sense of our limitations and the feelings of insecurity and fragility that accompany the construction of an identity and may deceive us into believing we are stronger than other people. Being beyond our control, this type of identification may represent a narcissistic compensation against the loneliness our work subjects us to, which you are starting to experience, and against the uncertainty of not knowing. *Exclusive* identification with an author or a theory has two consequences: on the one hand it blocks the development of free association, which is so important in clinical practice but also in theory—the polyphonic internal debate—and as a result rigidifies the analyst's internal position, with a bad effect on the way he or she listens; on the other hand, it contains the insidious danger of enclosing oneself in an endogamous and self-referential dimension that is reproduced across generations and tends to rule out creative comparison both on the clinical and on the cultural and institutional levels. Building a good internal democracy means accepting otherness and keeping one's curiosity about it alive. The unconscious is itself otherness. What we are striving to do is acknowledge it inside ourselves, in the patient, and in the analytic couple in the multiple forms in which it reveals itself.

Identification *with* a group is the opposite of the work *of* a group and work *in* the group, which is the most important tool for comparison and development of thinking. The internal democracy we aspire to is nurtured by this mode of exchange and represents a fundamental ingredient of the formative process, the most powerful antidote to the dimension of the familiar and endogamous. Indeed, it is in the group that we encounter otherness of thought and of how we approach clinical material and read theory, dealing with the "uneasy coexistence" (Ogden) of different and contrasting points of view. This helps us to come out of our self-referentiality, bear doubt, and come back to ourselves with something more or something different. This is a new dimension that was less explored and received less attention when I was in training and that needs to be carefully cultivated and fostered. This type of experience expands when we pass from the domestic context to the international. In that new environment the group perimeter expands, and an unknown, foreign aspect is added both in terms of people and language, which brings more strongly into play the sense of our analytic identity, above all for anyone who is still going through their own training.

In my opinion, international experience—in careful doses, of course—should be part of the formative process and be supported by training analysts. I stress this because it seemed to be missing from my training, and when I did it, it was a bit "single-handed," without the support and active participation of my teachers. The international dimension stimulates very strong feelings of otherness and foreignness in comparison with the familiar atmosphere of your training institution, but at the same time it gives you the sense of a wider community and a network within which we are and in which we recognize ourselves. The pedagogical climate expands and compels you to move out of the reassuring sphere of what you know. Remembering what happened for me when I had the experience of an international context, I associate it with the recovery of an adolescent dimension: the candidate leaves home and ventures into a wider space than that offered by her original nuclear family. Going out into the world is very exciting, and yet it is in this very transition that one has all the more need to feel supported by parental analysts, supervisors, and teachers.

When the institutional container expands to include supranational institutions, an ambivalent transference is provoked. In fact, while on the one hand this kind of participation represents an expansion of the trainee analyst's maturational process and is invested with high levels of curiosity, becoming a place for creating strong links and giving life to positive transferential movements, on the other hand it means encountering a boundary, a boundary set by foreignness, including the foreignness of a language, and by the re-dimensioning of the processes of idealization linked to one's development and identity as a member of a professional society, with manifestations of negative transference. Both these transference manifestations should be welcomed, acknowledged, and worked through in one's personal analysis, in seminars, and in supervisions.

The two dimensions, the international one and that of the group, oppose the idea of training as a "theological seminary," as Kernberg called it, and they are still the best antidote to the danger I mentioned earlier, of endogamy and familism, which represent a "narcissistic degeneration of the mechanisms of affiliation" (Ruggiero).

We only exist in relation to the other. Your effort must be directed to meeting otherness, that of the group of colleagues, both the closest and the most distant, the otherness of the patient and his history, the otherness of theoretical multiplicity and that of external reality and the socio-cultural context around us that enters our consulting rooms. The various levels of otherness, and how you accept them, contribute to the construction of your analytic identity and will characterize what you become. Elias Canetti, more poetically, wrote of "the power to contain very many things within oneself no matter how contradictory they are, to know that everything that seems irreconcilable nevertheless subsists in its own environment and to feel this without losing oneself in fear, and instead knowing that one needs to call it by its own name and meditate upon it."

Pontalis speaks of the "test of the foreign," which he associates with the otherness that lives inside us. He states that the "privilege of migration" is what characterizes analysis as an essentially migratory discipline: from one language or dialect to another, from one culture to another, from one knowledge to another. In this migratory capacity, in the capacity for tolerance when encountering the other, doubt, and uncertainty, lies the heart of the analytic experience. I think the task/duty to migrate and learn to migrate is also good material for reflection, stimulus, and learning in relation to your formative experience and your training.

8 Otto F. Kernberg
New York, U.S.A.

Dear Candidate,

Not knowing you, only permits me to answer some of the many questions you may have at this point and to be cautious about unsolicited advice. To begin: it is well worth it to become a psychoanalyst at this time, when psychoanalysis is widely being questioned and criticized—sometimes with good reason (more about that, later). Psychoanalysis, I believe, is the most profound and comprehensive theory about the functions, structure, development, and pathology of the human mind. It also provides a spectrum of psychoanalytically based psychotherapies, including the classical or standard psychoanalytic treatment, and several derived, empirically validated psychotherapies. And it is a unique potential instrument for research on the mind.

How can you get good training? Ideally, select a psychoanalytic institute that is not too small, has at least some generally recognized and outstanding scholars in their field, good teachers, researchers, experts recognized beyond the boundaries of their institution, and generous with their commitment to psychoanalytic education. It helps when a psychoanalytic Institution is part of or related to a University Department in Psychiatry, Clinical Psychology, or Social Work. If you are not a psychiatrist, you definitely should have an adequate period of clinical training at a Department of Psychiatry, to learn about psychopathology of the entire range of psychiatric illness, differential diagnosis, treatment, and general notions about the relation of psychiatric illness to Medicine.

If the Institution of your choice facilitates your own selection of your personal training analyst, and, through whatever channel of information you have, your personal preference whom you would choose, even better. If you don't have that kind of information or possibility, it becomes even more important that your Institute have a good reputation as a serious, well organized, and effective educational institution—even if it also has a correspondent aura of rigidity and conservatism (more about that, later).

Your personal analysis, guided by a capable, alert, sensitive, knowledgeable, and open-minded analyst, will largely depend on you yourself! Your curiosity about the unknown in yourself, your openness to the unexpected in yourself, will guide you. You will not learn "how to" in your analysis: against your possible expectations to learn psychoanalytic technique from your analyst, you will find out that you learn psychoanalytic technique from your seminar teachers and, most importantly, from your supervisors. Supervisors may be assigned to you: try to influence those selections, get the best you can find in your Institute. And don't be shy in searching privately for great supervisors, even (or hopefully) outside the boundaries of your own Institute. You will have to continue with personal supervision even after graduation (if you really want to become an expert!).

I have just pointed out the need to expand your horizons individually, beyond your concrete obligatory educational program. Major tasks that you will have to achieve by yourself: (a) Develop your own, integrated theory of technique on the basis of all respective information, supervision, and theoretical learning you have received. The field is complex, divided into competing schools of thinking, and no truly integrated "textbook" of technique is available (in any language). (b) Try to become a guest student, for some time, at an Institute with a definitely different theoretical and technical orientation than your own. You will have to try to arrange this for yourself without getting into trouble in your own Institute. (c) Read as much as you can, but selectively. Carefully study books before you buy them, regardless of who recommends them. You will discover how many repetitions and basically empty publications are thrown into the market. Read the leading texts of your own and of competing psychoanalytic approaches. A general, extremely helpful guiding system are the classical psychoanalytic dictionaries. I am referring to Laplanche and Pontalis (Freud's views, and classic French understanding); Auchincloss and Samberg (an American ego psychological, but very open overview); Salman Akhtar (an individual, critical approach); and Spillius et al. (a clear and comprehensive Kleinian approach). There are several others, but these four, in combination, should help to clarify different and controversial areas.

If you are not yet giving up on me, I also would urge you to become knowledgeable regarding the boundary sciences of psychoanalysis. (1) The neurobiology of the mind, the relationship between neurobiological and intrapsychic structures: Freud was fundamentally interested in this dimension, and surely, if alive, would, by now, have modified his theories significantly. (2) The social psychological field: the psychology and psychopathology of couples, family, and social groups, the application of psychoanalysis to these domains, and learning from them. (3) The relation of psychoanalysis to the humanities: Philosophy, Art, etc.

And, on top of all of this, you're learning should include specialized psychoanalytic psychotherapies, their indications, contraindications, and techniques! Here comes a major shortcoming of too many psychoanalytic Institutes: their neglect of psychoanalytic psychotherapies, their self-imposed limitations to classical psychoanalysis; and their neglect, if not direct mistrust and rejection of psychoanalytic research. These are major problems facing psychoanalysis today, and Institutes are just beginning to deal with them. You should be ahead of the game! Your professional practice should reflect an interest in a broad spectrum of patients: child and adolescent treatments, severe personality disorders, or even the present analytic approach to psychosis.

Finally, something about your personal life: psychotherapy starts where common sense ends. The richness of your personal experiences in love and sex, work and profession, friendship and social engagements will provide you with an expanded openness to your patients' experiences and conflicts.

Good Luck!

9 Stefano Bolognini
Bologna, Italy

Dear Candidate,

Being 70 years old doesn't impede me from vividly remembering both my early objective condition and my subjective experience when I was a Candidate: My childhood and youth are still absolutely alive in my mind, and I remember things exactly as they happened.

So, I allow myself to start an inter-generational dialogue with you, hoping to be able enough to put myself in your shoes.

However, without a doubt, I see not only some similarities but also some objective differences between my psychoanalytic era and yours. I'm deliberately using here this hyper-amplifying term "era", meaning "long historical periods," because in our field very remarkable changes took place after a few decades.

When I had started my training analysis (1976), psychoanalysis was still well represented in the universities and had considerably established its presence and prestige inside the academic and cultural environments in many countries. A cultured middle class (the classical breeding ground for our activity) existed more or less everywhere in Italy, and the appeal of our treatment was in the air. The number of our competitors (other kinds of therapists, trainers, life-coaches, etc.) wasn't so huge as it is presently, and, more generally, people were much more interested in their own interior evolution and growth than they are today.

On the other hand, we the Candidates were much more limited in our vision of psychoanalysis both as a scientific method and as a profession, because our contacts at that time had been usually circumscribed to our own local Institute, with scarce or no information and contact with the rest of the psychoanalytic world. We had been provided with our theoretical and technical tools merely by having read Freud and some pioneers like Abraham, Ferenczi, and Melanie Klein and by the lessons and scripts of our national leading masters, who were our only sources and identificatory objects.

There was no contact or very little contact with our colleagues from other countries, while today these contacts are blooming internationally, thanks to the IPA and to your Candidates association IPSO.

In my opinion, your current educational process is better than ours: more ideas circulating; more exchanges at several levels; less "religious" idealization of sacred, locally undisputable theories; and generally more room for new explorations in a wider open-minded environment.

What could be worse today for you instead in comparison to our previous generation's condition?

Roughly speaking, it seems to me you are having more difficulties in recruiting suitable patients in order to start from the beginning a full analytic high frequency analysis, because many patients today have serious, fundamental conflicts in their dependence on an object, so that learning to temporarily depend (and finally to creatively inter-depend) has become today a specific, crucial passage in their psychoanalytic process.

When I was a young Candidate, the classical analytic contract and frequency were accepted with no hesitation by the majority of patients, in spite of my evident youth and inexperience, and independently from their economic condition or with reciprocal, realistic adjustments to it.

Basically they had no special reluctance to depend on analysis, because the main issue at that time was very often an overwhelming Super-ego that made patients' lives highly problematic but which they considered a normal presence in their lives, and sometimes something they conflictually relied upon. *In our contemporary culture, the biggest obstacle is frequently the narcissistic Ego Ideal, which makes dependence on an object (so regularly equivalent to a parental object tout court) an unacceptable, humiliating condition.*

Maybe I am wrong, but I am inclined to imagine you will have in several cases to "create the analytic patient" step by step, starting the treatment as it is possible at the beginning, and working then for deepening the link for increasing progressively the psychic cohabitation with the patient, and hopefully for reaching a real analytic cooperation aimed to explore the unconscious: this is a new challenge in psychoanalysis, related to a changing human world.

Additionally, unless you live in a remote country, you won't enjoy the narcissistically inflating status of being a pioneer that many colleagues in previous generations experienced; on the other hand, you will have many more theoretical and clinical tools at your disposal, and you will have the opportunity to float in a wider community for confronting and sharing your experiences.

In short, if I compare my early situation as a Candidate with yours, I would say we had probably more grandiose idealizing illusions (such as being somehow "pioneers"; easily recruiting needy patients asking to be rescued via classical treatment; dealing with a univocal and undisputable, all-explaining theory) to be progressively reduced and realistically proportioned by experience. Although today you can have more consistent and refined analytic instruments, a more advanced professional community, and a different awareness of the contemporary psychoanalyst on how the human mentality, uses, interior organization, and availability to invest are rapidly changing in the relational attitude of the subject towards the object.

What instead remains substantially unchanged, in my opinion, is that analysts are in fact the only owners of the keys of the door to the unconscious and the only possible guide for patients needing deep and stable changes in their lives.

Isn't this enough to motivate you to become such a specialist, exactly as it was 40 or 50 years ago?

Dear colleague, I wish you to have this unique opportunity and to happily complete your path leading to this "impossible" but fascinating profession.

10 Cordelia Schmidt-Hellerau
Chestnut Hill, U.S.A.

Dear Candidate,

You've made a great choice when you decided to go for psychoanalytic training! To work with the human mind is endlessly fascinating. No two patients are the same, even if they carry the same diagnosis. To trace the particular defense strategies of your patients' ego when faced with challenge and opportunity, and to experience the emergence of their unconscious fantasies and infantile theories, will always reward you with awe and amazement. As much suffering as a patient may put on your couch or chair, to eventually access and resolve together the unconscious core-conflicts and beliefs that are at its root, will enlighten both of you with pleasure. And not to forget: which other profession would allow you to linger on dreams, to look at their intricate layers of meaning, and enjoy the beauty, wit, and even the archaic bluntness of their imagery? Because this complexity is what makes psychoanalysis such an intriguing profession, it is obviously a daunting task to study it.

When at the age of seventeen I read *An Outline of Psycho-Analysis*, I was instantly captivated by Freud's understanding of the human mind. His respect for the challenges and fixations of childhood development and their reverberations in the adult's life, his appreciation of the power of his patients' inner realities, his insight into the twists and turns of neurotic symptoms, and his compassion for the anxiety and pain they caused, deeply affected me. Reading how he explored psychic life and built his theory of the mind made me want to become a psychoanalyst. To this very day, I find Freud's thought processes most stimulating, and I recommend you read his work early and as completely as you can, and then—after having been steeped in later and contemporary psychoanalytic literature—once in a while reach back to his writings. However much of our current culture engages in Freud-bashing (decrying his work and his concepts as outdated and obsolete), try to judge for yourself. I promise, you will be surprised and inspired.

My decision to start psychoanalytic training in Zürich, Switzerland, was a momentous step. I felt as much excitement as trepidation, when I laid down on the analytic couch for my first session. And I felt similarly excited and apprehensive when I for the first time sat down as a candidate behind the couch, on which my first analysand had just placed herself. How to do this right?

Fortunately—as was the requirement in the Swiss Psychoanalytic Society (S.P.S.)—my own training analysis was already in its second year. I had attended some seminars, and a supervisor had helped me determine my patient's suitability for psychoanalysis. I was lucky because my first analysand was a "good neurotic," which eased my learning about the techniques of classical analytic work. I'd wish you were equally fortunate to start out with a rather classical indication for psychoanalysis, because it facilitates acquiring the basics of our craft. Variations to the classical technique and setting will soon enough come your way.

At the time, the S.P.S. allowed its candidates to freely choose their seminars from a variety of offers. The idea was that the unconscious would steer the choice of themes for which the candidate was open and ready. There was though a requirement to take a certain number of seminars on Freud, technique, psychopathology, and clinical courses before one could apply to become a member. I'm not so sure that we candidates let our unconscious make the choices with regard to the seminar subjects; rather, we liked certain instructors and flocked to their seminars, while avoiding others. The Freud-Institute in Zürich was rather small, and the candidates knew each other and built lasting friendships without being bound during the years of their training in fixed classes.

In order to finish candidacy and become a member, we needed to have taken the required number of seminars, have worked for a substantial time with two analysands under supervision, and with a third in an unsupervised analysis. The write-up of the latter case had to be distributed to the whole S.P.S. (not only to the members of my own but of all institutes in the country) and then orally presented and discussed (like the defense of a doctoral thesis) at one of the S.P.S.'s three annual congregations. To prepare for this challenge, I worked together with two candidate-friends who were grappling with the same task. Our mutual support and encouragement helped us to successfully get through this procedure.

As a young member of the S.P.S. I was elected director of the Züricher Freud-Institute, a position I soon shared with a colleague and friend who graduated at about the same time as I did. With lots of energy we threw ourselves into the organization of our institute, its course work and scientific programs. We invited speakers from other institutes and foreign countries to broaden our view of psychoanalysis beyond the prevalent ideas within our local and national psychoanalytic discourse. I had attended my first International Psychoanalytic Congress in 1993 in Amsterdam, and it had been a formative experience for me to realize that I was part of a broad international community of analysts, who were interested in and working on similar questions that I had just started to grapple with. Thus, as the director of the Freud-Institute and later as the Scientific Secretary of the Swiss Psychoanalytic Society I wanted to bring some of this international spirit to our local and national meetings. Over the years the attendance of international meetings and the connections with analysts from all over the world has considerably deepened my understanding of psychoanalysis in its different traditions, schools, and cultural colorings. Today as the chair of the I.P.A. in Culture Committee, I continue to invite colleagues from all over the world to think and work together on the psychoanalytic experience and understanding of the many ways our mind's creativity expresses itself.

Psychoanalytic institutes, societies, federations, and associations require a lot of administrative time, and sooner or later we all are asked to contribute to the workings of our organizations. As young leaders of the Züricher Freud-Institute, we felt we had good ideas about how to do things and what to do differently. Today I would say, we entered a sort of a generational struggle: some senior analysts wanted to hold on to their ideas, and we younger analysts wanted to introduce new ones. This is the natural way of how young analysts take charge, make an existing society their own, and adjust it to a changing world and culture, while senior analysts make sure that the essentials are not lost in transition. I believe these kinds of generational struggles are part of every institute's life. They can be carried out smoothly or passionately, or sometimes they merely smolder under the surface. Whichever way they go, constructive arguments keep a society vibrant—unless the capacity for compromise breaks down on either or both sides, leading to an unfortunate split of the society.

Discussions about psychoanalytic training are often polarized between those who feel that the requirements are too burdensome and those who argue that they are necessary to guarantee a high-quality standard for psychoanalysis. I don't believe that all aspects of these recurrent conflicts can be resolved by changing or easing the existing rules and regulations. Over the years I have witnessed and been part of many debates, in which training requirements were challenged as too anxiety-provoking, unfair, or complicated for the candidates. Usually the arguments both for and against such claims had merits and eventually led to changes aimed at making the procedures more user-friendly. But soon enough these new, hard fought-for changes were challenged again, leading to further changes and so on. Despite the fact that nowadays almost everybody who is admitted as a candidate will eventually graduate, you still may feel anxious. It is here where the organization of psychoanalytic training clashes with the psychology of its trainees. In my view, to claim that a candidate failed the requirements because the requirements failed the candidate misses the point. To face and master a stressful challenge—namely, the conditions for progression or graduation, whatever they may be at any one time—and to overcome the pertaining anxieties will be an essential part of your achievement. It proves that you can accept and hold a given frame and stand firm in the face of difficulties and perceived threats wherever they may confront you, be it from the institute's requirements, a combative patient, or adverse colleagues in your society.

It's a peculiar thing to be a candidate in a psychoanalytic institute. As much as you may have already accomplished in your private and professional life, when you enter the institute to begin your training, a subtle set of feelings sneaks up on you. You may experience yourself as more insecure when speaking to a senior analyst; your heart beats fast or you don't know how to behave when you meet your analyst in the hallways; you invest your supervisor with more than the normal appreciation and power—in short there are moments in the institute when you feel like a kid under grown-ups. I'd argue that this is part of the natural regression in the analytic process, and it's a good thing, nothing to be ashamed of. In fact, I hope you would give it some room and live it at least for some initial time (rather than skip it with a rush into committee work, which puts you together and on a par with senior analysts in your psychoanalytic organization). To experience these psychic peculiarities of being a candidate will enable you to retrieve and plumb the infantile ideas and conflicts that were activated in your training analysis and show up in the sudden onset of such transferential reactions. It's actually a sign of how well your analysis is under way.

Obviously, not only you but all candidates feel that way, more or less, and at times you may interact like siblings, bonding or competing with each other. Some of these feelings may be conscious but contained; others may be unconsciously enacted. As has been acknowledged in many papers, this peculiar dynamic is very specific for the atmosphere in psychoanalytic societies and institutes. And it can't be otherwise, because the relationships between candidates, analysts, and supervisors stir an enormous potential of unconscious feelings that crisscross the hallways every step of your way. It's complicated for you as a candidate, and it may be complicated for your analyst as well, because the analytic relationship you both are engaged in is so different from anything beyond your personal sessions. And while an ordinary analytic patient usually does not run into his analyst outside the office, your training at the institute makes these encounters unavoidable. This situation may be uncomfortable at times, but it also enables you to retrieve and "redo" your growing-up together with the group of your candidate colleagues, your analyst, supervisors and instructors—a reprise that will establish deep-rooted ties with the members of your society. Want it or not, you may soon find yourself in a new (professional) family.

By 2000, my life had taken a turn. I had moved from Zürich to Boston. Having been a Training and Supervising Analyst at the SPS, the requirements for me to become a member of American Psychoanalytic Association (A.Psa.A.) and the Boston Psychoanalytic Society and Institute (B.P.S.I.) were rather formulaic. But I had to go again through the procedures of being certified by A.Psa.A. and then becoming a Training and Supervising Analyst at B.P.S.I. My new colleagues welcomed me with warmth and interest and perhaps some caution or even reservation. Naturally they may have wondered: Who is this new colleague? What ideas does she bring along? And I too had to struggle with my adjustment: so many things seemed different from what I knew. Now, having lived and worked in Boston for twenty years, I can say that B.P.S.I. is my institute; I know and appreciate my colleagues, and vice versa. In that sense I belong—and still I don't. I'm familiar but not family. I think immigrants never fully leave nor do they fully arrive; they remain in some transitional space. I want you to know this, because one day you may consider moving to a different place. It's not impossible, but it's not so easy either.

Writing to you made me think of my early years as a candidate and young analyst. Now I'm a senior analyst. It's nice to work with a host of experience to draw from. It helps one stay patient and relaxed in the face of difficult analytic moments. It also generates more pleasure in the small analytic discoveries, the seemingly minor though momentous accomplishments of a patient. I have never tired of doing psychoanalysis, and I hope to continue to enjoy my work for many years to come. Also, I love analyzing, supervising, and teaching candidates, accompanying them on their path to becoming psychoanalysts. It's very rewarding to experience candidates develop and grow and become independent valuable colleagues. I also take great pleasure in writing. All of this is good; it's exactly what I want to do. Still, sometimes it feels a bit strange to be moving along this senior status and seeing more and more younger colleagues taking over. Of course, this is how it should be, and I welcome the growing share of colleagues younger than myself—though next to my delight occasionally I feel a little surprised. Aging is perhaps the single most puzzling experience in my life. When I see you and your colleagues at our meetings, on panels, or in our institutes, it pleases me and it makes me proud of what my generation has accomplished, yet simultaneously it hints at the change of our place in all of this. In part we represent the past, and we are part of the present, while you are the future of psychoanalysis. We senior colleagues will do all we can to prepare you not only for your own professional life, but also for the task of keeping psychoanalysis alive, as a science; a form of treatment; and a local, national, and international organization. The better you can do this, the more gladly we will accept our share in the institutional functions to decrease. My hope is that you will earnestly and passionately love psychoanalysis, keep it interesting, let it blossom, and transmit it in all depth to the generations that come after you.

So again, it's great that you decided to embark on this life-long psychoanalytic journey.

Thank you and good luck!

11 Abel Mario Fainstein
Buenos Aires, Argentina

Dear Candidate,

If experience has one advantage, it is the ability to have a perspective view of our discipline, including its theoretical and clinical developments, which we continue to maintain but also question; our creative capacity throughout the psychoanalytic world; and our insertion into different regions, countries, cultures, and communities.

Additionally, years of working together with my colleagues has afforded us friendships in different parts of the world, as well as this enthusiastic invitation from Fred Busch to participate in this collection of letters. I am grateful for that. It will allow us to transmit part of our legacy to younger generations.

It is difficult to capture everything that has been said in a synchronous cut of each of our daily lives or, at best, at any given moment. For that reason, Freud gave importance to the psychoanalytic institution as a place in which dialogue with more experienced colleagues would train future analysts. Bolognini added to this by taking into account dialogue and exchange between colleagues as the fourth pillar of training. In other words, the transmission of psychoanalysis requires filiation.

In this regard, I am grateful to all of the I.P.A. community, as well as to our regional federation, F.E.P.A.L., and to my own society for the opportunity for these exchanges. However, I think that psychoanalysis today is not only the I.P.A. Being open to the contributions of other organizations, the university, and to colleagues, who do not have a defined affiliation, add value to my training. Ignoring them can only result in impoverishment.

Different cultures in distinct social and political systems and a plurality of theoretical models and practices add to the challenge of maintaining the core of our discipline. It is centrally based on the dynamics of the unconscious, child sexuality, and transference. As in the pioneer times of Freud, this plurality can be diluted and possibly lost.

One way of maintaining its vitality is, in my opinion, to encourage ourselves to rethink, to question each and every one of its concepts in light of the epochal changes as well as contributions from other disciplines. As an example: the Oedipus complex, in its strict Freudian version, is heatedly discussed today for proposing a heteronormative way out in relation to femininity.

I would like to highlight the importance that dialogue has had for me with those colleagues with more experience, as well as the sustained process of continuous training that I have undertaken and developed for more than 40 years. I have been doing this by attending weekly scientific sessions as well as regional and international congresses. Additionally, after forty years of practice, I completed a master's degree program in psychoanalysis at the Universidad del Salvador.

I am fortunate to have been trained in and to have been part of an institution that has been around for seventy-five years and has for the last forty-five years had a system of educational and academic freedom. Following the ambition of Angel Garma, one of the institute's founders, this has allowed for programs to be open to the interest of each colleague in training and to all those who desire to teach.

I recommend the experience, and if the institute in which you train does not have the aforementioned system, you can complement your teachings with people and topics of your interest at any time outside of the institute, even while looking for analysts for reanalysis or supervisors.

I think that my three personal analyses over many years has been the pillar of my own training. However, from my point of view, this is something that cannot be imposed; it should come from the motivation of anyone who feels a vocation toward our work.

I agree with Patrick Guyomard when he described the effects of the Antigone syndrome in our analytical societies. Endogamy favors deadly confinement. In my experience that also applies to groups analyzed by a small group of analysts with the same institutional robes, theoretical lines, etc., to the point of being considered "analytical families." Nothing could be further distant from what psychoanalysis is in the sense of crossing imaginary identifications and avoiding the effect of mass psychology.

Personally, I fulfilled the institutional requirement. Afterwards, however, I searched for a renowned analyst, although I did so outside of the institutional framework. I recommend that experience, also for supervising clinical cases.

Our training, as I said before, filiates us. However, we should be aware of the weight of imaginary identifications that, far from training us, create prostheses or false selves if we do not work permanently on disidentification.

In my experience, this should be favored by institutional devices allowing for the transmission of psychoanalysis, but those same devices should then be thought of for their possible unidentifying action.

This was at the core of my institutional efforts as it was in my own training, in spite of our knowing that it is difficult to implement when one is part of an institutional group that is based on these identifications. As well as the traditional devices, new ones, such as the Working Parties or multi-family psychoanalysis, have shown me their effectiveness in training. I would suggest participation in some of them as well and in the planning of new ones.

Regarding this matter, I would also like to convey to you the importance, in my case, that institutional work has had.

Early on, I journeyed through and experienced working in different areas, which led me to preside over my own society. I then chaired the Latin American Psychoanalytical Federation (F.E.P.A.L.). Following that, I became a member of the House of Delegates, the Board and the Executive Committee of the I.P.A., as well as several other committees, carrying out specific tasks in the latter.

In the same manner as the aforementioned dialogue between colleagues, institutional work, when it attends basically to its diversity, has, in my experience, disidentification potential. With this in mind, it is welcomed for those who enjoy carrying it out. We will also contribute to the development of our institutions, which are essential for the future of psychoanalysis, as they have been since the creation of the I.P.A. by Freud in 1910.

To finish, I would recommend experiencing community work in clinics, hospitals, schools, etc., since the future of psychoanalysis is, in my opinion, linked to taking its benefits to larger groups as well as thinking about its contributions to other disciplines and vice versa. Each of these areas has enriched me, making me rethink our theories and our practices.

Furthermore, if it is of interest to you and you are able to seek a university degree, either parallel or complementary to training, I recommend doing so. Not only will that offer you accreditation that analytical societies in general do not provide, it will also allow for the systematizing of the research of your topics of interest, thereby making them accessible to the entire academic community. Furthermore, within the boundaries of different disciplines, it will favor interdisciplinary dialogue, which is usually very productive and enriching to our theoretical and clinical practice. Personally, art, psychiatry, neurosciences, and institutions, in their interface with psychoanalysis, are still of interest to me when thinking about the clinic, which is the center of my professional activity.

I discovered my analytical vocation thanks to a professor of psychiatry who, while I was in medical school, led us to participate in meetings of a therapeutic community. My own analysis at that time helped me to strengthen my vocation. However, just as one of my supervisors in the psychiatry residency program had anticipated: 10 years following the completion of my analytical training, I began to understand what the practice of psychoanalysis was. Being able to tolerate that wait is part of what I suggest trying to develop. Institutional life and dialogue with other colleagues are invaluable aids for this objective.

We need to accept that there will always be something inaccessible but that over time we will be able to come closer to our object of study, though we will always privilege the possibility of mitigating the suffering of our patients over the search for the purity of our method.

A dear colleague once said that pure gold cannot be worked; it is stored in bank vaults and many people suffer deficiencies.

I hope these ideas help you with the work I trust enthuses you, as it has me to this day. It is very pleasing to do what one likes on a daily basis by following one's vocation.

12 Jay Greenberg
New York, U.S.A.

Dear Candidate,

I'll never forget the day, decades ago, that I learned I had been accepted by the institute I'd hoped to attend. After opening the letter—I told you it was a long time ago—I walked exuberantly and distractedly through the streets of my neighborhood, imagining a future that I had hoped for but that I had not dared to fully expect. It was a future in which I was guaranteed financial security or more, in which I could bask in social and professional prestige, and it was a future in which I would gain privileged access to—and mastery of—the secrets that explain the mysteries of what was going on with the people around me. And perhaps I would gain some access to my own mysteries as well.

In the years since that day, just about everything has changed, about the world, about me, about psychoanalysis as a profession and as an intellectual discipline, and about the place that psychoanalysis has in the world. The grandeur with which psychoanalysis was imbued (at least by me) is gone. It is possible to make a living in a practice that includes some psychoanalytic work, but that's about it. Professionally we are more likely to be outliers than superstars. And we have learned what every generation of analysts must learn, that psychoanalysis is not, after all, the royal road to anything; it is at best an arduous and perilous path that we and our analysands hope will lead to at least some relief from suffering and to a greater sense of self-awareness and personal freedom.

What surprises me about thinking of my life as a psychoanalyst in this way is that despite the tempering of my initial expectations and even despite the disillusionments, it all seems like good news, or at least most of it does. Of course, I wish that more of us could count on the opportunity to do psychoanalysis, and that there was wider public acceptance of its value. But I have also come to believe—strongly—that we are at our best when we think of ourselves as living on the social and cultural margins.

Saying this requires a word of explanation. We psychoanalysts are, without question, privileged, and, sadly, with only a few notable exceptions, we serve mainly the privileged. But I think that it is better for all of us, analysts and patients alike, that analysis no longer has the cache that it had in a golden age that we all imagine nurtured a previous generation and that may or may not ever have existed. I remember a supervisor from my internship in clinical psychology who divided the world into "the analyzed" and "the unanalyzed," a distinction that even at the time I thought of as pernicious and that reflects a kind of illusion that we have to reckon with in every treatment and perhaps in every moment of our personal lives as well. It is an illusion to which we are, of course, no less susceptible than our patients, or perhaps I should say than other patients.

With this in mind, let me say a few words about my own training at the William Alanson White Institute and how it has affected my sense of myself and of the work I do. The training would probably be characterized these days as "pluralistic," although the term and the concept weren't applied to psychoanalytic thinking until 1987, almost a decade after I graduated. Pluralism is a tricky idea; it can refer to an atmosphere in which there is openness to a range of perspectives through which organizations and individuals are willing to look at things. In some "pluralistic" institutes, both the organization and individual members are free to entertain different points of view, including points of view that are not native to themselves. Or pluralism can refer to a kind of cacophony, a sort of open-air bazaar in which adherents of different theories compete for business. All are tolerated, but there is no particular interest in working together or even in looking carefully at the convergences and difference among the various approaches.

My experience at White was of the latter kind of pluralism. Many ideas were allowed—we had Sullivanian interpersonalists, Frommian interpersonalists, object relations theorists, and even the occasional Kleinian or ego psychologist. That pretty much covered the spectrum of what was available in North America in those days, and it was very different from what was going on—or what we believed was going on—in "mainstream" institutes. In those institutes, as we understood them, there was a shared commitment to a particular way of understanding and of doing things and to a systematic way of teaching that point of view to candidates who, upon mastering that way, would be welcomed into a kind of inner circle. Membership would provide assurance that, however vexing the work might be, if they followed the rules they were on the right track and would be supported by others. And, of course, the inner circle would be a source of the occasional referral as well.

At White there was no conceptual "inner circle," no set of ideas that protected us from being told that we were getting it (whatever "it" was) absolutely wrong. From my vantage point as a candidate, there was a lot of noise and pressure and some stunning lacunae, all despite the high level of sophistication among my teachers and supervisors.

The cacophony has stayed with me over the years. Perhaps because of this, there's a kind of question I raise about what I do virtually every day; it takes the form of something like, "If this, what about that?" At its best, today's pluralism demands that we ask ourselves that kind of question, but despite the advocacy of various points of view, it wasn't quite asked in those days.

I think of that kind of pluralism in much the same way that I think about the changing status of psychoanalysis in contemporary culture. It's vexing to be sure.

It is commonplace to say that our clinical work exposes us to uncertainty on a daily basis; negative transference is a significant element of this, but it is far from the only one. Because of this, being invited into a social or professional in-group is tempting and can seem like a necessary reassurance. But if we can embrace the strain, it is in the lacunae that we are most likely to find our creativity and even ourselves.

I have tried to bring this sensibility to my work as a psychoanalytic educator. Every new generation stands on the shoulders of those who have gone before, but they also dig themselves out of the holes that we have dug for ourselves and for our profession. Our failures as much as our successes provide the culture within which new ideas grow.

In saying this, I don't want to imply that I am open-minded, saying that of myself seems both inaccurate and pretentious. I have my personal biases, and I would like to pass them on to you because despite recognizing that they are controversial, they do shape my beliefs about our work. For example:

I think that ordinary clinical work is the best source of data for developing psychoanalytic ideas. This means that while I might, on occasion, be interested in findings from neuropsychology, child observation, and other disciplines that I feel are adjunctive to my own, I don't feel any pressure to align psychoanalytic ideas with ideas derived from other observational vertices.

I don't believe that the clinical insights of our psychoanalytic ancestors should be discarded just because they worked within a conceptual system (libido theory, for example) or with a concept of the psychoanalytic situation (broadly speaking, a one-person model) that we consider archaic and even misguided. These were sophisticated, sometimes brilliant people who were passionate about psychoanalytic ideas and about their patients; we will always have a lot to learn from them despite the arrival of the fads to which psychoanalysis always has been and always will be susceptible.

I believe that being alive in the world is inherently and irreducibly difficult and that our minds are organized in ways that both protect us from the pain of facing those difficulties and prevent us from dealing effectively with them. For Freud, the Oedipus complex and its repression embodied that. Today we think of other, often related themes—loss, mourning, ambivalence, physical and emotional damage that has been perpetrated by others, the unpredictability of the future—and so on. In light of this, I continue to believe that, even as we learn more about the complex ways in which minds are formed and about the damaging effects of developmental trauma, we must continue to focus on the ways in which conflictual solutions to the challenges of being human compromise our ability to live freely and effectively.

As I write this, I realize that your psychoanalysis, the psychoanalysis within which you are growing up professionally, is very different than my own, even though it is also very much the same. I imagine, although I can't be sure, that you are less idealizing of the choice to pursue analytic training and that you're more realistic than I was about what a life as a psychoanalyst will be like. But that just covers the logistics. In a deeper way we share an ambition that can border on the grandiose: we aspire to make it possible for our patients to bear the unbearable. Perhaps the goal is illusory. Consider the extravagance of Freud's early claim, one that still shapes our sense of what we do, that his method could "make the unconscious conscious"! We should all think, long and hard, about what that means and about how close we come to achieving the goal.

But again, this doesn't strike me as entirely bad news. I doubt that it is or ever has been possible to be a psychoanalyst without feeling some regrets, about the pragmatic rewards of our profession, and, far more important, about the limits of the work itself. But living with and in the shortfall has forced me—I use the word advisedly—to remain open to and restless about myself. Perhaps one way to put this is to say that I am as moved by the incompleteness of my work as I am by what I learned in and from it. I am reminded of this incompleteness every day, when I am challenged by one or another of my patients who make it clear just how much I don't know about myself or about what I am doing. Oddly perhaps, it is never pleasant to notice this; the pleasure I take in the discovery is always retrospective and it invariably follows, perhaps even depends upon, experiences of shame or guilt. But when I recover from these feeling, I take satisfaction in becoming aware that there is always something over the next hill. I can't imagine a profession that drives this home as forcefully as psychoanalysis does, and my fondest hope for you is that you embrace and enjoy its challenges and its opportunities.

With best wishes for your future.

13 Heribert Blass
Köln-Düsseldorf, Germany

Dear Candidate,

You have chosen to become a psychoanalyst, and I imagine that your decision has emerged from various reasons, probably stemming from personal as well as scientific motives and goals. At least, this has been my starting point at the time of my application for psychoanalytic training, or education, almost forty years ago. I think that almost every psychoanalytical candidate in the world is motivated by a combination of the wish for a deeper personal understanding, including his or her own unresolved psychic conflicts, and a basic curiosity in human nature. In a way, this mixture of personal and scientific motives may have some links to the four existential questions raised by the German philosopher Immanuel Kant (1724–1804): "What can I know? What ought I do? What may I hope for? What is the human being?" Especially with respect to the last question, it was Sigmund Freud who widened the scope of scientific perception significantly when he discovered and described the importance of unconscious meanings and infantile sexuality for human beings in general. As a young student of medicine, I was fascinated by reading Freud's writings, and sometimes still today I love re-reading his essays and books, even if in the meantime we have modified or changed several of his concepts. But reading Freud, not as a dogma but as a methodic introduction in psychodynamic thinking and ideas, is one of my first recommendations for you as a psychoanalytic candidate. Freud's dialogic style conveys already the essence of the psychoanalytic encounter where two people meet in one room and begin to establish an emotional relation as a tool for the gradual comprehension of the patient's inner world. Of course, you, as every analyst, will be an active and observing participant in this process, and you will be challenged with your own personality and psychoanalytical competence. Both factors are strongly influenced by your primary psychoanalytical education and your subsequent experiences in the following years of working as a psychoanalyst. It will provide you with the chance of lifelong learning, which is one of the advantages of our profession.

You may have noticed that I am a German psychoanalyst. This means that I have made my training within the so-called Eitingon Model, whose pillars are the triad of training analysis, theoretical seminars, and supervision. A lot of other psychoanalytical societies all over the world follow this model, too, but there are also other models of training, like the so-called French Model and the Uruguayan Model. The main difference refers to the form of personal analysis because in the French Model you have to be in personal analysis for several years before you can apply for the "formation," while in the Eitingon model you can begin your personal and training analysis after admission to the training. Of course, you can already be in personal analysis, too, but it is not required for the three admission interviews. But you have to choose a training analyst, or your analyst has to be recognized as a training analyst, whereas in the French model the function of training analyst does not exist. I mention these differences because we have a lot of stimulating discussions about the advantages and disadvantages of the three models in the International Psychoanalytic Association and I don't know what model you are training in. However, I would like to emphasize that your analysis or training analysis should definitely be a personal analysis. It depends not least on yourself whether and how you use your own analysis for a deepened and enriching approach to your own psychic life, even if your own analyst of course contributes just as much to it. From my own experience I can tell you that I have always experienced my training analysis within the framework of the Eitingon Model as a personal analysis and, as far as I know, have not withheld any association for institutional reasons. Of course, this is only possible if there is enough trust, and you should pay attention to the extent to which you can develop enough trust to foster openness in your analysis. It seems important to me to keep one's own analysis free of institutional considerations and limitations, because only in this way can a personal educational process unfold. In my opinion, this is also possible in a training analysis. It is not without reason that in international psychoanalysis there are various further terms for training, such as "Education" in English, "formation" in French, "formación" in Spanish and "Ausbildung" in German. Psychoanalytic training is more than the development of skills, although, of course, the learning of skills is also required. Overall, however, it is a personal educational process that involves an in-depth knowledge of one's own person and the mental life of others. In this respect, psychoanalysis can also offer help in mental distress, even if Freud has warned against a "furor sanandi." But for me, the aspect of possible healing is an essential part of psychoanalysis, even if it is sometimes difficult to achieve.

    This leads me to an important experience that I had especially at the beginning of my training and which you may also know: Nowadays there are so many different theoretical and clinical concepts of psychoanalysis that I was confused at first. And at my institute there were also some training analysts who were in more or less fierce dispute with each other. That wasn't so easy for my own orientation in the beginning. Perhaps you are also concerned with the question of which view of psychoanalysis is the right one. But then I found out this was the wrong question. It became clear to me that there was not a single true psychoanalysis. Rather, there are different approaches to psychodynamic understanding of mental processes, and sometimes it can be very helpful to change perspective. Against this background, it has broadened my horizon to learn about many different psychoanalytical concepts. And finally, I came to the conclusion that this has enhanced my psychoanalytic competence. I learned not to rely on too many certainties but to accept a recurring sense of insecurity as the inevitable and conducive catalyst of the psychoanalytic process. In this sense, you should not only follow a single supervisor or a special group of supervisors or a psychoanalytic "school." Rather take time to find out which forms of psychoanalytic understanding and working are appropriate for you. By this I do not mean that anything goes. Indeed, there are core characteristics of psychoanalytic listening and participation, of conceptualizing mental content, and of finding appropriate interventions that you should acquire in the course of your training. But for the development of your own sense of psychoanalytic competence, I think it is very important that you fill these three frames with a diverse learning process and gradually put them together into a coherent concept for your own psychoanalytic orientation. My experience has been that learning from many masters ultimately increases the opportunity to think for oneself, which does not rule out being more convinced of one or the other teacher than another. But it needs its own process of working through what is offered to you as teaching.

This leads me to the question of anxiety in psychoanalytic education. I think anxiety is unavoidable. Of course, I was also anxious about how I and my psychoanalytic work would be assessed by my supervisors and my fellow candidates. And I was also worried if I could understand my patients well enough. I still have this worry every day. But I would like to distinguish between anxiety as a helpful signal of never being too sure and anxiety as a fear of disapproval and exclusion. The latter paralyzes one's own feelings and thoughts. So, I would like to encourage you to be anxious in a caring sense, but not anxious in the form of submission. Be open to your teachers, but do not follow them blindly. Rather dare to discuss difficult analytical processes with them and hopefully find common solutions instead of either submitting or superficially agreeing and then doing something else. This includes dealing with mistakes. We all make mistakes in our daily work; of course, the severity of our mistakes is decisive. When it comes to mistakes in the sense of misdemeanors, that is, the violation of sexual or aggressive boundaries, an ethical approach is essential. Mistakes, however, in the sense of an initial misunderstanding of our patients may mean something different. When we are ready to acknowledge our mistakes and think about them, we can learn from our patients. So, it can be an essential part of your supervisory process to talk also about your mistakes, even if it should be connected with a sense of shame. I have been ashamed as I realized some of my mistakes during supervision, for instance, were too superficial or not really addressing the patient's emotional needs or choosing an interpretation that hurts too much, but in general I was lucky to meet supervisors who were willing to offer an atmosphere of acceptance that enabled me to talk about my mistakes. In my own work as a supervisor today, I also try to provide an atmosphere that allows for the discussion of potential mistakes and their relevance to the psychoanalytic process. I hope that you can also find such confidence in the relationships with your supervisors so that you can dare to talk about your errors and potential mistakes. Of course, and once again, this depends on the attitude of the supervisor, too.

If you are able to develop trust in your supervisors and the Education Committee of your institute, you should also not be too afraid of evaluating your psychoanalytic training. I have participated for several years in a working party of the European Psychoanalytical Federation (E.P.F.), in which we dealt with the question of when a candidate is ready to qualify. I would like to remind you how important it is to find forms of interventions that are consistent with one's own observations and conceptual understanding, regardless of the basic psychoanalytic concept chosen. If you agree with your supervisors that these are important criteria for the success of your training, you also have an opportunity for self-evaluation, despite all the uncertainties and as well taking into account the fact that our explicit theories do not always correspond to our implicit theories. This is the reason why we need an inter-collegial exchange about our work both as analysts in training and after training.

I want to finish with a remark about the scientific nature of psychoanalysis. This could be important for you, especially if you are cooperating with members of other scientific disciplines. As psychoanalysts, we don't have to hide or deny our belonging to the scientific world, even if today we are more often attacked with the argument that we do not meet scientific requirements. Some of us are trying to defend our profession by saying that psychoanalysis is a kind of art. I can partially agree to this comparison. However, I would like to emphasize much more the distinction between connotative and denotative theories of science. Psychoanalysis, with its hermeneutic approach, corresponds to a connotative scientific theory and does not have to follow an exclusively natural scientific claim. But of course, we can and should also participate not only in qualitative but also in quantitative research. Comparative studies, which followed this approach, such as a large study on chronic depression in Germany under the direction of Marianne Leuzinger-Bohleber (2019), have shown that psychoanalysis does not have to shy away from scientific comparison.

I think this is a good message for you as a psychoanalytic candidate in our contemporary times. I wish you all the best for your further psychoanalytical development.

14 Elias and Elizabeth da Rocha Barros
Sao Paulo, Brazil

Dear Candidate,

When we look back at our professional career in Psychoanalysis, firstly as candidates and then as clinicians and training analysts, there are three lessons we feel were formative and critical to us, and which we wish to pass on to you: (1) the value of developing an openness to the different schools of Psychoanalytic thought; (2) that a psychoanalyst should always strive to foster his or her own sensibility—and that this is something one cultivates; and (3) the importance of truly understanding the specificity and uniqueness of Psychoanalysis and of the psychoanalytic attitude, perhaps the hardest lesson of all.

Although we are Brazilian, we studied in France for three years and then were trained at the British Psychoanalytic Society. This was not only by chance, but reflective of an interest we had in experiencing different psychoanalytic cultures. We have come to believe that investing in a *kaleidoscopic approach* to psychoanalysis—that is, learning to work with different models of the mind and becoming open to different cultures and traditions—is of fundamental importance. To lock oneself into one cultural tradition is a sure way to impoverish understanding.

The second lesson we learned and greatly appreciate is that a sensibility is something one construes. "Sensibility" is an enigmatic quality that simply cannot be taught in a formalized way nor organized into manuals and protocols. It certainly encompasses things such as lived experiences, feelings, contact with one's most inner being, a capacity to sense another person's inner world, a disposition to wander through one's memories and inner emotional history, and a recognition of phantasy life. Perhaps, crucially, sensibility depends on the way in which emotions are processed through thought, and the ability to readdress ideas and feelings through a variety of angles and points of view. One can cultivate this through building deep interpersonal bonds with friends, partners, and family members and through finding time for literature and culture in general. (*Do not* restrict yourself to the cultural productions of a single country! This will only work against the fostering of a sensibility.)

But we should deal in greater detail with the third lesson we learned: to truly understand what an analyst is and does. This entails an appreciation of what the "analytic attitude" is.

Amongst Freud's greatest achievements is the invention of a unique mode of human interaction: the *analytic relationship*, which is something that must be thoughtfully, carefully, and gradually established by means of the *analytic setting and attitude*. This is a critical and cornerstone idea within psychoanalysis: the analytic relationship does not spring forth in a "ready-made" way. Both analyst and patient must work together towards delineating this ever-evolving relationship.

Like learning a new language, the acquisition of an *analytic attitude* depends on becoming gradually exposed to, acquainted with, and immersed in a new and foreign semiotic world. None of the other professions ask of the professional so much in terms of personal discovery and transformation.

It should be noted that, even though psychoanalysis postulates that the unconscious is ever present and ever active, it does not always manifest itself or make itself available for psychoanalytic scrutiny and observation. Similarly, when the analyst detects unconscious meanings in the patient's material, this does not necessarily mean that the patient is ready to receive and understand the analyst's comments or interpretations of this material. Timing is of the essence here, and being able to attune oneself to the ebb and flow of these situations is something we only learn through practice and hard-won experience.

For the reasons above, we see great value in André Green's active concept of *placing oneself in the position of the analyst*. To do so is to remove oneself from the trappings of common sense and the flow of everyday conscious life. The position of the analyst is to achieve a peculiar mental state—one unique to psychoanalysis—marked by free-floating attention and by a frame of mind akin to a dream-like disposition to capture meanings and foster creative symbolic language.

To place oneself in the position of the analyst is also to make oneself keenly aware of both *transference*, *reverie*, and *countertransference* and of the implications of these interpersonal processes. To do so means to reconceive of oneself as not solely a receptor of communications and projections but also as the driving force and trigger that induces these communications and projections. This is not an easy concept to grasp and may seem alien and counterintuitive. The novelty brought out by the *psychoanalytic* conception of transference and countertransference is that processes of fusion and splitting are at play in such a way that the clear-cut distinction between "the patient" and "the analyst" captures but fleeting moments of the interaction. There are times where "patient-and-analyst" constitutes a fused dyad, for example. And communication is thus infused with complex resonances. For the analyst to conceive of him or herself as the trigger force that sparked a particular communication is an artifice that helps bring attention to the way in which unconscious material colors the analytic situation.

We believe that the transformation of discourse into clinical material was the most significant and difficult thing we learned in our training.

Let us try to convey this in action by means of a clinical vignette. Claudia (patient) arrives late at her session and quickly apologizes:

> P: "*Ugh, traffic was hell today. I'm 20 minutes late. I didn't want to miss a minute of my session.*"

We might at first think it only natural for the analyst to acknowledge that indeed traffic was unusually bad that day and console the patient by saying that the important thing is that she did arrive, that she showed that she valued her analysis through her apology and comments, and that all is not lost (after all, there are still 30 minutes left in the session). All of this would represent a way of listening to the patient's communications and of reacting to them in a way that is benevolent, tender, welcoming, and full of empathy. But psychoanalytic listening should not limit itself to the promotion of a heartwarming environment. The analyst should strive to amplify the possible resonances and meanings of experiences. One should be alert to the fact that even an offhand comment on lateness such as Claudia's initial remark might open a channel for the analyst and the patient to access deeper layers of unconscious material.

In the clinical situation above, the analyst decided to not give in to what would be a natural and comforting response. Instead of soothing Claudia's anxiety about her lateness, the analyst chose to let that anxiety take its course and see where it would lead through associations that might appear. Claudia then said:

> P: "*I wanted to come here today because I had an important conversation with my boyfriend. I told him that we have been together for a long time and that we need to decide what our aspirations are, where our relationship is headed. Something prevents him from truly understanding what I'm trying to tell him. He tells me we should just enjoy our time together, that if we decide to get married that decision should arise spontaneously. He tells me he isn't ready to make decisions about kids and marriage. I think this is all immaturity on his behalf.*"

This allowed the analyst to venture an observation/interpretation:

> A: "*The traffic jam today sparked in you feelings that might have been already simmering in your mind. You had something urgent to tell me and could not stand traffic keeping you from trying to grasp the meaning of the conversation you had with your boyfriend. A sense of urgency lingers within you: you need to understand where this relationship with your boyfriend is flowing to because you feel you don't have all the time in the world. You want to make some decisions and not live a life outside of time. You feel pressured to make choices and face obstacles that are not entirely under your control just as traffic is outside your control. These obstacles stop you from arriving at a place you want to be in life.*"

What we see here is the analyst embracing and absorbing a trivial comment on traffic as a direct communication to him/herself of potential unconscious content. This is, of course, a way of listening and grasping things that is a deliberate strategy of psychoanalytic technique. The patient's initial anxiety about being late was not dealt with on a concrete and conscious level. With patience, the analyst waited to see what would develop from Claudia's initial comments. And her language was explored and expanded symbolically: getting "stuck in traffic" became a metaphor for being "stuck in life," and missing out on her analytic hour became a metaphor for a feeling of time running out, of being late to arrive at a place in life she feels she wants to get to. So, we see that the analyst does not take language on its face value (the referential meaning of words) but on its connotative and evocative aspects as well.

Claudia reacts to the analyst's interpretation in the following way:

> P: "I am very worried about my father. He is ok, but yesterday he underwent a number of clinical exams that were not on his usual routine checkup examinations. Nobody has said anything to me, but I detect a heavy atmosphere at home: there is something they're not telling me, or something I'm not supposed to know in order for me not to get too worried or bother my parents with annoying questions. This has always been the case in my family. It isn't easy to distinguish between what is just a matter of not pestering me from unnecessary worries from what is an attempt to stop me from placing difficult questions that may raise the issue of death and dying."

In this communication we can perceive how we learned along our training and life to take into account that many dimensions of timing are present in a session. In a sense, the communication is indeed about worries regarding her father and her history with her parents (the "there and then"), but could these musings not also be understood in terms of things going on in the "here and now" of the session? From the point of view of the "there and then," Claudia might be speaking of and reliving a number of enigmatic and/or traumatic experiences—an overwhelming feeling of "not knowing," of a mystery lingering in the air, a sense of the presence of the fear of death, of being treated like a child who cannot handle the difficult aspects of life, the dread of losing her father etc.—that were/are indigestible, both in the sense of "a hard pill to swallow" and in the sense of "not being metabolized" (not finding adequate means for mental representation). From the point of view of the "here and now," Claudia might be alluding to an encroaching sense of danger (a possible serious illness connected with a relationship that might not survive), a feeling of her vitality being "diseased" and mortally wounded by broken dreams, of having her capacity to think being drowned out by uncertainty and mental noise.

15 Daniel Jacobs
Brookline, U.S.A.

Dear Candidate,

I've divided my letter to you into sections. Let's start with:

Not knowing

Your analytic education is an exercise in uncertainty—and in learning to tolerate that "not knowing." Not knowing what your analyst *really* thinks of you. Not knowing how you will pay off your educational loans. Not knowing whether you will have an analytic practice after so much effort, an effort that leaves you wondering if you should be at home with your family instead of at seminars. Uncertainty is the rule of candidacy. Competing psychoanalytic theories can also confuse as much as they clarify. And how about the lack of clarity as a beginner in how to analyze? How does one even get to do analysis, find a patient who is willing to undergo intensive treatment? It seems to me that many of you may be taking classes and discussing theory and technique without having an analytic patient, without perhaps having been in analysis long enough yourself to appreciate the process. That makes it hard for some of you to have the necessary conviction that a patient could benefit from an analysis. Without personal knowledge springing from your own experience, it is hard to convince another of its value. And if one has an analysand, that raises uncertainty as to whether he or she will stay in analysis long enough to provide the needed credits toward graduation.

I haven't even mentioned the inevitable feelings of envy and competition in relation to other candidates and faculty. At any institute, gossip and rumor abound. What is one to believe? For example, a classmate at my Institute bought a sports car that coincided with the sudden ending of his training analysis and candidacy. There were rumors his analyst had given him an ultimatum: "choose analysis or the car." Others wondered if my classmate was being irresponsible, taking on an additional expense while being behind on payments to his analyst. Or maybe, for the candidate, the sports car was a preferable form of treatment. We were unsure what to believe.

Shame

When I was a candidate, I had a patient who suddenly announced he was going to terminate his analysis the following week. He didn't, but I was stunned by his announcement. Not only because I realized I had paid too little attention to a growing negative transference, but because I was amazed by his degree of apparent freedom. He had no connection to analysis other than seeing me. He was not in the mental health field: he knew no one in our field, and he had told no one he was in analysis (a secrecy, I later understood to be the effect of an intergenerational transmission of trauma). He could walk away and no one but he, my supervisor, the progression committee, and I would ever know. My patient's unencumbered freedom to choose seemed very different from the way I felt as a candidate. If I left my training, I would have to explain my exit from the institute to classmates, friends in the field, and supervisors. And the thought of changing training analysts has its own uncertainties. Like in a second marriage, if you are unhappy again, there's definitely something wrong with *you*. It's easy to feel that if something goes amiss, it is somehow the fault of your inadequate analysis, your adolescent rebelliousness, or your incompetence.

The key to getting though training and beyond is to keep an eye on that sense of shame. Shame at what you don't know. Shame about, at times, wanting to quit the institute and perhaps the field. Shame when a patient leaves you. Shame may prevent you from writing up your cases, because you feel you are a beginner and as such will be exposed to criticism. (Not that experience spares you from that!) Shame may make you hesitant to speak up in class or ask a question you feel is too simple. (They rarely are.) Or you may feel shame in not having found a case or in losing one. Shame is often defended against through criticism of others—the institute, supervisors, colleagues—or through withdrawal of investment, or through dismissing theorists who are too difficult to understand. I hope you will find ways to talk with other candidates about the possibility of feeling shame during analytic education. It is often too private an emotion.

Value

With all that I have said, you may well wonder, "Is analytic training worth the time, the expense, the nights away from family?" My answer is emphatically, "Yes!" Psychoanalysis is one of the best ways of countering "the forgetting of being." It helps you understand the ways in which you limit our own humanity and how you can deny your own freedom of thought, feeling, and expression.

I have had three different analytic treatments, each incomplete in its own way, each teaching me a great deal about myself, and each beckoning me to keep enlarging my understanding of myself and others. Each analysis conveyed to me the value of continued self-examination. To give your patients the instruments for self-analysis seems to me one of the greatest gifts you can bestow. My first analysis helped me clear up conclusions arising from childhood experiences and the conscious and unconscious fantasies about mind and body that arose from them. That analysis helped me decide to go to medical school and become an analyst. My second analysis, a training analysis, focused almost entirely on my Oedipal conflicts. We counted the ways I retreated from them. It proved very helpful but did not focus sufficiently on traumatic infantile experiences that helped shape those Oedipal conflicts. It took a woman analyst to address those early pre-Oedipal experiences. Each analyst brings his or her own perspective: there is no shame in changing analysts or going back for another round (hard to imagine when you are a candidate). I tell you this in hope you will hold psychoanalysis lightly, always being free to ask how certain theories or techniques, certain supervisors, and your own training analysis are helping you, but also, what the limits of each are.

Case Reports

Of course, you will be expected to "write up your cases." This expectation becomes a major stumbling block for some. The fear of exposure and concern about criticism leads many to procrastinate. There can be so many rationalizations for delay: no time, no ability, no wish to do it because you think it a requirement that should be eliminated. I have always been suspicious of the suggestion that a candidate's report is confusing because he or she lacks "writing ability." Very often, the difficulty lies in the candidate's difficulty in thinking clearly about the case. One of the goals of analytic training, it seems to me, should be capacity to clearly explain one's work verbally and in writing. That should be a requirement for graduation. Writing mentors should be available for those who are struggling. There is no shame in being asked to re-write a case. Disappointing? Yes. Aggravating? Yes. But you can learn a great deal by rewriting about where you are confused or where there is not enough evidence for your hypotheses.

Perhaps the difficulty some candidates have in writing is, paradoxically, that they approach it too seriously, plowing through their voluminous process notes in search of inspiration. Here is my advice: try treating your write-up like a play or a symphony. Theater: Two strangers meet in an office. Each wants something from the other. What happens next? How does their relationship deepen or does it? As they continue to get to know one another, how does that shape what they say to one another? When do they fight and for what reason? When do they make up and how? And what has happened to each before the curtain comes down. You are writing a clinical report that is akin to writing a play or a short story with a beginning and middle, if not an end. Then once the arc of the story is clear, you can embellish with process material. Or you may compare it to a symphony: An opening theme announced by your patient, its development with the surprising arrival of the horn section or kettle drums, and then the bridge to a second theme, and so forth.

Whatever you write, it will be your own creation based on observation and your own psychic make-up. Even the best report, like a dream, is an invention to be met with a willing suspension of disbelief. A case report, to my mind, resembles a poem with its own truths—"an imaginary garden with real toads in it," as Marianne Moore wrote. Of course, suspension of disbelief is not the same as the incredulity that I sometimes feel in reading our literature. On occasion, the descriptions of patients' difficulties and their resolution seem to tax my willingness to believe. These accounts have no rough, real sharp edges, no splinters felt under one's skin. Little is left unfinished or still dangerous. These reports become highly varnished pieces of immoveable furniture that sit stubbornly in one's mind, blocking the way to further understanding. The symphony unfortunately is only a pop tune, the psychoanalytic drama: a teatro buffo. Sharing your work with others can help prevent that from happening.

I have found giving drafts of my writing to others to critique invariably improves it. When I wrote up my cases for certification, I met with four colleagues for a year, meeting every other week. Each of us, in rotation, gave the others one of their case reports to read before our meeting. When we met, the report was critiqued. When all had presented, we circled back to the original presenter to see how he did with his revisions. Round and round we went, each of us presenting 3 cases. It was a marvelous experience. As we talked about our cases, it became clear each of us had a unique approach that could be characterized: perhaps a consistent emphasis on pre-Oedipal material, or an avoidance of the patient's anger or a quickness to interpret aggression, etc. Our characteristic way of analyzing became apparent and was very helpful in recognizing our strengths and limitations. I am currently in a writing group with four senior analysts that has met for years. We help one another prepare papers for publication. We have learned to be honest without being hurtful. That ongoing support for the difficult work of creation has been invaluable.

Getting Involved

At the time I trained, mercifully for me, candidates were not invited to be on Institute committees. I could keep myself out of the politics of the institute, its administration, and its rivalries. Committee work can initially be seductive. It is a way of feeling like an analyst, without having analyzed many patients. (I later succumbed to lots of committee work, some of which I enjoyed, much of which I regret.)

It is harder, I think, to become a good analyst without a lot of experience. As a candidate and after graduation, I made income secondary to opportunity to immerse myself in practice, taking on as many analytic patients as I could at whatever fee they (and I) could afford. I think it best to focus your efforts on treating patients, reading the literature, being analyzed, and obtaining supervision. Concentrate on building your practice. Committee work will always be there.

While in candidacy, I found a small group of fellow classmates I could trust and formed study groups with them. I learned as much from peers over time as I did from supervisors. And their support and friendship helped in the stresses of candidacy. As a candidate and after, I began to attend meetings of the American Psychoanalytic Association. Feeling like an outsider, at first, I decided to join small study groups where I met colleagues from other institutes across the country. They provided broader perspectives on psychoanalytic education and practice. They also became a source of referrals.

Authenticity

You can only be you. Don't try to be anyone else—not your teacher, your supervisor, or your analyst. Listening to and learning from them is one thing; being them is another. It is hard in the midst of learning a new skill to feel confident enough not to imitate. For some, it is a necessary first step. Over time, through your analysis, by reading, thinking, discussing cases, and meeting with other analysts, you will develop an authentic analytic voice, your own particular way of conducting analyses and talking with patients. And no one can copy it. Your own analytic way of being will develop over time. It took me quite a while to find my own voice and, for better or worse, one that is different in many ways from that of those who first taught me years ago. For the most part, I have enjoyed the journey to becoming who I am. I hope you will take pleasure in your own analytic venture. Best wishes.

16 Eike Hinze
Berlin, Germany

Dear Irina, dear Mark,

It is a strange feeling to write as an old German analyst (79 years old) to an unknown candidate, but it's a challenging and fascinating experience, too. I can let my fantasy float and go back through the decades of my psychoanalytic life. Do I have anything to say that might be helpful for you, Irina, Mark?

To express my thoughts in a differentiated way, it would be much easier for me if I could write in my own language, German. But English has become the world language of science. So, if you are not a native English speaker, in order to communicate with colleagues from other countries under the umbrella of the I.P.A., you have to feel at ease in this language. I know many instances of psychoanalytic groups where colleagues stayed silent because they did not speak English sufficiently well or because they felt ashamed to express their thoughts in what they thought was very bad English. I am familiar with these feelings myself, and it took me a long time and much effort to overcome them. A much-esteemed colleague of mine used to open international conferences with the encouraging statement that the official conference language was "bad English." It takes a certain amount of shamelessness to express one's differentiated thoughts in a foreign language. Writing these sentences, I still feel slightly uneasy, even at my advanced age, when I am aware that I could express my thoughts in German more elegantly.

Of course, if you, Irina and Mark, happen to be native English speakers or otherwise fluent in this language, these considerations do not apply. In this case please stay aware of language difficulties your colleagues who are not native English speakers may experience. And learn another language. Getting acquainted with a foreign language immensely helps to empathize with the special flavor psychoanalysis has in this cultural and linguistic realm. You will learn the different approaches to psychoanalytic practice and theory. Thereby you will get acquainted with central questions and problems of contemporary psychoanalysis. "Is there one psychoanalysis or many?" (Wallerstein). I invite you to seek contact and exchange with international colleagues. This inevitably has the consequence of being confronted with different ways of practicing psychoanalysis and theorizing about it. On the one hand, this encounter is an enlivening and enriching experience. On the other hand, however, it may lead to confusion and helplessness. "Does anything go?" (D. Tuckett). Is there any solid ground of our science? One way to escape this dilemma may consist in rigidly adhering to a specific psychoanalytic school, most often the one that is the preferred version in your institute.

Here I would like to express my second advice. You are still young. Stay alive, curious, and critical. Insist on these prerogatives of young age. Don't stop questioning theoretical inconsistencies you encounter in your training; keep questions alive. I know that learning the practice of psychoanalysis entails identification with one's teachers. Developing these building blocks is an indispensable element of learning. But these identifications need not be lifeless stones in a flow of development. They should be cornerstones in a process of development. Fixed and lifeless identifications may lead to the well-known adherence to certain psychoanalytic schools. They finally paralyze free and creative thinking. In my view, thinking in terms of "schools" belongs to the past and smells of medieval scholastic thinking. Don't be discouraged if psychoanalysts of your institute identify critical thinking with the acting out of unresolved personal conflicts in the course of your personal analysis. One of the greatest dangers threatening psychoanalysis from within is rigidity of thought.

Delving into psychoanalysis and the unconscious world is a life-long challenging experience. That does not mean to concentrate obsessively on psychoanalysis. On the contrary, leading an extra-analytic life with other interests and activities is indispensable for enjoying psychoanalysis as an enduring journey into the world of the unknown. Life as a candidate can be very hard and exhausting. You have your daily job as a medical doctor or psychologist. You may be living in a partnership, within a family with children. Perhaps you work scientifically in the university. At the same time, you have to be in a time-consuming personal analysis, attend theoretical seminars, and finally, conduct your own supervised analyses. Psychoanalysis is an impossible job, as Bion wrote. This applies even more to psychoanalytic training. Being engulfed by the strenuous life as a candidate sometimes may seem not to leave any space for other thoughts, activities, or initiatives. On the other hand, being immersed in the exploration of your own unconscious may liberate energies and open up new internal spaces giving your life new directions and dreams. I think you should try to maintain and develop your interests and activities outside psychoanalysis, although the training may devour so much of your available time and energy. We need friends, partners, family, and a social circle that is not exclusively psychoanalytically oriented. Also, do not neglect your body. It is not very encouraging to observe aging analysts who cultivate their back pain and other syndromes connected with low physical activity. We have a sedentary profession and need some physical compensation.

There is a specific characteristic of psychoanalytic training compared with other academic curricula. We are embedded in a group of other candidates. This sometimes creates a bit of an adolescent atmosphere combined with other regressive aspects of psychoanalytic training. In these years of intense personal development, we often get to know each other thoroughly. In my life, deep relations and friendships had their foundation in this period. Although our profession is characterized by a somewhat solitary life not distracted by many activities other professions offer, we are in a rather specific way engaged in constant group activities. This is also true for training. But during our whole life as an analyst we depend on well-functioning groups to sustain and develop our analytic attitude and balance. As there is no baby without a mother, as Winnicott stresses, there is no analyst without a psychoanalytic group in which he is embedded. Often the colleagues of your own institute form the core of these groups. But as I already mentioned, it is extremely valuable to look beyond the horizon of your own group.

After the long years of training, there comes the time of your final evaluation. You will be elected member of your society and of the I.P.A. Notwithstanding the sometimes seemingly eternal years before, all of a sudden you are thrown into a different aggregate state. You feel joy, satisfaction, relief, but you may also experience kind of a void. You no longer belong to the group of candidates. You have not yet found, however, your way into the identity of a member. I still remember this moment very intensely. Which aims shall I now follow, and which trajectories lie ahead of me? For so many years the aim of successfully passing the final assessment structured my analytic life. And suddenly I did not see anything ahead of me. My personal solution was the following. After some time of retreating into my practice, I started to take over functions in my society, began to teach, and wrote my first papers. Psychoanalysis offers so many opportunities for collaborating in various scientific and professional activities. Such activities can be extremely rewarding. Of course, this means a lot of work. But this is an indispensable aspect of our life as psychoanalysts. We need feedback by our colleagues. Without this constant input, we run the risk of drying out and losing our creativity and psychoanalytic competence. This sounds a bit threatening but should not obscure the fact that being a psychoanalyst, although it may sometimes be burdensome, can be a satisfying life-long experience of meeting in-depth oneself and other human beings.

17 Alan Sugarman
San Diego, U.S.A.

Dear Candidate,

My career as a psychoanalyst ranks as one of the two most gratifying aspects of my adulthood. Being a father is the only one that ranks higher. As a candidate, you are just beginning your career as a psychoanalyst. I assume that you are excited about it. Otherwise there would be no reason to make all the sacrifices and to put in all the hours that candidacy involves. Inevitably, you are also worried about many things. Some of the things that I worried about were my mental stability, my clinical ability, my capacity to develop a psychoanalytic practice, paying for training, the time training took away from my family, and so on. Please be assured that not all your worries stem from neurotic conflicts or primitive anxieties. Many of them seem universal to being a psychoanalytic candidate. Despite the reality basis of many of these worries, however, it is important that you find ways to manage them so that they do not interfere with your wish to become a psychoanalyst and to have a psychoanalytic practice.

What I am about to say is not meant to minimize the reality of the emotional, financial, and temporal costs of training. Training does take time, it does stir up a multitude of difficult emotions, and it is quite expensive. Nonetheless, I have watched classmates and colleagues of similar talent and life circumstances become so focused on these issues that their approach to training, and later their practice, ultimately prevented them from having the sort of career they wanted. Many say, and it is true, that psychoanalytic training makes one better at everything one does clinically, not just clinical psychoanalysis. Nonetheless, most of us seek the training because we hope to spend a significant part of our workday practicing psychoanalysis. I have always spent at least half my day doing analysis since I was a candidate by not allowing these external realities to interfere with my goal.

For example, the time demands are truly daunting. Nonetheless, I embraced candidacy and being active in my local institute from the time I began training. I volunteered for committees or projects, attended local scientific meetings, and took part in the various social gatherings at my institute. My wife and I had just relocated to San Diego when I began my formal training. For us, the institute became a home where we made friends, found support, and even found friends for our toddler son with the children of other candidates. Making my wife feel as much a part of the institute as me helped her not to mind the time I devoted to it. To be sure, I did set some limits. Finding that doing concurrent adult and child training was taking too much time away from my son, I took a leave of absence from the child program. To my surprise, the leaders of the program modified the seminar demands after a few months so that I could rejoin the program. I do not think they would have been so surprisingly accommodating if I had not already demonstrated my investment in the institute. The moral for you in your training is that you will only get back as much as you put into it.

Putting in time also means attending the national meetings of A.Psa.A. In addition to time, attending these meetings costs money, both for travel and from lost income. Nonetheless, the meetings have played a major role in my education and subsequent career. *Attending these meetings exposes one to orientations and perspectives one might not learn at one's home institute*. Most of our institutes have one prevailing orientation and way of doing things that a candidate may assume is the manner in which every analytic institute thinks or operates. It is truly eye opening to find that there are many ideas about theory, practice, and training out there in the broader psychoanalytic world. This principle holds even more true for attending I.P.A. congresses. But international travel can be even more daunting during candidacy in terms of time and money. It is worthwhile, however if you can manage it. Several past presidents of A.Psa.A in my generation began attending I.P.A. congresses as candidates.

Attending these meetings also surrounds you with others who have the same level of excitement about thinking and practicing psychoanalytically as you do. For decades, I found that I always seemed to convert a therapy case to an analytic one after attending national meetings. There was something about the excitement and stimulation in the formal and informal discussions that allowed me to get past my resistances and preconceived ways of thinking about my patients. I could then see some of them in a new light. My technique also improved because of these meetings. It is not uncommon for all of us to fall into certain unexamined ways of working with and thinking about each patient as we go through the day. Attending the meetings and listening to a great deal of clinical material, presented by many other analysts, inevitably leads to the self-reflection that makes us all better analysts. Finally, attending meetings often acts as a networking device also. Analysts from other parts of the country frequently have to refer patients in your hometown. It has always been common for me to receive calls (and more recently emails) asking if I can see a patient who is a family member of a patient of the analyst living elsewhere. Such referrals tend to be more open to an analytically oriented treatment than the run-of-the-mill person contacting us for consultation. Thus, attending these national meetings is an excellent way to make others think of you as someone to whom they can refer.

This last point bears on another lesson I learned and would like to pass on. Having an analytic practice is never easy, and it always seems like the past generation had an easier time finding analytic patients. There is some truth to this fact as cultural and societal changes seem always to go in a direction away from the psychoanalytic approach we all love and find to be more effective with our patients. Nonetheless, an analytic practice remains obtainable even today so long as one keeps in mind the truism that analytic patients do not call us, saying they want psychoanalysis. Rather, people call us wanting help. *It is incumbent upon us to show them how and why psychoanalysis is the treatment of choice.* Usually this involves beginning to see them at a less than analytic frequency and deepening the treatment gradually. As this occurs, increasing to analytic frequency happens naturally. One also must be able to emotionally connect with patients and explain to them, *in plain English,* how you understand the causes of their problems and why your treatment approach has the greatest likelihood of helping them. It is essential that you do not burden yourself unnecessarily with a blank screen approach that comes across as cold, distant, and unempathic. It also is necessary that you learn to translate our complicated theoretical jargon into everyday language. I find the intrapsychic conflict model easy to translate and use to show patients how conflicts between their wishes, anxieties, and conscience contribute to the symptoms and behaviors that trouble them. Others might find other models more useful. It does not matter what model you use so long as you are adept at translating it into words that resonate with your patients.

These ways of developing analytic patients will not be useful, however, unless patients are calling you. That leads to another tip. Do not sit in your office and wait for the phone to ring. Marketing is essential. *We all have different ways to do it, but it is essential that you get your name in front of others as a capable and available clinician.* Today, websites and social media are being embraced by the younger generation. My younger colleagues report great success at gaining referrals by using technology in this way. For me, my most comfortable way to market myself was to give talks or to teach. I always presented talks to parent groups about topics of interest to them. Likewise, I began to offer extension courses at my institute when I was a candidate. These activities proved quite successful for me. Others prefer socializing with large networks, relying on the truism that people tend to refer to their friends. It does not matter what approach you use so long as it fits comfortably with your personality. The crucial thing is to make yourself known to a broad segment of the potential patient population.

Let me now switch to problems to watch out for in training. One of my biggest regrets was the pressure I felt to conform to certain ways of thinking and working in order to have the approval of the powers inside my local institute. During my candidacy, I wrote two analytic papers extending a current theoretical model of interest to me. Unfortunately, my instructors were highly critical of this model, and of me for preferring it to the ego psychological model emphasized at my institute. Consequently, I put those ideas aside after the two papers were published and came back to writing, using the preferred model. In the last five years, those early ideas of mine have become quite current in psychoanalytic developmental thought. It appears that I actually was quite prescient thirty years ago. *This discouragement of innovation is a serious problem in psychoanalytic education.* Do your best to think critically and stay true to yourself if you believe that your ideas hold water. Obviously, you need to do so without being provocative or closed to other ways of thinking about things. But if you have taken time to truly understand what your instructors are teaching you, and you think that your different ideas have merit, ask that they be discussed on their merit, not just dismissed.

The same holds for ways of working clinically. We all have different personalities, and it is necessary to work with patients in a way that fits with who we are. Some of us are quite at home with a blank screen model, and others need to talk and interact more. It is possible to remain technically neutral even if one departs from strict silence or anonymity. Find the way that works with who you are. Otherwise, you risk being experienced as distant, aloof, or uncomfortable by your patients. I remember feeling that I could finally work the way that felt right once I was appointed a T.A. As with my writing, I had felt forced into a way to work that seemed unnatural and constraining. I became a much better clinical analyst once I no longer had to be approved of by authorities. Be prepared to explain to your supervisor that you are uncomfortable with working in the way they prescribe if your way seems to still fit within a psychoanalytic framework. Supervisors, in general, are becoming more tolerant of candidates thinking independently these days as we clarify more the most useful ways to supervise.

Obviously, the caveat about the above is to be sure that your way of working is not simply a way to enact unresolved conflicts. The best way of being sure is to immerse yourself in your personal analysis. It is important that you find an analyst with whom you feel comfortable being brutally honest about the workings of your mind as well as the ways you work with your patients. Unfortunately, this does not always happen in one's training analysis. If it doesn't, seek another analysis when you can. For me, my third analysis, when I was already an established analyst, is the one that truly helped me to know and master my deepest conflicts. As expected, my clinical work improved remarkably. For this reason, my parting words will be to remember Freud's suggestion that we should all be reanalyzed periodically. Do not shy away from another analysis if you find that you are getting in your own way at any point in your analytic career.

18 Paola Golinelli
Bologna, Italy

Dear Candidate,

Now that you have listened to numerous words, theories, and clinical cases, who knows if what you are left with as a sort of everyday vade mecum will be made up of some simple recipes, to keep you company, to console you in the—let's hope!—many hours at work.

People say that what sticks in our heads from many analyses, and perhaps from one's own training, is sometimes an apparently banal phrase, or a small gesture. There was the analysand who recounted how she remembered only one interpretation from her long analysis. Having reported in a session, almost in tears, how she had involuntarily torn a blouse to which she was particularly attached, her analyst had whispered in a small voice, "*There are excellent tailors who know how to sew up even the worst tears.*"

Of my own training I remember the gratifying atmosphere around the work of developing fundamental experience for then going on to practice a profession that I have always thought is fabulous, even if also "impossible" on many accounts.

I remember times of enthusiasm, but also those of discouragement when the patient's fatigue seemed to add itself on top of my own.

During a session with my second patient under supervision, I found myself thinking that I could feel he was greatly troubled, and I would have liked to say something of a useless, consolatory nature, the kind of thing I would have liked to hear myself. That was a thought to keep hidden from my supervisor, as if to say, "It's fine for you to tell me how it's done, but if you only knew how much trouble we're having, two little children, poor Hansel and Gretel here alone, frightened by our own ambitions, far away from our goal." Like Gretel, I would have liked to take him by the hand and comfort him, to tell him that we would have made it: we two young ones in a world of expert and apparently confident adults, escaping from the marzipan house of the witch-theory, who at that time was not placating my anxiety nor telling me what to do with him.

Every analytic couple encounters emotional squalls along their analytic path, alternating moments of collaboration and times of various modulations in their asymmetry. Every couple has an experience of solitude, even if its members know they can turn to someone more expert than they, the supervisor, and, further on in their professional life, to colleagues.

During the years of my training, I found myself thinking that at times the work of supervision (and analytic work, too) seems like the relationships we see narrated in the classics or in initiation films, where the old cowboy passes on his knowledge to the young one, never failing, free from momentary failings of the wisdom and skills acquired in the field, and the young one follows him faithfully, apart from some inevitable and "healthy" intemperance.

However, at various times it did happen that I felt more in the conditions described in some old westerns when, having to cross through enemy territory, the protagonists must put themselves in the hands of a native guide, even if he is suspected of being two-faced. He is in touch with the "hated" parts of his Self, while unable to express himself in the noble language of white adults. And yet the travelers will have to stay on his good side, because he has direct knowledge of the territory, he notices tracks and sniffs the air, and he knows the native language, which may be rougher but is still essential for getting in touch with the darker, more regressed parts of the Self. Sometimes there is no other way to get out of the narrows and reach the yearned-for destination than that of trusting in your "native" Self, accepting that you can make mistakes, that you might meet with your supervisor's momentary disapproval, with all the fears of unfortunate consequences that come from it. Sometimes there is no other way to save one's own personal creativity and start using it. There may be times then when one feels like the inexperienced explorer in new territory, who has to trust others and entrust oneself, and other times when one feels rather rough-hewn, but present at the front line, next to one's patient and needing to choose a path, without too much hesitation.

As a candidate, it seemed to me (but I believe that at that time it was a very common experience among my training colleagues) that learning analytic technique meant basically to acquire the skill of doing interpretations—for us initiates, that mysterious and marvelous thing, which to our inexperienced eyes represented the real analytic "instrument." Much time has gone by since then, not only for me, but also for analytic theory and technique. If I were to say now which is the analytic tool *par excellence*, I would have to go on at length and include more than one.

I will turn once again to a story and use it as a metaphor—an old science fiction story. It is lowbrow literature, full of utopias and dystopias. I still love to read this genre, along with "high" literature and art in general, as they are all indispensable ingredients for stocking the storehouse one can draw from when doing analytic work. They have often come to my rescue, especially in moments of doubt or uncertainty. The story tells of a deserted wasteland that offers no more means of sustenance nor guarantees for the future. An old grandmother entrusts her grandchildren with a chest, which she has always had at her side; it is her legacy. To find a new land, they will have to endure an arduous journey, but they must never abandon the chest, for any reason. The grandchildren depart; they encounter adventures of every kind, conflicts and fatigue. They are tempted to abandon the chest, to open it, to destroy it. They get to the point of desperation at times, when the temptation to open the chest is titanic. They end up cursing it, because it gets in their way, it is heavy, it slows down their progress. They fantasize about its contents. And yet they never betray the promise made to their grandmother, despite the burning curiosity to know what the chest contains: might there be treasures enough to make up a fortune, or just a dying old woman's odds and ends? Only upon arriving safely will they open it. It is, of course, empty, but by now it is clear that the charge of transporting it has saved them.

Every analyst takes on the burden of the old grandmother's legacy and implicitly accepts that along the journey, theories that were once loved may later appear to be obsolete, or even "dead," but the important thing is to carry out the task.

What it is that each of the pair—donor and heir—puts in the chest will be subject matter for that unique and unrepeatable analysis which that specific pair will have done in that given moment, but I believe that each one, the patient and the analyst, will include their necessary illusion, hope, and desire. On the patient's side, there will be the desire to re-read their own history with a relatively less-burdened approach to the future, compared with before and previously unresolved tangles. On the analyst's side, there will be a revisiting of their theories as well of him or herself, leading to a rediscovery of the meaning in being an analyst and the desire to continue being one while negotiating its ideal aspects. Accessing all the personal creativity the analyst can conjure up, the journey will be brought to its end. That treasure chest we call the unconscious, "an infinity inside us" to call up Matte Blanco, is ubiquitous, mutable, dynamic. It is born again of its own ashes; it is never definitively discovered or known; and it re-presents itself over and over again, with new nightmares, both private and collective ones. Our task is to try to decipher them.

Good luck, dear candidate, and *buon lavoro*!

19 Allannah Furlong
Montreal, Canada

Dear Candidate,

The first time I met my analyst, I realized I wanted her to become my analyst. She gave one or two lectures in a course on psychoanalytic psychotherapy I was taking. In a strange twist, we even shared a taxi with other car-less participants part of the way home on one of those evenings. Paul-Laurent Assoun (1995) claims that in a "coup de foudre," there is a thought that is experienced as an affect. The French "coup de foudre" better describes the thunderstruck daze I was in than the English "love at first sight." This emotion is carried by a hidden anterior thought relative to a lack in the self, such that the subject discovers an answer to a question she or he was unaware of asking. It was probably some weeks or months later that I screwed up the courage to ask for a consultation. After she said scarcely anything in response to my initial outpouring, I remember another taxi ride back to my hospital office, in a state of shock, convinced that she was going to reject my appeal to become her analysand.

Looking back on it since, Assoun's intuitions ring true. I can see how incredibly narcissistic my choice was: she seemed to be everything I wanted to be. For a long time, each detail of her appearance and behavior that surprised me was always a sign of difference from the idealized mirror in which I wished to hold her: blond rather than brunette, left rather than right-handed, scrawly endorsements of my monthly checks (back in the days when banks used to return cancelled checks), dog rather than cat owner, a maternal tongue other than mine. It is also ironical—given how important her body was to me—though indicative of how transference can color perception, that it was not until years after I had completed my analysis that I "saw" that she had a quite generous figure.

I consider myself lucky to have been able to choose my analyst, to have been able to freely follow the folly of my idealization and fixation with someone who accepted to be "used" by me (Winnicott, 1968), or as Roussillon (2009) would put it, with someone who agreed to be an "object malleable," an object I could distort in symptomatic ways in order to better perceive my neurotic motivations. In the institute I eventually joined, a candidate's personal analyst did not have to be a training analyst. In larger institutes, particularly nowadays where various "minorities" may have some representation, enough variety of training analysts (in sex, in color, in speech, in character, in sartorial choice, in cultural background) can allow freer rein to the unconscious motivations driving the choice of one's analyst. But in my youth, in our relatively small town, there was only one female training analyst, and I did not want to be her analysand. It was clear that the person of the analyst was as critical to me as the process of the psychoanalytic experience. On the one hand, this personal factor seems essential to such an intimate experience, and I would hope, dear candidate, that you too will have the opportunity to indulge your private madness (Green, 1986) to the same extent as I was able to do. But it also brings home the observation that psychanalysis could not have been an activity I could have engaged in with just anyone. It had to have been a joyful created/found, longed-for/discovered encounter in order to plumb the deepest parts of my being (or so I believed at the time).

Freud wrote about countertransference as part of the "personal equation" of the analyst. There is also for many people who become analysts a personal equation in *their wish to become a certain kind of analyst*. This factor plays a role in the bond drawing people together in groups of a particular theoretical bent, though it too needs to be analyzed if the group and the individuals in it are to evolve. In recent years, I have been repeatedly struck by the relevance to psychoanalytic institutions of Jan Assman's study of *The Price of Monotheism* in which he examines the historical and cultural significance of the "Mosaic distinction" between true and false. Though, as Freud insisted, monotheism is a "progress in intellectuality," it also requires a conversion, a revolution, a radical turning away from the old gods to embrace a new singular fidelity to the one true god, in the present case, the conception of one "true" or "best" analytic identity and practice. Thus, there is an inevitable dark side of monotheism according to Assman, which leads it to the temptation of absolutism and denigration of difference. This is without a doubt an apt description of the forces at work in my personal adherence to a specific analytic tradition incarnated by my analyst, as well as in the commitment of many of my colleagues. And I have witnessed the dark side of these highly invested ideals in the self-exclusion of several talented members of my local society who did not feel adequately appreciated by the amorphous majority or who were actively blocked in their career aspirations by the passivity of that majority. Certain authors and certain questions can be put aside by the loyal disciples as unworthy in a complacent attachment to what is professed by the admired local theoretical "leaders." As one of these colleagues remarked out to me, there is a sociology and politics of dominant ideas in groups such as ours. Even when we believe the analytic ideals to be "true," there are power plays behind who is anointed to incarnate them. Moreover, that the history of psychoanalysis is strewn with the unintegrated debris of multiple passionate schisms is further attestation of the pertinence of Assman's preoccupation. I like where Assman ends his book: "I want to sublimate the Mosaic distinction, not revoke it.... We need to hold fast to the distinction between true and false... if these convictions are to retain their strength and depth. But we will no longer be able to ground this distinction in revelations that have been given once and for all. In this way, we must make the Mosaic distinction the object of incessant reflection and redefinition" (p. 120).

These reflections bring me to an unexpected suggestion. Perhaps our psychoanalytic institutions need committees or mechanisms of concern for the development of the psychoanalytic careers of their members. With tongue in cheek, one might think of the business model of client loyalty or adherence, yet what I have in mind is a different kind of seduction. The commitment of the majority to each of its members has long been an important aspect of control and conformity in organizations, which is obviously something I am trying to question. Nevertheless, if we could twist the formula, I find truth in the feeling that individual analysts need to feel desired by the community not for their conformity but for their otherness, because I have so often witnessed downward spirals of depressive self-devaluation and withdrawal among persons rejected in the process of training analyst status, or of election or inclusion in a given committee or seminar, or in a conflict with another member of higher analytic status. What might we call my imagined committee: a membership-continuity or a membership-inspiration (Laplanche, 1999) committee? Oddly, since I am a fallen away Catholic, I am reminded of the parable of the wayward son if the story be taken as a wish to include differences in a joint effort of psychic work. I am not the first to wonder (c.f. Celenza & Gabbard, 2003) whether even in the case of ethical transgressions, the community might find healthier outcomes by resorting, where possible, to avenues of restorative justice rather than to punitive measures.

To conclude, dear Candidate, I encourage you to pursue your pathway to becoming an analyst. Psychoanalysis is just as intellectually exciting as any other modern scientific pursuit as well as allowing its practitioners glimpses of the human heart and mind rarely fathomed elsewhere. Yet in the necessary process of being malleably used by patients in myriad ways, the work is difficult and draws upon the best and the worst in ourselves. In order to survive as analysts, we need to constantly work on our true and false distinctions, to value the never-ending inclusion of the unconscious in all walks of life, and to support each other in this common challenge. Many are called and many need to be chosen.

20 Barbara Stimmel
New York, U.S.A.

A challenge and a privilege...

Dear Candidate,

Let me start by describing that which I believe must be accurate. You are a sophisticated adult with an impressive education, some number of years as a professional in your field, clinical or not, eager to join our fervent subset of thinkers/practitioners, fortified by the ability to accept the humbling experience of returning to school as a psychoanalytic candidate. I encourage you to sit back and enjoy this "regression" in the service of the ego!

Writ Large

The history of psychoanalytic education in itself is worth considering. Our body of knowledge is not fixed but vibrant, constantly influenced by culture and context resulting in "schools" that reflect different countries, cities, even institutes. There is powerful controversy among different theoreticians, dramatically different techniques among clinicians, and various models of education for its students. There has been uniformity and conformity, but also resistance, rebellion, and rejection within our institutional halls. This apparent foment actually pretty routinely is understood to be a mirror of the intellectual passion, pride, and pleasure that our studies and work bring to us. You are invited to learn the combination of multiple models set within a noticeably singular dedication to your and your colleagues' education amid the strength and vitality of our profession.

So here you are re-entering the world of tutelage with all its demands, sacrifices, and unavoidable disappointments. These will be compounded through the inevitable transferences that *abound* in each and every analytic institute, classroom, supervision hour, analytic session. This is not to scare you, rather it is an invitation to relax in the face of newly awakened dynamics that not only characterize education but also family, politics, all human interactions. There is comfort though in being surrounded by others in the same boat, others who will have in the past experienced much of what you are now thereby offering living proof that this is a doable enterprise and happily, yet others who will help see you through.

Inevitably, all of us writing to you in this book have been analytic candidates – we have been analyzed, supervised, educated; we graduated, and now teach and analyze other candidates. We have served in many capacities in local, national and international psychoanalytic associations thereby leaving our imprints on the profession. We, each in our own way, understand with humility and empathy similar experiences that you will encounter. None of us can do much more than impart our knowledge through the imperfect compromises of our own complicated selves. Therefore, mine is but one set of reflections on your journey. With that caveat in mind, mix my thoughts, experiences, wisdom with the rest, do some sifting, tasting, juggling and I wager you will be ready to forge ahead with the knowledge that you can do this, and that its rewards will continue unfolding throughout your career.

Writ Small

The first, largest, and longest-lasting context of this journey is the intertwined, essentially inseparable, nature of your personal treatment and your more-or-less public education. Your analyst, in her/his behind-the-scenes way, will be a foil, an ear, an antidote, an accomplice, a support, a strain along with many other forms during your years in candidacy. She is most likely a member of your institute and is possibly the analyst/supervisor of some of your co-candidates, she sits on the committees that comprise the educational/political arms of your educational setting, has some prominence in the field or none that you can discern: all of this and more will constantly impinge on the analytic experience interacting with all else that gets churned up. Sit back, you are in for an exciting ride.

But do be prepared for turbulence because you are studying within a very complex community (which one is not?), and those around you will be caught in their own transference throes. For many reasons analytic institutions can be tricky, touchy teapots with many tempests brewing. My simple suggestion is that you tread carefully, not fearfully, and use your analysis to help keep what is most important clearly in your sights. All the while take the opportunity to look very closely at yourself, your surroundings, your colleagues, and the profession itself with increasing subtlety and appreciation. If you do, edification and enrichment will ensue. And then soon enough, you will be in the older generation helping those coming after navigating these (not always choppy!) waters.

The classroom is a complicated place because being a student after having finished all that, perhaps long ago, can be a struggle. It will not be a surprise to you that inescapable issues in student/teacher relations will come to the fore. Hopefully, much of the time the admixture of theory and technique, class and consulting room, will add elements of surprise, even excitement, such that the content triumphs. I am not myopic, certainly—different instructors will be poor, ordinary, and good—but some will be great; I promise.

Your supervisors comprise yet another kettle of fish! Their varying styles can and, I dare say, probably will confuse you at times. Sometimes they will hear similar material in very dissimilar ways; they will offer diametrically opposite interpretations; technical suggestions will come bouncing from different corners of the clinical room. The best supervisors will remind you that theirs is but one way of working. Also, they will remind you that your task is to listen, learn, distill, incorporate, integrate, but form finally your own clinical identity. This will happen for you slowly and satisfyingly as you come to see that your increasing knowledge of psychoanalytic theory and practice is an ongoing interaction with your deepening self-awareness and capacity for change.

Allow yourself to learn from those who want to teach. For the most part, they will be there to excite and inspire your intellect, your enthusiasm for the work, and to encourage your developing skills as a practicing psychoanalyst and a contributor to our larger scientific world.

Additionally, the status of candidate often can be more than that of student. You will have the opportunity to become involved in the life of your institute through committees, candidate organization(s), (locally, nationally, and internationally), as well as make some of the most important friends in your life. In the end, I advise you to hang back and watch those "running the show." Given that they were here before you, and thereby know a thing or two, you can often learn much from (some of) them. Remember though that it is likely true most do not have particular skills in administration, probably not having had much experience beyond their turns in office, chairmanships, etc. Be patient; this is compensated for by their devotion of time and effort to your education, to the field, and to your future.

Most important, though, is that you use these settings to learn from and emulate your mentors, while being careful not to idealize them, or their roles.

Writ Personal

I entered candidacy with no clinical experience. I saw my first patient as a nascent therapist/analyst. This experience girds my conviction that psychoanalysis is a clinical method that can be learned by anyone ready and eager to help others understand their own minds. If, like me, you come from another part of the professional universe, do not worry; you can become a very fine analyst someday. If you are a clinician already with much experience behind you, do not worry; you will not have to unlearn anything; rather, you will have the opportunity to discover myriad new ways to listen. And whichever your pre-candidacy situation, your patients will be among your best instructors; be ready to learn.

I was a candidate a long time ago when the American and International psychoanalytic organizations were pushing and pulling their way beyond outmoded and unfair practices. It was a heady time. My institute was one of three initially accepted into the International Psychoanalytic Association from the U.S. even though not in the American Psychoanalytic Association. This was the beginning of a new and pluralistic (academic degrees, theoretical/clinical models, organizational structures) era—overdue and welcome. In those early days of begrudging but inevitable commingling of formerly unfriendly colleagues, some pretty wonderful things were accomplished.

My involvement in these developments overlapped my candidacy and my graduation into membership. Then years later when already an officer, on the faculty, and a training analyst in my institute; on committees and a training analyst in the I.P.A.; now a member of A.Psa.A., sitting on its program committee, I began child analytic training at a different institute than my own.

Going "back to school" while being involved in teaching, supervising, analyzing, and leading was somewhat disorienting, demanding, and certainly strange! I made this unusual choice of beginning a new career path twice, but each instance was very well worth it. And then, Otto Kernberg invited me to be N. American Associate Secretary of the I.P.A. Board during his presidency. My small institute, for years shunned by the American but eventually joining the I.P.A., had prepared me well for the bigger universe of psychoanalysis. And what I encountered amid all the different accents in language and the consulting/teaching arenas was how much we, from all around the world, were committed profoundly to our profession remaining healthy, helping others, and most important, inviting next generations to join us. And that of course, includes you.

I refer to those days not to wax nostalgic but rather to suggest that it is highly likely that you also will have a time and place to have an impact on our profession. There are so many avenues along which to do that, including perhaps the most powerful of all, in your practice. It is there that you will help hearts and minds mature, love, and work, and their possessors will indirectly spread the fruits of psychoanalysis allowing it to continue to flourish and grow.

My last thoughts inevitably center on that left unsaid, questions I could answer (personal and professional), advice I could offer if we were able to sit down with all the time we would wish. But short, way short, of that, I want to say that my days as a candidate grabbed me by my arm—and never let go. I was thrust headlong into a felicitous collision with thrilling, enriching, challenging discoveries awaiting me in this grand educational endeavor. I am not ignoring the headaches, clinical conundrums, compelling demands, and prodigious energy required to juggle demands of an out-of-phase career shift. My children and husband, my larger family (including my pets!), my health, and other pleasures all were in continuous competition for my exhausted attention. I cannot remember the clamoring rest, but there was more, as surely there will be for you.

As in some of the best analytic hours, I will end where I began. It is "a challenge and a privilege…" for me in attempting to be of some help to you. And for you to encounter and master this rich, rewarding, remarkable way to make a difference in the world.

Good luck and, Enjoy!

21 Abbot Bronstein
San Francisco, U.S.A.

Dear Candidates,[1]

I want to start with what it is essential and necessary to remember: Psychoanalysis is a great field and a great profession—rewarding and stimulating intellectually and personally, offering something remarkable to the people who are our patients and our students and ourselves. It is also exhausting and complicated, expensive and demanding, unsettling and disruptive.

Doing clinical psychoanalysis is not what we imagine it to be when we start and the answers we personally seek and professionally need are far more elusive and complicated than we imagined. If we feel we have found them, keep looking.

My own effort to do analysis was anything but a straight line, and I imagine that is so for most candidates and analysts.

In North America becoming an analyst was not easy for someone who had chosen to not go to medical school. That has changed for political, economic, and social reasons in the United States. In London, Europe, South America, and now in the States, that is no longer the barrier. Other barriers now exist, no less difficult to traverse and overcome. And then there are the personal, external, and internal hurdles.

For me, starting out in math and science, wanting to be an engineer, shifted when I realized I didn't understand theoretical math. Physics was easy; I could see it. Theoretical math not so much. So, I took a year abroad in the 1960s to Israel. This is what my draft board would allow. I studied archeology, and literature and the book of exodus, art history, and one abnormal psychology course where we read Little Hans, in Hebrew! Yet it made sense to me. This thing called the unconscious was for me more like physics and geometry. I could see it, understand it.

Finishing college, I volunteered at Sheppard Pratt Hospital with chronic schizophrenic patients as an aid and "researcher" before going to graduate school in Clinical Psychology. Sullivan had said we were all more human than otherwise and talking daily to the men on these long-term wards convinced me. In graduate school, getting involved in analytic research in New York and then in San Francisco, working with thoughtful intellectual and clinically original therapists and analysts, opened up what was for me a world of stimulating dreams and ideas. It was something I felt I could see and know about. Working with patients in multiple-times-a-week therapy, in graduate school and then during pre and post-doctoral fellowships, provided the exciting entry into how the theory was imperfect but extraordinary in its explanatory power.

I had a father who was a linguist, a mother who was a teacher and interested in science, an uncle who was a psychoanalyst who had moved to work with Melanie Klein in London, and a close friend of the family who was another remarkable analyst, who one time in public after I had introduced him, reminded me how I used to ride my bike into his hedges all too often. I thought these were merely incidental to my choices, my interests, and where I would find myself professionally!

I had symptoms and anxieties and dreams and an unconscious it turned out. These unconscious thoughts and phantasies had a kind of concrete existence, a life not of their own, but integrated into my life. Choices were not as freely made as I thought.

I was greatly relieved when I read a paper by Phyllis Greenacre or Edith Jacobson, I think, on analysts in training and how they all should struggle. If it was easy, something was wrong. The easy part was not something I had to worry about! The ideas that you would have anxiety, struggles, conflicts, difficulties, and that it was okay and even expected helped greatly.

Then came analytic training! I had to go through one of 2 routes if I wanted to train at that time in San Francisco or in many places in the states. Either one became a research (C.O.R.S.T.) candidate or one bootlegged training, getting supervision and seeing cases frequently and getting into analysis with a good analyst. I was set to become a research candidate when life intervened. I was diagnosed with a life-threatening illness, and I put off the entire idea of formal analytic training at all.

But I stayed in my analysis, continued in multiple supervisions, read everything I could, and worried if I would see my child turn three much less as an adult.

I did survive. By then a lawsuit allowed psychologists to apply in a specific category that was non research for full training. Something called the Gaskill amendment allowed for a special admission through the institute locally and then approval by the American.

I did attend the San Francisco Psychoanalytic Institute, graduated and realized I was still pretty lost clinically. I stayed in supervision with 2 supervisors who had been mentors during my training and began working with the British Kleinian group in London (just randomly!) and started supervision and study groups that lasted the next 25 plus years, opening up a way to work clinically that was different and yet familiar and similar.

So, what do I recommend and hope for you, as candidates and the future of this wonderful, complex, and troubled field we have chosen? How does one begin to face the psychic pain in oneself and in the patients we are working to help? How do we stay balanced in our personal and professional lives? How do we manage the disruptions to our lives when patients die, move, fail, breakdown, attack, or idealize us?

In a field in which we are taught not to advise, because of the real clinical risks of giving advice, here is some advice.

First, believe in the unconscious. It exists and works in not such mysterious ways. One teacher of mine said knowing one has an unconscious is the one criterion for a psychoanalyst to develop.

Read, study, and envelop yourself in the work of past and present psychoanalysts. Write if you can, and even if you can't, try. It forces you to clarify your own ideas. Being creative is different from being original. We can create interpretations and have creative ideas about psychoanalysis and patients, and they don't need to be only ours, or new to the field. Teach and supervise psychotherapy and analysis. See patients, as many as you can, as often as you can. Lower your fees to be able to do as much analysis as you are able to do. 4–5 analytic cases ongoing, after training is a good number! 2–3 ongoing cases these days in training is a good place to start. Remember you are a psychoanalyst in training and then a psychoanalyst, not a psychologist, social worker, psychiatrist, or professor of English literature. You may be that too, but you are a psychoanalyst with a special area of expertise and the tools to do the kind of work you are trained to do.

See patients 3,4,5 times a week, and use the couch. These are tools that help with that process we call psychoanalysis. Get help frequently and for a long time—a very long time. This profession is only "impossible" if you try to do it yourself. It is not easy, and it is difficult to know how much we don't know; yet it is essential if we are to become and evolve as psychoanalysts.

Get a good analysis and be able to use critical thinking regarding that process, as well. It was said by many that the first analysis is for the institute and the second for you. NO! Both, all, and every analysis is for you. It helps your family, your patients, but mostly it helps you. It is training but not to become an analyst as its primary goal. But it does help in ways that are both direct and amorphous. But it helps you with your life, and that is good. It provides you with knowledge of the pain of depression and confusion and paranoia and despair. It shows you how difficult change is and how much time and work it takes to achieve the changes sought after within each of us. Your analysis shows you the limitations of yourself, your mortality, and the limits of the help, however far reaching it may be.

Analysts often when they write thank their patients for teaching them. They do it in a unique way, but I think it is only one of the groups of people we should remember to thank, who teach us, support us, and help us thrive in a taxing, chaotic, and engrossing field. Our students, when you are candidates, teach as well as learn. Your critical thinking skills and experiences help your analysts, supervisors, and colleagues learn. Never forget your friends and family! Without their support and tolerance of our internal chaos and struggles, we would not be able to manage. Take care of your patients, but also your children, partners, parents, and others. You learn more from them than one imagines.

Lastly be patient with yourself, your colleagues, your analyst, and your teachers. This process in all ways is difficult, rewarding, and brings up conflicts and anxieties that we don't understand.

Analysis is a wonderful process to be able to participate in for ourselves and our families. I would urge you to guard it, protect it, and also realize its significant limitations all simultaneously.

As one teacher said, he was a little jealous at the developments that have been made and how my fellow candidates and I would be able to move the field in ways he couldn't imagine and was unable. We didn't need to be dependent on the past, but he felt we could build and learn. We could hopefully start from where he ended, benefit from his experiences, and move forward into the study of the mind in ways that will continue to excite and provide better outcomes for ourselves, our field, and most importantly our patients.

Note

1 I want to thank the candidates, other analysts who have trusted me to be their supervisor, my supervisors and teachers, and my analyst for the help in understanding the idea that one cannot do this thing called analysis alone.

22 Cecilio Paniagua
Madrid, Spain

Dear Candidate,

The editor of this original and timely book, Fred Busch, asked us to write a short chapter on personal reflections about our experience of becoming psychoanalysts. To this purpose, I will expound on some of my memories and conclusions in the hope that they will resonate helpfully with the anticipations and struggles in some of you.

After finishing my medical studies in my hometown, Madrid, I went to the U.S. with a Fulbright Scholarship. After a Rotating Internship in which my vocational bewilderment became quite evident, I decided to do a Residency in Psychiatry, the clinical specialty less similar to the ones I had been exposed to. All I had read about Psychiatry was taxonomic, phenomenological, and organic. My references on psychoanalysis were most nebulous. I was accepted for training at the Jefferson Medical College of Philadelphia, and there my good luck started. My professional identity became gradually less diffuse as I listened to the teachers and instructors who happened to be psychoanalysts. That's where it dawned on me what I wanted to become when I "grew up." The deep, broad, and systematic way of thinking of these professors provided at last a cohesive frame for my juvenile scientific and humanistic sublimations.

Later, while working as a psychiatrist in hospitals and mental health clinics, I enrolled in a psychoanalytic program. As a Candidate at the Baltimore-Washington Institute, my personal and professional interests solidified as I learned theory through clinical observations from teachers, most of them ego psychologists. I found the seminars' readings captivating.

Because of family reasons, after graduating in 1986, I returned to my old Madrid to live and practice. Of course, I was aware beforehand of the prevailing anti-American antipathy among the Southern European intelligentsia; however, I did not expect the degree to which I would end up feeling like a foreigner in my own turf after being a foreigner in the U.S. The Madrid psychoanalytic group was initially sponsored by the Paris Society and was subsequently influenced by analysts emigrated from Argentina, mostly Kleinians and Lacanians. From senior colleagues I had to hear about the "shallowness" of ego psychology.

At the Asociación Psicoanalítica de Madrid I taught Freud and Technique seminars, becoming a rather popular teacher. I was a Training and Supervising

Analyst at my local society, but no Candidate chose me as a personal analyst. I supervised only one young colleague from another country. As Secretary of the Education Committee, I tried to change our Seminars system, proposing that classes be made part of the curriculum on topics like "Child development," "Theory of the instinctual drives," "Ego psychology," "Mechanisms and forms of neurosis," "Analyzability," "Technique," and "Principles of Psychotherapy." I also put forward the thought that the Freud seminars, the only obligatory ones until then, could be made thematic instead of chronological. My proposals were thoroughly rejected with the main argument that Candidates were all University graduates who did not need to go back to "High School-like teachings." The Eitingon model was considered antiquated. The minimization of the seminars' centrality in training was due mainly to the idea that for Candidates the acquisition of expertise should revolve very predominantly around their personal analysis and clinical supervisions. To no avail I reasoned that this apparent imbalance may deprive future analysts of a fundamental means to learn less transferentially colored independent views on their profession (c.f. Busch, 2019).

In 1998, after 12 years of membership in the Asociación Psicoanalítica de Madrid, I resigned from it, remaining the only Active Member of the American Psychoanalytic Association in the city. My failure in adaptation was painful, but also had unexpected positive results for me. During those years at the Madrid Association, I had a first-hand opportunity to compare different theories of technique—my preferred area of interest—discerning once and again the misleading appearance of common understanding. I learned a lot about mine and others' use of rationalizations and intellectualizations in our conceptual abstractions. To this day, I remain amazed by our inveterate tendency to transgress rules of sensible correspondence between the observational language and the theoretical language.

I ended developing a most gratifying clinical practice apart from the official analytic milieu, and more importantly, I had time for productive reading and cyber-communication with respected scientifically minded colleagues. My dedication to the investigation of dynamic psychology increased with time, and I was capable of publishing nationally and internationally more than any of my psychoanalytic countrymen. My love for our protoscience grew exponentially, and I felt progressively fortunate and happy about my vocational choice. My professional identity and convictions became stronger away from the quasi-sterility of programmed meetings and excessively theory-driven presentations. I achieved a definite feeling of soundness in my evolution, and the Angst of my youthful years was left behind. Now in my mid-seventies, my interest in the advancement of psychoanalysis as a semantic science has remained unabated. From my reminiscences I will summarize now what I think may possess some educational interest for you.

Exposure to different traditions and languages represents, no doubt, a highly enriching experience. However, doing analysis in a different tongue necessarily implies limitations due to the diverse subcultural assumptions, the potential for significant misunderstandings, and the inevitable affective sieve that verbal expressions have to go through. Let me underscore here the reminder that "denotations" are not the same as "connotations." Of course, these facts do not nullify analysis as a form of treatment in these circumstances, but they affect its efficacy.

I am a defendant of dynamic psychotherapy as a practice different from analysis. I think that those who maintain that everything an analyst does is psychoanalysis delude themselves, idealizing their trade, possibly doing a disservice to a good number of patients. I recommend that for many neurotic cases, focal dynamic approaches capable of obtaining "good enough" results should be considered before prescribing four-sessions-a-week treatments (c.f. Dewald, 1973). My later professional experience in an environment less affluent than the one where I was trained may have sensitized me about this point.

Future analysts need to acquire a repertoire of psychotherapeutic strategies based on expert assessment of pathologies and complex situations. Candidates have to learn why and when the triad "anonymity, neutrality, abstinence" is indicated, that is, to what extent these are useful or risky. Certainly, Candidates should not end their training thinking that "major surgery" is the only effective solution for neurotic conflicts. I think that the humanitarian *"guérir parfois, soulager souvent, consoler toujours"* can suffice.

In my opinion, long classical analyses are indicated, first, for personality disorders with highly maladaptive character traits that leave the patient doomed to repeat throughout his/her life grossly self-defeating patterns, passing significant pathology onto future generations; and second, for individuals who need to acquire thorough knowledge of their unconscious tendencies and vulnerabilities in order to carry out their professional work, that is, psychoanalysts.

Dedication to psychoanalysis implies a considerable degree of patience, tolerance for uncertainty, endurance of critiques, and economic sacrifice. *I believe that analysts ought to be driven by a great degree of idealism in order to face these challenges.* Fascination with the disciplined research of unconscious psychic phenomena has to be paramount during their training. I will quote here Anna Freud's reminder in her 1967 short text on "The evaluation of applicants for psychoanalytic training": "If you want to be a real psychoanalyst you must have a great love of the truth, scientific truth as well as personal truth, and you have to place this appreciation of truth higher than any discomfort at meeting unpleasant facts, whether they belong to the world outside or your own inner person" (in Kappelle, 1996, p. 1213).

The choice of a personal analyst and supervisors is of the greatest relevance. Knowing information about their reputation is advisable, of course, but I would suggest that you follow also your own intuition. An old saying goes, "Teachers teach not only what they know, but also who they are," and internalizations with the latter will be important in the development of your career. In your personal and self-analysis, you will have time to explore the transferential determinants of your choices.

As for seminars, it is convenient in our age of pluralism to be exposed to past and extant theories, becoming adept at what De Urtubey (1985) called "metapsychological polyglottism," always trying to discern in the understanding of arduous concepts what is complexity and what prolixity. Grasping the meaning of different notions requires a questioning attitude on what authors view as evidence when making their inferences. I agree with Boesky's (2015) statement that "Seminars in our institutes discuss comparisons of the various theoretical models but mostly ignore their epistemological premises" (p. 66).

It is essential to develop one's own verisimilitude criteria and technical preferences after long listening and interrelating of distinct theoretical ideas. We should have an open mind "but not so open that the brain falls out," in the words of an older American colleague. We can arrive at our own judgments and style without abandoning respect for the experience of senior analysts. Simultaneously, we should pledge never to swear on the pronouncements of any master (*"Nullia in verba iurare magistri!"*) but to pursue the exploration of psychic truths even when these seem divergent from the teachings of admired classics (*"Amicus Socrates, sed magis amicas veritas!"*).

One should learn about one-person and two-person contemporary approaches, navigating between the conviction of objectivity and pretense of imperturbability on one hand and the belief in fusional understanding on the other, or between excessive skepticism and gullibility. For the exploration of the intricacy in unconscious compromise formations between drive derivatives, defensive counterforces, and self-representations, not all theories of technique were born equal. My personal preference in clinical work is resorting to a series of approaches that facilitate *interpretations by the analysand* of his/her own associations, which may confirm, amplify, or disconfirm the analyst's conjectures. In my experience, the close-process technique proposed by contemporary ego psychology seems the most appropriate for the purpose. However, in the "systematic study of self-deception and its motivations" (Hartmann, 1959, p. 22)—my favorite concise definition of our endeavor—all analysts need to reach their own conclusions as to what is the most truthful research methodology and the most effective approach for their patients.

Best wishes, young colleague, and welcome to what many of us consider the most interesting profession in the world.

23 Ellen Sparer
Paris, France

Dear Analyst-in-Formation,

Writing about "becoming" a psychoanalyst is as paradoxical as writing about being in analysis. How shall I write about what is essentially, for me, a personal journey, fueled by one's personal desire and experience? At the same time, once admitted to a Psychoanalytic Institute, this "becoming" is also contained within an Institution, with its unique and specific demands and requirements. "Becoming" thus becomes framed by both internal, psychic reality and external, Institutional reality.

We call it "formation" in French as it is a constant process of shaping, molding, and transformati—not to an external mold, but rather a keeping alive, we hope, of the inner psychic work begun during analysis. The "aim" as such, of the formation, if one can speak in such terms, ultimately, is an appropriation of an analytic function, in great part learning to distinguish a psychotherapist function from an analytic function.

In order to move from the couch to the armchair behind it, you will need to have elaborated "enough" of your own psychic world, both the oedipal pole as well as the narcissistic one. You have hopefully thought and analyzed your wish to become a psychoanalyst, with its identifications, rivalries, and murderous wishes toward your own analyst. You know enough about your psychic world to be able to speak about it, its impact on your present, and the impact of events of the past on your current life. The transference of your patients will test the mettle of your psychic functioning, so it is indispensable that your personal analysis is well under way.

These are some of the elements we are looking for in the three interviews when an applicant applies to the Paris Psychoanalytical Society. Facilitating this move, from lying down to sitting behind the couch, maintaining analytic truth, honesty and ethics is also, in some way our "goal"—if it makes sense to speak of a "purposive idea" during the years of formation.

I hope you are impassioned by the work of Freud whose architecture of the mind, so carefully constructed over the course of decades, remains the most complete structure of the psyche. One of the tasks of your formation is learning to read Freud. What do I mean by this? Every article Freud wrote was written in a context, and as the years passed, the later texts should be understood in relation to previous reflections and theorizing. What other articles was he working on when he wrote a given text? What notions had he touched upon sometimes years earlier and then came back to develop? The footnotes are often invaluable clues of how future elaborations modified earlier propositions.

I would like you to understand his followers within the context of his oeuvre and historical events. Psychoanalysts have moved from one area to another; the languages and the translations from the German have influenced what is important in different analytic schools. And then I hope that you can use your own creativity to extend the clinical and metapsychological structure.

I am struck at how rapidly I have come to my "hope" for you. This letter could be reduced to one line: I hope you find your own path, but in all honesty I do have some convictions about what that path entails. For me, for us, formed in the French model, one's analysis is always a personal quest. It can only be during the course of that personal endeavor that one discovers or perhaps confirms one's desire to become a psychoanalyst.

Many colleagues will tell you that the current state of the world and psychoanalysis' diminishing place in it is a great problem for you. I can only partially agree. Psychoanalysis has almost always been under attack. But I will come back to what I consider to be the greatest dangers in your formation a bit later.

In my early twenties, despite the outward appearance of success, I found myself in difficulty with my life and my relationships and began my first analysis. It was during those years of analysis, graduate and post-graduate work, and the possibility that I'd had of working with some extraordinary analysts, that my own desire to follow this path clearly emerged for me. Only to be confronted with the quasi-impossibility for the psychologist that I was to be accepted for "training" at a psychoanalytic institute in the U.S., unless I was willing to agree that I would only accept "research" patients in analysis. I floundered for a while and worked, and then, in one of these serendipitous events of life, had the opportunity to move to Paris. Paris, the home of so many great psychoanalysts and of a Society (in fact Societies, but my heart was set on one, the Paris Psychoanalytical Society, the S.P.P.) that did not hold my lack of a medical degree against me.

What had brought me here? External events in my life? The possibility to become a psychoanalyst? I began this letter by talking about two realities, Institutional-external and Psychic-internal. We very much hold to the conviction that each Analyst-in-formation must be free to choose his/her path or journey in becoming an analyst, yet, fundamentally, how much liberty do we have from the inner psychic drives that push us in one direction or another? At the same time, if there is one thread that hasn't changed since I've become an analyst at the S.P.P., it is the importance of one's personal journey.

We do not have "classes" at the S.P.P., in the sense of academic years; one's application is made whenever the candidate feels ready, after a minimum of three years on the couch at a minimum of three sessions per week with a member of the S.P.P. or the I.P.A. This is because an analysis is a personal endeavor to be undertaken with the analyst of the candidate's choice, regardless of the analyst's place in the Institutional hierarchy. And yes, many people at the S.P.P. are in analysis during their "formation."

The minimum "requirement" for "validating" the formation is two supervisions, one individual, and one collective (group) supervision. Each analyst in formation is free to choose the supervisors with whom s/he would like to work, although the admitting committee may request that the person begin with individual or collective supervision.

Seminars are taken at the candidate's discretion, although we recommend seminars on reading Freud, initial consultations and beginning treatment. Active participation is important.

So, what is difficult about being in "training" today? I could respond in terms of the material reality, specifically the difficulty of finding analytic patients today or even to invest in a "career" whose tenets are so far removed from the current cultural atmosphere. The question of culture comes closer to an issue that is generally present—and problematic—during formation, specifically, the feeling of many candidates that they are being infantilized. This experience should, I think, be understood in relation to a concomitant feeling, that is, of idealization. By this I mean idealization of the Institution. Both of these must be understood psychically in order to avoid the very common projection onto a so-called "reality" of an infantilizing Institute.

Becoming a psychoanalyst at an Institute inevitably puts you in a psychically "infantile" place. You are entering a world in which you hope to find and to take your place both in an analytic genealogy and a group to which you have aspired, unlike the legacy into which you were born. What will happen in this group is very much similar to what Freud described in his text on Group psychology. The unconsciously idealized father (and mother) will ineluctably be awakened as will the alliances and rivalries with the analytic brothers and sisters. What will happen in this group will provoke certain transferential elements encountered in your personal analysis, which is part of why your analysis should be well under way.

It is very likely that you will find yourself caught between an increasing identification with your "group" and at the same time putting it in the place of an ego ideal. This could place you at risk of seeing the Institute as persecutory. The imagos that will be awakened may be maternal or paternal depending on your history and psychic makeup. Working this through so that you avoid a painful dis-idealization of the Institute/Society is crucial, without which you may choose to disinvest, decathect libidinally your Society. Becoming a psychoanalyst requires continuously working and elaborating your inner life and also your life within the group or Society to which you will hopefully become a member.

24 Harriet Wolfe
San Francisco, U.S.A.

Dear Candidate,

I wish I could meet you in person. In writing you that, I realize my preference for in-person dialogue is a segue into something I'd like to talk with you about: the challenges that develop in psychoanalytic training during transitions, the challenges related to change.

This is a time of transition in psychoanalytic education. In the context of advanced technology, questions are arising about how the formation of an analytic identity is best achieved and whether technologically mediated training is comparable to in-person training. This is a question that, during your career, you will likely be asked to consider.

I pursued psychoanalytic training from 1986–1994 in San Francisco, California. My institute used, and still uses, the tripartite Eitingon model. I had a training analysis that was very helpful to me. I was in my early 1940s when I started and only wished I could have learned about psychoanalysis and found an analyst sooner. My classes varied greatly in terms of faculty members' ability to teach. Instructors ranged from analysts who conducted a seminar as if it were a clinical session and an opportunity for free association, to expert communicators regarding the history and meaning of theory and the array of potential interventions with a control patient. My supervisors were excellent. I got to choose them, and I could change supervisors if it seemed warranted and would be helpful. We formed a candidates' association that eventually was given a place on the Board of Directors.

In today's training world there is a controversial push for greater openness to remote training, also called distance/mediated/internet training. The variety of language used to describe remote training reflects the unease among many psychoanalytic educators who are uncomfortable with analytic treatment (and especially the analysis of candidates) occurring outside the frame of two bodies in the same room. There are strong opinions but little actual data to make a reasoned choice on the matter. There is clinical literature on the non-verbal communicative aspect of the body in treatment—everything from borborygmi to unconscious contortions and mannerisms. This literature supports the view that it is important for the analyst to have an in-person exposure to the patient and for the patient to have that exposure to the analyst. There is also literature that asserts screen relations—or the virtual image and voice in internet-mediated exchanges—are unable to provide the three-dimensional depth required to sustain a psychoanalytic treatment. You may, however, know people who feel they are benefiting greatly from mediated treatment.

Whatever the answer to this complex question might be, new technologies inevitably change the world, and this includes psychoanalysis. Resisting change in favor of a conservative or even nostalgic ideal is a poor strategy and one that could never protect our discipline. A lot has changed, for instance, since I started training over 30 years ago, including *everyone's* access to "distance" relationships. Given my age and past experience, I have to consciously resist a tendency to generalize about internet-mediated communication as two-dimensional. My adult daughter, the current candidates in San Francisco, and my patients who work at companies like Google all constantly use technology to communicate in business and in personal relationships. I think there may be a generational difference in the experience of and conditions for intimacy.

When I was a candidate, remote training was not available, but there was definitely remoteness. It had to do with the social/professional hierarchy that separated Training Analysts, regular graduate analysts, and candidates. There were restrictions on who could attend our monthly scientific meetings, for example. Scientific meetings are now open to all types of members—community, candidate, and graduate analyst members—and also interested students and other visitors. Most members see this shift as a positive move away from elitism as well as a recognition that analysts-in-training are mature clinicians who do not require protection from their elders. Others see it as a loss of intellectual influence on the part of the most experienced members, the Training and Supervising Analysts, who no longer attend in the numbers they did when attendance was restricted.

I think this loss in Training and Supervising Analyst participation reflects a resistance to change that is inevitable, complex, and very hard to work through. Yet, change is precisely what we aim to accomplish through psychoanalytic treatment. When we consider change in terms of our organizations, however, it challenges us in unconscious as well as conscious ways and often puts questions of power and authority front and center. Such dynamics can become more influential than clinical judgment or scientific investigation.

I would like to tell you a story. It is a composite, not a confidential communication, but all the elements are true. A senior candidate whose wife had recently lost her job, the mainstay of their family income, forfeited his first control case because his patient's spouse was accepted to graduate school in another part of the country. The case was full fee and was going well, but reality had intervened, and the candidate would lose the case 21 months into the treatment. The candidate knew the case had to continue for at least 24 months to be credited toward graduation, and both he and his patient were eager to continue their work. He appealed to his supervisor for permission to continue the case by Skype. His supervisor knew that distance training was not permitted and said he was sympathetic to the situation but could not approve it. Besides, in his view, Skype treatment was worthless.

The candidate was dismayed and sought support at a higher level. He went to the Director of Training who had the same views as the case supervisor: Skype treatment was not permitted nor considered valid. So far, no one in authority had inquired about the case, the nature of the work, or the nature of the patient's problems. There was no opportunity for appeal of the decision. The candidate and his patient elected to continue by Skype, which the candidate could not tell the Institute. The candidate did not get credit for the case. He was unable to find a full fee case during the next year and could not afford to work with very low fee patients. He ultimately dropped out of training because he felt the Institute was unresponsive to patient and candidate needs.

The themes in this story are sadly familiar. It is a story about rigid, inflexible rules and authoritarian attitudes. I offer the details to illustrate that the nature of authority is complex. There are many organizational layers involved in education, and, in a time of transition, it can become confusing who is in charge of what. Even when the locus of authority is objectively clear, participants in psychoanalytic training may resist change and view it more as an undesirable loss than a potential gain or opportunity.

There is a tendency to link the old, known approach to training with certainty and quality control; a new approach is an opportunity one day but a major threat the next. The first question about authority in times of transition is: who has the power to say yes or no? Secondly, there is the challenge of flexibility. When is flexibility an opportunity, and when is it a threat to quality control? Thirdly, and in my mind both most important and most vexing, what are the implications of putting the existing model of training above individual patient/candidate needs? Does refusing to consider an exception reflect a predictable organizational regression in the face of uncertainties during times of transition?

Whether distance analysis is a good development remains an open question. Whatever answer we might personally endorse, change is upon us. It is the relationship to change that I want you, future analysts and leaders, to consider.

When structures or standards change, two things happen: (1) uncertainty becomes a source of anxiety and potential regression; and (2) communication and dialogue within and between the elements of the organization become extremely important. The leadership task becomes one of providing clarity and vision and reminding participants on all levels of their roles and the opportunities that change represents. A leader may recognize an opportunity to point out regression, but interpretation in the context of organizational change is a delicate matter. One risks being seen as biased, manipulative, or even reckless when one addresses an unconscious motive within a work or educational setting.

Psychoanalysis is an approach to thinking and education that emphasizes reflection and understanding. It becomes a contradiction in terms when rules regarding the psychoanalytic training model take on an absolutist quality. The preservation of a certain model rather than the establishment of policies and procedures that reflect attention to individual training and clinical needs is inconsistent with fundamental psychoanalytic principles.

The allure of rules is that they offer a sense of security and stability, especially during times of rapid change. At best, rules promote healthy functioning and improve output. They make us better. At worst, rules become a bastion against important new thinking like an orthodoxy that can only perpetuate itself.

Somewhere in between seems right. Quality control is essential, but we have a potent, well-tested analytic method and ways of understanding human nature that merit organizational confidence. In my view, flexibility in the face of shifting technological and cultural change is not a specific risk to psychoanalysis or a harbinger of a slippery slope. Flexibility, as I see it, is an approach reflecting an overall attitude of curiosity, discovery, and openness to new thinking and willingness to face challenges without excessive fear.

Dear Candidate, we need your help in exploring the pros and cons of flexibility in the goals and standards for analytic training. Please be active participants in the conversations at your institute while you live through the process! Also, participate in the national and international conversations, now so much easier thanks to communication technology. An open and transparent educational system promises to allow greater emphasis on scholarship, research, and collaborative thinking, all good for the future of psychoanalysis.

25 Maj-Britt Winberg
Lund, Sweden

Dear Candidate!

You are facing a major change in your life. It might be compared to the other programs you have already participate in, from high school to university, or maybe not.

Sometimes I think that Psychoanalysts, just like scientists, choose to stay as a student for the rest of adulthood. We are looking for a pleasure-filled play space, which gives us satisfaction in an "aha" experience.

The enjoyment in it attracts. We know that we can experience this again and again in patient work, in supervision situations, and in meeting with colleagues, students, and candidates.

From now on, you won't see a movie, read a book, or sit down for a dinner conversation with the same mindset as before. You will also have a new three-dimensional view of what you see and get to know.

At dinner parties, when discussions arise, you may be the "boring person," pointing out that there is another way to look at the issue. Last time I was at a dinner, a discussion regarding the appropriateness of building a new prison, near a certain place and the resistance of doing it, came up in the dinner conversation and I could not refrain from giving it another dimension. I hypothesized that it may be about people's unconscious processes, the fear of doing something not allowed, or identification with those in prison, more than the location of the building itself (Freud, 1905).

Do you want to go through that change? Yes, of course you do, is my answer. It is absolutely wonderful and incredibly enriching. It gives a goal of discovering the meaning of life, which few are exhilarated to experience.

It's like science, but in this research, it is in the service of humanism. You will be introduced to something new and exciting, but as an adult.

At the time when I was on my way to this change, I was not particularly aware of what would happen to me. I had, like you, an education, work experience, and a family with small children. I thought that I had created a pathway for my life.

But in combination with my own analysis, theoretical knowledge, and my daily work with patients in analysis and supervision, I was privileged to experience a change in my adult life. The big changes I thought had already occurred in my life, like education, work, birth of my children, and existential adult issues, were not the last ones.

Dear Candidate, another change is waiting now. Obviously, you can make a protest and say, "But change is part of life." But these changes in your life, if you choose to move on in your education to become Psychoanalysts, happen on a conscious level, or sometimes on the unconscious level that then becomes conscious.

You can evaluate your thinking and make decisions based on a conscious level that gives you a tremendous freedom. Sometimes it also leads to sorrow. You make conscious decisions, but those decisions are not always accepted or appreciated. But when you have finished deliberating the various possibilities and limitations, make a long-term decision. It might sometimes not be the best for you. But on a conscious level, you might remain on your daily job, which does not really please you. But you allow it, to be able to make changes as you wish by just being attentive and patiently waiting to see the outcome, as a scientist and Psychoanalyst.

When I stepped over the threshold of my own Psychoanalyst education, I had some inner fantasy that I would step into a society like an English gentlemen's club. Scenarios with intellectual conversation in small groups, where members sat in Chesterfield chairs and smoked cigars. I was educated in Denmark, an equal country, where women also smoked cigars, to my great fascination when I visited Denmark during my childhood.

"Elegant women sat in tearooms and smoked cigars!"

All these fantasies came naturally to shame, but they still come easily, I notice, as I write this. During the first year of my education, I was disappointed that these intellectual conversations did not go as smoothly as I had thought they might and that I would not get answers to all my curious and "hungry" questions immediately.

I also suffered from a serious illness a few weeks into my education and needed surgery and treatment. I am Swedish and, as now, lived in southern Sweden. Therefore, I was able to attend my education in Denmark. At that time, the Oresund bridge between Sweden and Denmark did not exist. Transportation was via boats. Travel like this, of course, was time-consuming. So, this period in my life included not only my studies, but periodic hospital treatments due to my disease, time spent with my small children, frequent travel between the countries, and my own analysis, supervision, patient work, and theoretical seminars. Why did I do this, I wonder now. All this trouble.

I don't know is my answer. Of course, there must have been a driving force. But it wasn't for career or fame. This is not so common in our country; it exists, but not in the same way as in the rest of the academic world.

It was probably the curiosity and seeking for knowledge, an intellectual challenge, but the one that exists in academia as well. In the psychoanalytic world, you are to a greater extent your own examiner, and you are driven by a belief in change, and a curiosity, but in your own chamber. To eventually bring you out to a larger context, of course.

Now when I summarize the past, I can see that it was just that which made me who I am, but maybe not in Chesterfield armchairs with cigars.

I have had this conversation with myself several times and also with colleagues, candidates, students, and friends. As in psychoanalysis, things have to take time, and it must take time. That is how lasting change comes about.

My conviction is that we have a very important profession, precisely in this inert work of change in the service of humanism. We must convey the lustfulness of knowing the wings of freedom, of being allowed to think freely and independently.

I would not be fair if I gave a picture of wealth mentally and literally. It's not like that. On the contrary, being a psychoanalyst rarely yields material wealth.

It also happens that you finish your work for the day with a heavy feeling of having a major depression on your shoulders. The day looks grey and without joy. It is the downside of sometimes carrying much of the suffering of others, but it is a material, a psychoanalytic material. After a while, you can usually chisel a light in the tunnel. You take a bike ride, get new perspectives on the problem and the weight of another denomination. You may decide to do something over the weekend to take a mental break. You can meet a colleague or supervisor to discuss the problem; you may have already identified the patient who is giving you the weight or the material the patient is presenting.

You choose to work in a profession that sometimes gives you a physical weight but also an intellectual challenge. The problem can be solved.

Dear candidate, when I teach, part of what I try to convey to you is very simple. Read Freud!

Maybe you start to sigh, a bit bored, or maybe you have read it already!!

Do you know what? Freud is the Christmas tree that you then decorate with all of your own knowledge. You must have the fundamentals, otherwise it will be difficult to grasp.

Read Freud uncritically, as a fiction. Experience the amazing thing about human beings and living, which he managed to capture. Long ago I told this to candidates who immediately gave a rejoinder, "but Melanie Klein writes ..." (or what they just got in mind). Then I always reply with a "Stop," let Freud stand for himself! Let the knowledge sink in, read uncritically, and then when you have him there naturally, hang on to the other theories, and evaluate and compare how the development has looked.

My latest teaching was about the "Instincts and their Vicissitudes" (Freud, 1915), so if you have a desire and become curious, please read it, uncritically. See how Freud pleasantly starts to think about objects, not as they later developed into integrated objects, etc.; the designation of objects, and how it slowly develops a thought that we use today. I hear the fantastic wings of history; we have got this pleasure, this opportunity, and this fantastic theory. Give it that chance. Be uncritical before decorating the Christmas tree.

For what was in my imagination then? The meeting with colleagues, I can see now, has come to fruition. But it will be a Worldwide meeting. Maybe not every day, week, month, but all the more rewarding and enriching when it arises.

Now when I have this opportunity to look back, I see a necklace of experiences and knowledge, of which I am incredibly grateful.

So, Dear Candidate,

If you want your life to change in this basic direction, don't hesitate. You are facing a wonderful life change!

> "Sure, there are goals and meaning in our journey—
> but it is the pathway, which is worth the effort."
>
> Karin Boye
> "I rörelse" The poetry collection; "Härdarna" (1927)

26 Arlene Kramer Richardson
New York, U.S.A.

Dear Candidate,

I feel very fortunate to have found psychoanalysis and to be an analyst. I am one of those individuals who tried other professions before experiencing analysis and becoming one. Certainly, there are other professions that are more rewarding financially, but for me nothing was more captivating than analysis.

Becoming a psychoanalyst works well for those of us who have experienced our own analysis, felt very much helped by the experience, and find any other work boring, senseless, or impossible to stick to after trying for some time. Myself, I rejected an offer to become an insurance actuary even though the recruiter insisted that I could have a house in an exclusive suburb, a car and driver, and a luxurious life with an early pension. I tried elementary school teaching, college teaching. Nothing stuck. Actuarial work seemed to be boring; I could not spend my life doing that all day long. Elementary school was fun, but too exhausting; I could not go so many hours being on every day without even a bathroom break. College teaching was more fun, but I could not get a job in New York without establishing myself elsewhere first. And I would not leave my family. Then I got analyzed. During my analysis I tried psychological research design and university teaching. Jobs in research required writing grant proposals, tailoring them to the federal mandates for research. Boring. And academia required sitting in faculty meetings to discuss who got priority at the copy machines. Boring.

So, there was nothing left but doing for others what had been done for me: psychoanalysis. This was infinitely interesting and has been so for all of the fifty years I have been in practice. Actually, I was very lucky to be learning psychoanalysis at a time when psychologists in the United States were not accepted for training in the psychoanalytic training institutes of the American Psychoanalytic Association, except for the one in Topeka, Kansas and a few others. Like other unreasonable laws, this one spawned bootlegging. Psychologists got analyzed by members of the American Psychoanalytic Association, or by European refugees who, like Freud, believed that "lay" (nonmedical) analysis was legitimate and worthwhile.

A group of ten psychologists got together and hired teachers from the New York Psychoanalytic Institute to teach us the courses they taught at their institute. But we paid them, which the institute did not, and they did not have to evaluate us. We evaluated them by re-hiring them, or not. This freed them to teach as they believed rather than hewing to an official line. We each had our own analyst and hired our own supervisors. We even hired one of their most valued members to read through the Standard Edition with us, all the volumes, all the footnotes. At the time, we were the first to do that, and I do not think there is a single institute that does that today. It was fascinating to see the development of Freud's thought and the development of the field over the course of Freud's career. We understood the concepts in terms of the context of the times in which they were written, the experience of the early analysts, and the particular issues that interested the field. All of us stuck with the six-year experience. Some of us became psychotherapists. Some became psychoanalysts. Some became members of local psychoanalytic societies and institutes. Some became members of the American Psychoanalytic Association and the International Psychoanalytic Association. Those memberships led to national and international contacts with colleagues that led to patient referrals and enlarged our practices.

Could such a group work today? Maybe only in a big city. But even if you join an established institute, it is possible to ask for courses that interest you if you can get a group of like-minded people together to learn. A group is important because it will allow you to get referrals, find analysts for your patients' relatives and friends who want or need treatment, and for challenges to your own ideas so that you do not become hide-bound. Even after you do the required course, you will have the benefit of studying together especially if you include colleagues from other institutes and even, via the internet, in other states or other countries.

Psychoanalytic learning takes place in your own office, in your study groups during and after training, in teaching others, and in reading poetry, novels, history, and philosophy. It takes place in seeing and analyzing movies, plays, operas, paintings, and sculpture. It takes place in dealing with conflicts with friends and family. And, sometimes, used with restraint, psychoanalytic knowledge can help you understand and empathize with your children.

Once you begin to think like an analyst, every experience that touches your feelings, evokes empathy for others, or arouses your anger, sadness, fear, or any strong emotion and causes you to think about your feelings yields analytic knowledge. So, you can continue to learn and develop analytic skills as long as you can hear, articulate, and think. This makes our profession one you can practice into old age. You do not need to retire as long as your mind is working well. That obviates the need for a big pension. For me the time spent analyzing is the most stimulating and satisfying time I can imagine. When people ask me when I will retire, I say that I will do it as soon as I think of something I would rather do.

27 Gohar Homayounpour
Tehran, Iran

Dear Candidate,

As I ponder over this letter I am writing to you, my line of associations leads me down two different roads. The first, *Après-Coup*, looks back at what my own candidacy was like, and the second path takes me to that which I would like to transmit to our candidates here in Iran, to those at the Freudian Group of Tehran, and to you.

What is highlighted, looking back at my own years of candidacy, is the desire that I continuously had to connect with analysts, supervisors, and teachers outside of my own institute. Even when your training is at the best psychoanalytic institutes, it is inevitable that each institute has its own specific culture of strengths and weaknesses, of trans-generational traumas, of symptoms continuously repeated and acted out, of secrets, and its own unique origin story. If you merely stay within the confines of your own institute, you are bound to get caught within all these forms of resistance and to repeat it all with the next generations of candidates when you become an educator and an analyst yourself. But if you also extend your desire to the outside world, outside of your own institute with other supervisors, teachers, and analysts, it will feel like magic. New blood will flow through the veins of your developing, psychoanalytic mind; you will be much less in danger of ever losing sight of the never-ending nature of the process of becoming a psychoanalyst; that it is always and foremost a continuous "becoming." As you reach beyond your institute, separating yourself, courageously transforming and becoming outside of your immediate family or even in faraway lands, you will be able to aid your institute to transform itself right beside you, for you will bring to the institution all the souvenirs of your adventures.

This brings me straight to my second line of associations, and our own candidates here in Iran where, because we did not have many psychoanalysts, our candidates had no choice but to reach outside of our own group to get supervision and analysis, and we had to invite many colleagues from all over the world to teach them. This, I can proudly say, has had the most enriching effect on our candidates.

There is a danger too that I should mention, which is that our candidates might fall into the trap of becoming "Jacks of all trades and Masters of none," which I find is often a general problematic of contemporary psychoanalysis, so this danger needs to be acknowledged and elaborated as well.

It does not seem that in contemporary psychoanalytic education, at least for the time being, this has led toward an integration of theories, although it has on some occasions. Mostly it has led to the imitation of various parts of different theories, and not to what one would call an internalization. In such cases I don't see the liberation, integration, and creativity that could come from such a way of being. Instead it leaves a sense of lack: a lack of an internal sense of who the candidates are and of what they can become as analysts.

Another significant line of thinking that I try to communicate to our candidates is that you have to genuinely believe in the unconscious. We keep on *doing* things for our patients and candidates because, deep down, we do not believe in the unconscious. We have to move from doing to thinking and being, and this is the only way to develop a psychoanalytic mind (Busch, 2013). But if you keep *doing*, how are you ever going to learn to just be and to listen to the whispers of the unconscious?

Just to offer one example, I am a member of a few psychoanalytic referral mailing lists, using which I have tried to conduct a small research, out of my own curiosity, over the last five years. The results show that referrals are almost always asking for medication-subscribing psychiatrists and seeking out various forms of psychotherapy, yet always insisting that it should be supportive psychotherapy, couples' therapy, or help with a specific previously diagnosed condition and so on.

On very rare occasions a psychoanalyst is looking to refer a patient to an analyst for psychoanalysis! However, we have to remember that these lists are only for psychoanalysts! Perhaps we might be led into thinking that patients are not interested, and therefore adopt the capitalist approach of the "customer is always right." I have heard recently that in two very important psychoanalytic institutes, they recently hired a publicist in order to attract candidates such as yourself, as these institutes have been suffering from a lack of interested candidates for years. The publicist, being a publicist, asked them, "What is your brand?"

I think the more we try to sell psychoanalysis as one would sell Coca-Cola, the more we dig our own graves. Psychoanalysts are eliminating psychoanalysis, not because we are not democratic enough, not because we are expensive, not because we are "old-school," not because people are not interested in long term treatments (certainly these critiques could have been applied on other historic occasions as well), but mainly, I feel, because sometimes psychoanalysts don't believe in the unconscious; for resistance is prevailing over the shadow of their once-upon-a-time wish to get to remember what they already know.

Dear, dear Candidate, we have become too accommodating to attract customers, and all we have achieved is the loss of analysands. We have lost our mysteriousness, inevitably associated with the uncanny unconscious, and as we tried to become clearer and clearer, we have entered the world of evidence-based prose and of lost unconscious fantasy. But Psychoanalysis is a poetic discourse, and so, as Freud informed us very early on, if one day you are talking about psychoanalysis and people are agreeing with you, that means that you have not done a good job explaining psychoanalysis. Psychoanalysis *par excellence* is disturbing, psychoanalysis is subversive, and it must remain as such. The moment we try to normalize it, clarify it, observe it, and perceive it, we lose the unconscious. I tend to think that in the mainstream, psychoanalytic training has been gentrified in the name of neuroscience and medicalizations, foreclosure of sexuality, and unconscious fantasy.

Psychoanalysis is not customer-friendly, and it should never become so.

But I am not one of those analysts who envisions psychoanalysis as doomed. Psychoanalysis will survive because of you, dear candidate.

Psychoanalysis will survive because the unconscious is not going anywhere. No matter how many new tricks and forms of resistance are found to wish it away, psychoanalysis will survive with your precarious desire for this strange, inexplicable profession; for your transference to the unconscious; and for your desire to say the unsayable. Please don't try to be too gentle with it, try to dream with it, try to dream it. Find pleasure in its strangeness, in your own strangeness, in that of your patients in the unknowable, and in the inevitable mystery of this very possible profession that we call psychoanalysis.

And you are always invited to visit us in Tehran, where the Freudian Group of Tehran will welcome you with Persian hospitality.

P.S.: Please read Freud and read him well.

28 Ines Bayona
Bogata, Columbia

Dear Candidate,

> There is no real time,
>
> is your own time,
>
> what is real
>
> (Ines Bayona)

Psychoanalytical identity

Time... Couch... Yourself... Live-Life...

I am at the time that not long ago, I was a candidate, ten years. Time enough to realize what being a psychoanalyst has been for me, personally in my inner and outside world, in my mind, and my body; all of it in my psyche; and especially with my patients at my private consulting room, a very enriched, almost indescribable experience, indeed unfinished. There would always be something to do, share, learn, experience, and at the end, transform. All is just within "TIME" and about "yourself."

I have just come back from three weeks of a challenging academic experience. An invitation to be a conference participant in Russia, Moscow, where there is "hunger" for psychoanalysis, the enthusiasm of all type of professionals is indescribable, while in other places of the world and sadly between colleagues there is the rumor that psychoanalysis is dying. I was alsoat the I.P.A.-London 2019 Congress. Listening, exchanging, and participating in panels, conferences, I.P.A. committees, and working groups with colleagues from all over the world; visiting Freud's Museum; the Tavistock clinic; walking the streets and parks where a part of psychoanalysis continues its development (from 6 June 1938 up to today), without forgetting the origins on Berggesse 19, Vienna (up to May 1938). My knowledge, my mind, and my soul are in tears of appreciation, thankfulness, and emotion.

I could not imagine a better opportunity to accept this invitation and write this personal letter to you, My Dear Candidate. I cannot imagine being in my everyday life without my psychoanalytic practice and academic world and without my society and being part of an international psychoanalytical community.

While you read me, you must be asking yourself, "OK Ines, but HOW, and then WHAT?"

Well my answer FOR YOU, MY DEAR CANDIDATE: "Feel and capture within yourself YOUR OWN Psychoanalytical identity."

With all the structure you received during these years of psychoanalytical training, *keep transforming it into your own psychoanalytical training for life*. And all this depends on you, neither the institution nor your colleagues nor the international community. It is you, with your wish and desire in mind, that will determine the way you can capture the feeling, knowledge, and experience.

There are no "psychoanalysts;" there is "you as a psychoanalyst." There is not "a TIME" to finish the training; in a way, it is "your own time" and hopefully you will never finish the process of transforming yourself as a psychoanalyst. It always should be "to be continued"; there isn't "The End."

The How. Let me try to share with you My dear Candidate my way of doing it: enjoy and suffer every moment. Keep your enthusiasm, curiosity, illusions, the unfinished hours reading and writing, papers, supervising, patients, study groups, and from my point of view mainly: "the couch." For yourself going back to it in different times of your personal life and the one for your patients. And you are right there listening, holding, understanding. Yes "the couch," a couch full of tears, fears, furies and disillusions, idealizations, frustrations, insights, dreams, sharing loves and unrequited loves, dreams and silences, and also feelings of happiness and peace, should always accompany any analyst within respect, neutrality, ethics in one way or the other, and not just the analyst in training.

Since I was a Candidate, this has been my main task: "Feel and capture MY Psychoanalytical identity on the couch and outside the couch." The Institutes do their best, but "the best" has to come from you, Dear Candidate.

Through Freud's proposal and I.P.A. fundamentals, "supervision, theory, personal analysis" is how we end being a psychoanalyst, but not enough from my point of view. *Not enough to develop your own psychoanalytical identity*. I just remember one of my great professors using the following metaphor: "to be able to compose and play Jazz, you had to know the music fundamentals, then you are free to create your own music." Pretty much the same is true of analytical training and to be and develop your psychoanalytical identity.

Psychoanalytical identity is not just being one more psychoanalyst in the world after the training is over and to call and name yourself "I am a psychoanalyst."

WHAT is Psychoanalytical identity? From my perspective, and experience while I was a candidate and since then, it is YOU being a psychoanalyst, and this is what I will like to share with you. It is your own way of working with your patients; your own mental psychoanalytical model to view the suffering, love, and productiveness of life; your own way of writing psychoanalysis; your own way of including your personal life and the way you live life; your own way of treating your patients and yourself on and off "the couch"; and following my professor's metaphor, "the way you compose your jazz music, with theoretical background, and constant creativity."

My Dear Candidate, I would like to write and share a little about what I mean when I say, "including your personal life and the way you live life." Because this is what really will make you be "you as your own psychoanalyst and develop your psychoanalytical identity."

First of all, and very important, I want to make clear that it has nothing to do with sharing your personal life with your patients. No, please do not take it this way. It does have to do with your inner and outside world in relation with your everyday practice and how you integrate them in your mind and with your patient's speech and life. This is the way you make your psychoanalytical practice hand-crafted, creative. I will explain carefully and try to put it simply, to be able to communicate what I mean. It has to do with your inner and unconscious life and with your conscious and outside life; the way you live life in these two worlds of your own, and the magic and creative way you interweave it with all the training, theory, supervisions, and personal analysis.

Some time ago, during one of my vacations, I was visiting a museum where the original Guernica by Picasso is shown. I enjoyed the visit to the museum and admired Picasso and the Guernica. I have "parts" of Guernica's replies in my consultant room. Also, I was traveling by train and saw beautiful sunflower plantations. At that time, I thought about a patient, who had a very difficult but touching history. In one session, she gave me a paper sunflower. Sometimes, this patient described the way she was feeling that day by using that art display. When I was at the Museum, in front of the Guernica's, the sunflower plantations came back again to my mind, and also to my patient. There, I realized how much I was able to understand about her, her painful work on "the couch," when these three images came together in my mind "Her – Guernica – Sunflowers" within my own feelings while I was standing there at the museum. After this experience, I wrote a very productive paper for a psychoanalytical symposium, and the analysis on the couch moved differently, our analyst-patient relationship grew stronger. This is an example of how you can interweave your lived life with your psychoanalytical formation. The creative way of using experiences similar to the one I just shared, is what makes you be "you as a psychoanalyst with your own psychoanalytic identity."

Besides all the other things I mentioned earlier in this letter to you, there are other very important and valuable tools that will help you desire, develop, and transform your psychoanalytical identity.

When I was in training, I read the book *Psychoanalysis: The Impossible Profession*, by Janet Malcolm. In a way she is right with the title of the book; she is also passionate and defiant. The way I read this book is that I had to be creative as a psychoanalyst so it would not be impossible. Other books like *The Man with the Beautiful Voice: And More Stories from the Other Side of the Couch* by Lilian B. Rubin; *Mis claves para Ser feliz, (My clues to be happy) Sigmund Freud* by Sebastian Dozo Moreno; *El día que Nietzsche lloró (the day Nietzsche cry)* by Irvin D. Yalon; *Salome, her life and work* by Angela Livingston, and *Unorthodox Freud: The View from the Couch* by Beate Lohser and Peter M. Newton have been stories that keep my self-identity, keep me motivated, and help me to remember that my psychoanalytical identity has to be under transformation all the time, for me, my patients, and my choice on how to do the work. Besides, I could go and tell you what each of these books had left me and gave me to keep transforming my Psychoanalytical identity.

To finish this letter to you, Dear Candidate, I would like to share Freud's words from the book *Leaving today: The Freuds in Exile 1938*, from the Freud Museum London. A letter from Freud to his friend Max Eitongon from June 6, 1938, the day he arrived in London after his exile.

"The feeling of triumph on being liberated is too strongly mixed with sorrow, for in spite of everything I still greatly loved the prison from which I have been released."

Whenever the training is finished, it will be with sorrow but liberating, like Freud's feelings at the time of the exile. Again, it depends on you, like it was for him, to continue your psychoanalysis development, transformation, and identity, as Freud and Anna Freud continued in London to develop and keep writing. Freud, although being a refugee and very sick, was able to finish his last paper "Moses and Monotheism" (May 1939). He never stopped living his life and integrating and interweaving the life he lived with his profession.

Dear Candidate, I wish you the best on YOUR OWN way finding your Psychoanalytical identity. Remember, it is always on TIME with Your Self.

29 Donald Moss
New York, U.S.A.

Dear Candidate,

Beware the group. Beware the theory. Beware the supervisor. Beware the profession. Beware the meetings. Beware the case conference. Beware Freud, Klein, and Bion. Beware the relational turn. Beware the new. Beware the old. Beware contemporary. Beware classical. Beware ego psychology. Beware Lacan.

You will be under aggressive scrutiny as you navigate your way into becoming a psychoanalyst. The scrutiny will come from both within and without. You will wonder who you really are—what is authentic about you and what is merely cover; what is real and what is defense; what is strength and what is symptom.

Powerful forces will exert strong pulls on you. Change. Stay as you are. Be true to yourself. Come this way, be this way, think this way, do it this way. They will cite their own authority as evidence of their strength, their strength as evidence of their validity. Beware that logic. Be alert to the tension you feel as you encounter that logic. The group will use it, and the theory will. The classical, the new, all of them will use it.

You will wonder whether and when you should mount what kinds of energies in your own defense, to whom and to what you should ever devote your loyalties. Can you rely on yourself? Under pressure, can you really rely on yourself? Or, might it be better, after all, because you are, inarguably, new to this game, to turn elsewhere, to the ones who've been around, Ogden, maybe, Feldman, to all the available sources, all the pluralities, the others, the readymades, the previous, the proper? Wouldn't at least some of them be a better place to turn? You, after all, who, really, are you?

I want to tell you about two formative moments in my training. I was stunned, floored. In each of these moments, as though, while running freely and with abandon, I had smashed into an invisible wall. In neither moment was I badly damaged, though. In fact, I prospered from both. Most of all, these moments exposed me to my own naivete. They provided me with surprise, the crucial precondition for any kind of learning. Here's what I think I learned: in the world of psychoanalysis, along its prescribed paths, there exist these kinds of invisible walls. In fact, I think there are many. They aren't the same for you as they were for me. But I'm certain you will smash into some of them. So, I say to you that proceeding with abandon as you become a psychoanalyst may not be a good idea.

Be cautious, dear candidate, be wary.

> Here's a moment from the third year of my own training: We were a class of ten. We were working on Termination, and a classmate was presenting case material intended to exemplify a properly handled moment. I piped up, saying, basically, that something in the session didn't seem properly handled to me, that in fact something important had been missed. I was the only one who piped up in that way. The instructor, a very senior nationally known fellow, looked around the seminar table. I remember the look on his face, a look familiar to me from primary school, the look of certainty on an authority's face, certainty mixed with righteousness. Well, he said, nine of us see the material one way; one of us sees it another. He smiled. None of my classmates said anything. End of discussion.

Cruder than most moments, and thus more memorable, this experience nonetheless represents an ongoing corrosive force that was, and perhaps still is, present and defining in our Institute training regimens.

> Here's another, more wrenching perhaps, maybe less crude: I was a psychiatric resident in a psychoanalytic hospital. Ted, my best friend in the residency, and his girlfriend Annie, were close to my wife and me. On the same day, Ted and I were notified that we had each passed our licensing exam. That evening, I was on call in the ER. Ted came in with Annie slung over his shoulder. She had taken an overdose of Barbiturates, writing a note: Ted, now that you've passed your exam, you won't be needing me anymore. We worked on her, but she died. I went back to Ted's apartment with him, hanging out at the kitchen table until dawn when I had to get back to work. Ted made me promise not to tell anyone about the suicide. He wanted to do it. I promised and Ted kissed me, very warmly, as we hugged goodbye. The next day I found out that that morning Ted too had killed himself. He had gotten the barbiturates from our hospital's pharmacy. They wouldn't have given him those pills had it been known that Annie had killed herself. Of course, the staff and patients worked hard, separately and together, to make sense of what had happened. In the staff meetings, I was surrounded by senior psychoanalytic clinicians. They seemed to know what the proper emotional response to all of this should have been. To a one, they targeted Annie. We were to be furious with her for taking Ted from us. I, of course, had done the right thing. Who could have known? The problem for me, though, was that I wasn't angry at anyone. I also wasn't certain that I had done the wrong thing. In fact, I wasn't certain about any of it. I was, however, surrounded by others' certainties. I remember how often I heard the phrase: "You must be feeling…." and then something would follow. Not once did my feeling correspond to what I must have been feeling. I didn't know what to do. I wasn't saying much. I felt neither guilty nor innocent, neither angry nor forgiving. This had happened, that's how it

seemed to me. I couldn't talk to anyone who had actually been involved. They were both dead. The certainties around me started to take on a screeching, noisy aspect. I wanted to find someone to talk to. A supervisor recommended an analyst, a man I had never met, never heard of. In our meeting, as I was telling him what had happened, as I was going over it, he didn't say anything. What he did, though, after some time, was to momentarily close his eyes, as though, for a second, what he was hearing might have been too much to bear. He opened his eyes and maintained his silence throughout our meeting. The time had been mine, not his. It was an enormous relief. I stayed with him for ten years, in what, for me was a transformative psychoanalytic treatment.

I feel I learned important lessons from those ten years of experience, how lost I was at its beginning, how, without knowing it, I was looking for refuge—for a place, or a person—where I might find the kind of stillness I needed. I learned how damaging psychoanalytic certainty can be, how distorting, and how seductive. And I learned how enabling, restorative, and empowering a quiet and clear psychoanalytic presence can be. After the suicides, surrounded by certainty, I wasn't seduced. I somehow knew something was wrong that couldn't be apprehended quickly. I needed, and found time, needed and found the chance to proceed slowly. Later I learned that Freud had, in fact, referred to psychoanalysis as "slow magic." And indeed, it is slow magic.

I think most of us are capable of resisting the siren calls of certainty. The site of that capacity has nothing to do with insight or introspection. Instead, it marks our starting points, our origins as conscious beings—our most native, most private, site. This site and what it generates are beyond the reach of interpretation. No one but you belongs there. It's yours alone.

Access to that site is the pre-condition for any of us to become decent psychoanalysts. Forego access, let strangers in, and we forego our chance to do the kind of work I think we all might want to do.

This, I think, is one of the goals of analysis, to help other people regain access to this site, to clear it of ancient presences, to restore it to its original condition of dignity, decency, and directness—to restore its privacy, and to therefore restore the promise of generative relations with others. This native, private site allows us all the possibility of dignified and somber judgment, dignified and somber thought, dignified and somber love, and, of course, the delights of undignified, exhilarated, erotic play.

The opportunity to pursue that goal, to pursue it armed with more than a century of sustained thought, thought that began with Freud and that continues all around us, is a great gift. Enjoy it, dear candidate, this gift that, if you are careful, will continue, without end.

30 Virginia Ungar

Buenos Aires, Argentina

Dear Candidate,

I am very happy to have this opportunity to write to you and tell you about my own experience in analytic training.

First, I would like to congratulate you for your decision to train as a psychoanalyst. This, of course, implies a commitment for a number of years and, as you will by now have realized, an investment of time, effort, and money. Taking that decision requires an amount of courage to start out on a road that is not the easiest among the options on offer in the field of mental health.

I am not here referring to an intrinsic difficulty in this postgraduate course but to the demands that it places that you leave aside other options you may have for the little free time enjoyed by a young professional working in the field. What's more, when you start out on the path to becoming a psychoanalyst, you soon realize that it is also a way of living, a way of being in the world. We know that the work conditions involved are not easy in many places, but, in spite of that, you have chosen this path, and this decision draws an affectionate glance from me.

Let me tell you now something of my own story to give you some idea of what I feel today, many years later, about the journey I undertook. I started analysis when I was 18, encouraged by my father who was a radiologist. If you are surprised, I should explain that I was born, studied, lived, and worked in Buenos Aires, Argentina, and this was toward the end of the 1960s, a time in which psychoanalysis developed a lot there. My first interview was with the father of one of my schoolmates, José Bleger, one of the greats of Argentine psychoanalysis. This experience left a great impression on me that remains to the present day, and it was the precise moment that the journey started I am trying to relate to you now.

Bleger referred me to an analyst, and I had personal analysis with her for seven years. I had started Anthropology at university, but after two years I decided that I wanted to be an analyst myself. At that time, you could only train if you were an MD, and so I left Anthropology and entered the School of Medicine at the University of Buenos Aires. To my own surprise, they were wonderful years and I enjoyed studying all the subjects and had a great group of classmates, in the process getting to see a side of life that I had not previously known because much of these studies were carried out in a public hospital in Argentina.

Even if I went on to specialize when I graduated, I soon realized that I preferred to listen to patients than examine them.

Making a small digression from my tale, at the end of my third year I got married—quite early by today's standards—and had two children, the first born before I finished at the School of Medicine.

I then graduated, worked for a couple of years in professional healthcare at the hospital and saw patients in a consulting room with good supervisors, having started to study Freud with I.P.A. analysts in my student years.

For that reason, at the age of 28, about three years after finishing my personal analysis, I asked to do the admission interviews at a society that had just been set up called the Buenos Aires Psychoanalytic Association. I had already started my training analysis, and I was accepted and started psychoanalytic training with a group of colleagues that I studied together with for four years at the A.Pde.B.A. Institute.

These were very intense years: studying a lot and going to analysis, supervisions, and seminars. Now, looking back, I can see how difficult the process was and, at the same time, how unique and singular the training experience itself was.

I was very young. I worked with patients half the day, and I had two young children. I remember constantly juggling training and study with the children's school days, ballet classes, sports, and appointments with the orthodontist, not to mention when they got ill so that everything had to be cancelled. Weekends watching them play as I studied or wrote papers for seminars also come to mind. As I said, a huge effort was needed, and I was lucky enough to be able to count on my family to help in the care of my children.

As history cannot be written as the events described are taking place, it is only now that I can see the unique opportunity that I had in my life that allowed me to be four years "immersed" in psychoanalysis, very dedicated to my studies, supervision, and my analysis at an intense pace.

The group I was in at that time had 24 candidates and was the first to go through the institute. We formed a bond in our enthusiasm for the new institution, which was recognized immediately as a Provisional Society because of the number of founding members with high levels of experience and prestige in Argentina and abroad. We struck up solid friendships and studied together, but we also spent weekends, holidays, and trips together with children and partners. We had good experiences, and some sad ones too. There, friendships were sown that remain to this day.

Just one personal point: I started to attend local, regional, and international scientific meetings early on, and this opened up my mind in a way that only recently, in the position that I now occupy in the I.P.A., I realize was the start of the journey that brought me to where I am today.

I don't want to give an idealized picture of my training, however. Again, I say that there was a lot of effort and dedication in those years, and time scraped from wherever possible, especially family life. I had excellent teachers, and some not so. I had wonderful supervisors who were as generous as they were demanding. My colleagues said that I chose the most difficult ones, but from them I learnt during my clinical experience so much about psychoanalysis. Above all, however, and being faithful to Bion, I learnt through experience what it is to be dedicated to a task and to have a passion for psychoanalysis.

Now, I'd like to tell you some memories from that time that come to mind as I write. My first supervisor, Darío Sor, a very well-known expert in Bion, told me towards the end of my second year of supervision that he was going to evaluate me the next time we met. The following week, I arrived, and he said he would start the evaluation. A bit worried, I got ready to listen. "My dear doctor," he said, "you are not afraid of the unconscious." I waited to hear what came next, and he said, to my surprise: "That was your evaluation." It was only years later that I realized what he wanted to say to me, and I understand it better because supervision is one of my favorite professional activities. For me, it is a privileged space in which to transmit psychoanalysis.

I worked with children from the very start, and it was thanks to this practice that I was able to understand what I feel to be the most precious element of my clinical experience: contact with the most archaic, most infantile, and most creative points of human beings. These are areas that are not always open to easy access and reveal themselves in children in play.

Dear candidate, with this in mind, I recommend that, at least once in your professional life, you experience psychoanalysis with a child. You will thank me for the recommendation.

Another memory concerns Dr. Benito López, who was my supervisor for 11 years. He honored me with his friendship and was one of the most talented and generous people that I have ever met. Unfortunately, he died young. I had already finished my training when I worked with him, and it was he who introduced me to Donald Meltzer. My meeting with this exceptional analyst changed not only my psychoanalytic outlook, but also my vision of life, the world, and, especially, myself. I will never tire of giving thanks for the opportunity to meet him and organize with colleagues four of his visits to the Buenos Aires Psychoanalytic Association. I also studied and had supervision with him and shared unforgettable moments in Buenos Aires, Oxford, and other places around the world.

But now, I must return to the reason why I am in contact with you, dear candidate, not forgetting to tell you that I did my training during the last military dictatorship in Argentina, years that were the darkest and most horrible in the history of my country. Analysts disappeared, I lost friends, many teachers emigrated, and those of us who stayed lived for years in constant fear. That was not the best context in which to practice psychoanalysis, but institutional life provided us with contention, helping us even with readings about war.

Dear candidate, the moment has arrived to place myself in the present, glancing to the past but also focusing on the future. Training has changed in many ways. Even if, with the position I hold today, I have access to a broad panorama of contexts, I would like instead to tell you about what I see in my own institute.

Today, in terms of theory and clinical practice, training has become pluralistic. When I trained, we principally studied Freud, the classical authors, and some others and, in my institute, Klein and the post-Kleinian authors were also important.

Since then, the range of theories that are taught has widened. Now, the candidate is able to choose the teachers presenting their courses and the relationship is more open and there is a fluid and horizontal interchange.

Before finishing, I would like to say that both of us—the student and the teacher—must make an effort to always remember that you and your colleagues are doing postgraduate studies and, as such, are already our colleagues. Even if there will be something asymmetric implied in both the analytic relationship and the teaching and learning, we for our part must not treat you as children and you for your part must fight not to slide into that position. This is why I prefer to call you "analysts in training" and not "candidates."

To finish up, I only wish that you are able to enjoy and take the best advantage of this immersion in psychoanalysis. These are circumstances that may never present themselves again.

31 Arnold Richards
New York, U.S.A.

Dear Candidate

I think I can assert that from a very early age I wanted to become a psychoanalyst. My earliest lexical memory is reading about the death of Freud in the Yiddish Forward. Psychoanalysis combined for me, and many of my cohorts, the virtues of both science and the humanities. It is a field that one never tires of. The clinical and scientific challenges never end.

During my training at the New York Psychoanalytic Institute, some of us referred to it as the Church of Rome. It was the bastion of Freudian orthodoxy. It had a distinguished faculty that included a group that emigrated from Central Europe just before World War II. They had been trained by the cohort who had been analyzed by Freud or analyzed by others who had been analyzed by Freud or his close followers. We were very fortunate because the faculty, who were a Who's Who in psychoanalysis at the time, included Hartmann, Lowenstein, Mahler, Young, George Gero, Ruth Eissler, Martin Stein, Lily Busell, Charles Brenner, Jack Arlow, Otto Isakower, Herman Nunberg, Ken Calder, and Charles Fisher.

In 1989, the Encyclopedia Britannica published an article I wrote, "Psychoanalysis: Burgeoning and Beleaguered." When I started my analytic training in 1964, psychoanalysis was burgeoning. In the article, I referred to this time as the psychoanalysis of plenty—there were plenty of candidates and plenty of patients. Not only was psychoanalysis, as Auden wrote, a climate of opinion, it was also, at the time, the most important therapeutic approach.

I feel very fortunate about the time that I entered this field. The experience of being a candidate and the challenges that a candidate faces today are very different from what they were then. On the positive side today is that in the American Psychoanalytic Association, unlike in the past, non-physicians are welcomed. There is also the positive impact of psychoanalytic pluralism. I finished my training before Heinz Kohut published *The Analysis of the Self*. Melanie Klein, Winnicott, and Bowlby were not included in the reading lists for my classes. There was to some extent a stultifying Freudian orthodoxy at the N.Y.P.S.I., advocated by the European emigres but opposed, to some extent, by some of the Americans, particularly Jack Arlow and Charles Brenner.

However, the organizational rigidity and the structure and polices of exclusion remain to this day in some institutes. Candidates are naturally interested in graduating, advancing in their institutes after graduation, and being in a position to get referrals. Opposing institutional rigidity can, and likely will, work against a candidate. There is no easy solution to this situation, and I am not sure what advice I can give. Certainly, diversification of affiliation can be helpful post-graduation. But I do know of several analysts who have had to move to another city to find a more congenial home. In the end, we need to try to be true to ourselves, to our principles, and our beliefs. And it is important to remember that this is part of the best analytic attitude.

In the years after my training, I have been very proud of my success in nurturing the writing of younger colleagues, candidates, and students. Psychoanalysis offers many pleasures and satisfactions—treating patients, teaching, and politics. Every analysis is a voyage of discovery for the patient and the analyst. The analytic couple learns how the mind works, and this knowledge fosters healing and life change. The field's intellectual and clinical satisfactions remain for a dedicated few. Whatever the hardships involved in training for this profession and in its practice, the stakes could not be more significant. In a segment on P.B.S. about psychoanalysis that I produced, we interviewed Charles Brenner. When we asked him about the importance of what the analyst does, he said, "It can be a matter of life"—pause—"or death." To all prospective candidates welcome.

32 Ellen Pinsky
Cambridge, U.S.A.

Dear Candidate,

When I was a candidate, my friends and I used to play a game that goes like this:

> Imagine that the entire psychoanalytic literature is destroyed tomorrow. Psychoanalysis vanishes, but you can bury a time capsule to be dug up after a few hundred years. Into that capsule you can put some papers—a handful of short works, or excerpts from longer works, ten or twelve brief pieces at most, that people of the future might use to reconstruct psychoanalysis. What do you put in the imaginary capsule?

So, here's an assignment: Create your own imaginary time capsule. Your capsule's contents won't be the same as anyone else's. Also, the composition of your capsule is not static but will shift over time, necessarily so. The dynamic process is the point: your reading, questioning, mulling the texts—appreciating, and learning from, the always changing contents. Some selections for your capsule may remain, some will settle in for a while, and then you'll remove one or two to make room for something else.

In the process of creating, and re-creating, your capsule, you are not only tracking your own development as a psychoanalyst, you are also preserving the discipline. Perhaps most important, you are writing a letter you would send to future generations of aspiring psychoanalytic students, in this way connecting you to past and to future. (I think here of Freud's melodic sentence in "Creative Writers and Day-Dreaming," about phantasy, or daydreams, and the function of a child's play: "Thus past, present and future are strung together, as it were," Freud writes, "on the thread of the wish that runs through them" [1908, 148].)

Here, for guidance and encouragement as you work on your capsule, I offer the following, from a different realm:

> "If France were destroyed tomorrow and nothing remained but this film," once wrote the critic Richard Roud, "the whole country and its civilization could be reconstructed from it" (1980, 841).

That audacious assertion about Jean Renoir's masterwork, *The Rules of the Game*, asks the viewer to think about an encompassing work of art: What is the film's power to epitomize, in one hour and fifty minutes of playing time, an entire culture—to compress an essence, across a range, from germinating seed to full flowering?

In simpler words, how does the film work? How to think about it and articulate it?

Can Freud's remarkable "talking cure," too, be epitomized or preserved in such a seed? Can you capture that psychoanalytic essence in your own time capsule?

The main idea is for each person to design (and re-design) a personal, particular time capsule. It's not about a list, but about a process—an individual who is learning over time. For the record, I'll divulge my own capsule: a combination of standard, canonical ingredients and idiosyncrasies, its contents not yet sealed, never finalized. Over the years I've added and removed works, but certain things are always there: for example, Hans Loewald's paper on therapeutic action (1960), Paula Heimann's "On Counter-transference" (1950), Winnicott's "The Use of an Object" (1969), and Freud's brief narrative about his toddler grandson known as "Fort-Da" (1920, 14–15). Sometimes I include Freud's "Creative Writers and Day-Dreaming" (1908), or James Strachey's "The Nature of the Therapeutic Action of Psychoanalysis" (1934), and sometimes more recent pieces: for example, Brian Bird's "Notes on Transference" (1972), Betty Joseph's "Transference: the Total Situation" (1985), Ida Macalpine's "The Development of Transference" (1950), Irma Brenman Pick's "Working through in the Countertransference" (1985); or, I'll add a paper, maybe two, by Melanie Klein, John Klauber, or André Green. The combination is always shifting, some occupants transitory, some never removed.

It's always useful to argue why a particular piece of writing is indispensable to reconstructing psychoanalysis. But for me, as maybe not for some, Freud always takes up a lot of the capsule, with two of his briefest papers never removed, and competing for first and second place: "Remembering, Repeating and Working-Through" (1914) and "Observations on Transference-Love" (1915). In these two closely linked short essays (barely twenty pages in all)—rich, maddening, impossible to exhaust—in these two gorgeous pieces, I still find the foundation.

But if I have to choose, "Observations on Transference-Love" reigns alone at the top of my list. Freud's essay is the quintessential document—defining the clinical setup, charting its dangers, providing ethical precepts for guiding treatment, and, perhaps above all, in the context of those ethical questions, confronting the immense power and necessary strangeness of the transference: that form of love, or attachment, that fuels the psychoanalytic process.

After all these years, I still revise my capsule. Recently I added Selma Fraiberg's beautifully written (and prescient) "Ghosts in the Nursery" (1975)—I hear in it an echo of Freud's "summoning up a spirit from the underworld" (1915, 164)—and also included Loewald's "Transference and Love" (2000 [1988], 549–563), an especially rich companion piece to Freud's 1915 essay on that fundamental subject. Loewald writes eloquently there of "the communications between patient and analyst, each being moved by the other" (562). My selections, as you can see, emphasize, and re-emphasize, the importance of the concepts of transference and counter-transference, with their elaboration over the years. I'm drawn also to the writers who understand infancy and childhood. I especially value thinkers who illuminate the nature of the therapeutic relationship: "What is the place of love," they ask, "and what kinds of love, pass between the two people in the treatment room?"

To repeat once again, the time-capsule game etches the importance of the literature, whichever pieces a person chooses, and also aims to bring in the humanities more fully. It's the choosing and the re-choosing that matters. The aim is to keep something alive, not only the individual analyst's development but the evolving, and increasingly jeopardized, discipline itself. One's capsule, with both its permanent occupants and the ever-shifting other bits, is a way to illustrate (or track) growth, change, and development for a student analyst, and for every analyst over a life-time of learning. That's my view, as an educator.

I encourage you to fall in love with the writers, to treasure the texts, to read, read, read. Be curious, learn the language, try on different theories, but at the same time be suspicious of jargon and bandwagons. Strive always to use plain words. The unconscious, after all, nestles in the body, not in polysyllabic technical terms.

Let me conclude with my most recent capsule addition is a passage by an especially fine writer and master teacher. Here is Ella Freeman Sharpe, almost a hundred years ago, on "qualifying" as an analyst:

> In any reading for analytical qualification I would make compulsory the following books: Nursery Rhymes, the Alice books, Hunting of the Snark, Grimm, Andersen, the Brer Rabbit books, Water Babies, Struwelpeter, Undine, Rumpelstilzkin, Peter Ibbetson, Greek Myths and Tragedies, Shakespeare's Plays.

Were I an arbiter of training, I should set an examination on those books as a final test by which the would-be analyst should stand or fall. My final examination for qualification would run on these lines:

> Quote in full a verse in which "London Bridge is falling down" occurs.
> Give briefly the story of three blind mice.
> If the mice were blind, how come they run after the farmer's wife so purposely?

Account for the cutting off of their tails.

Illustrate what unconscious drama is being staged when a patient thinks of himself as one of the blind mice. What inference concerning the health of the ego do you draw from the fact that the tails were cut off instead of the mice being killed?

"Somewhere in that list of immortal stories we shall all find an unconscious phantasy of our own. To understand even the tale of the three blind mice is to have a conception of what those crystallized terms id, ego and super-ego really mean in terms of the drama of life. Faced by a cross-examination on children's nursery rhymes in terms of psycho-analytical theory, with an application to the struggles going on in ourselves or in our patients, would any of us do more than scramble through it? To pass it creditably would mean that one had a good chance of being a creditable technician" (1930, 256–257).

Sharpe's examples recall Renoir's *The Rules of the Game*. If as Richard Roud says, that film contains the necessary seed, it is not by pronouncing large ideas, or explicit historical clichés, but instead by details: of manners, of cuisine, of gadgets, social amusements, and customs of adultery in different social classes.

Sharpe's test for qualification accords with another brief passage on psychoanalytic education: Freud's imagined "college of psycho-analysis" (perhaps Freud's own time capsule?), a school where the curriculum for analytic students would include: "the history of civilization, mythology, the psychology of religion and the science of literature. Unless he is well at home in these subjects," writes Freud, "an analyst can make nothing of a large amount of his material" (*The Question of Lay Analysis*, 1926, 246). How thrilling for me, a former middle school English teacher, not only to find that Freud is himself a wonderful writer, but also to see how deeply he values the humanities.

Finally, dear Candidate, one more thing: Your time capsule needs to include a nursery rhyme, children's story, comic strip, and fairy tale or myth of your choice. Enjoy!

33 H. Shmuel Erlich
Tel Aviv, Israel

Dear Candidate,

Although we have never met and hardly know each other, I feel the need to write to you, to share some of my own experiences (alas, too long! The years go by too quickly...) which I hope will mean something to you and to tell you why I feel so close and involved in what you must be going through. I hope you won't mind if I get a bit personal, because it is an important part of the story: It is all so very personal and not merely professional.

Talking to a candidate like you invariably raises in me the questions I faced when I applied, was accepted, and began my training in the Israel Psychoanalytic Institute. One big question was: Why in the world do I need this? And that was even before I knew what I was getting into. I was fortunate to have an excellent psychoanalytically oriented training as a post-doctoral at the Austen Riggs Center, and when I returned to Israel, I was regarded by many as a psychoanalyst. I quickly realized, however, that the people with whom I shared a common language were all psychoanalysts, so I decided to complete my training, applied to the Institute and was accepted.

In the first place, therefore, the answer to why I needed this is at this level: to be with the people I would have a great deal in common with. To be frank, and as you may already have experienced yourself, it is true that even within the Institute, and later in the Psychoanalytic Society, I have more in common with some, less with others, and very little with a few others. But even this taught me an important, if humbling, lesson: people always are different from one another in everything they do or belong to. This is so even within a family, where people differ in so many ways. And yet, again as in a family, there is a commonness that holds and binds them together, over and beyond any discrepancies and disagreements.

Something else I discovered over the years, and again the family metaphor serves me in this, is that I (and most of the colleagues I know) are in this psychoanalytic venture not for any financial gains (there aren't any) nor for getting the esteem of those outside the field (there is rarely anything vaguely approaching it, more often one gets the astonished response of why belong to something extinct, esoteric, and irrelevant) but simply for the love of it. Believe me, it is a rare privilege, a great pleasure, and immeasurably worthwhile to spend your life engaged in something you love.

You may well ask: What is there to love? The training can be exhausting and burdensome, the reading often hard to understand and rarely enjoyable, the people I see in analysis can be so difficult and not easily likeable, and what they project onto me is sometimes so obnoxious or plaintive that it is nearly impossible to take. Well, all true. You must already have come across the aphorism, "The impossible profession." But let me take these complaints (or realistic observations, if you prefer) one at a time to see what they may hold for you.

Let's start with the reading material. You are of course quite right in saying that a great deal of what you read is difficult to comprehend. There are several reasons for this. First, psychoanalysts are not necessarily great writers. A few are indeed, and it is a great pleasure to read them, except that even then you should be careful not to fall for the beauty of the prose and maintain an impartial judgment of its psychoanalytic merits: Is it original or a rehash? Does it contribute in any way to the expansion of what we know, or does it serve to enhance the author's own ego? Does it engage with what might be called psychoanalytic core ideas, or does it "expand" our horizons to take in barely related ideas, be it spirituality, mysticism, or romantic notions? This may sound overly judgmental, but I believe it is crucial if you wish to get at what I called above the "psychoanalytic core," because holding on to it is what will give you the perseverance and endurance you will need.

An important exception in this connection is reading Freud. Admittedly, it is a very personal predilection, so let me explain. I came to Freud somewhat belatedly, having had more of an ego-psychology training coupled with an interpersonal background. Occupying the Freud Chair at the Hebrew University of Jerusalem for fifteen years, I offered courses on the development of Freud's thought that were open to university-wide students. I continued to teach Freud in the same way at the Institute, and for many years now I offer a seminar to members of our society, many of whom are experienced and seasoned analysts, in which we systematically read and discuss Freud's writings. What I found in all these engagements is remarkable: I and everyone else simply enjoy it so much that it becomes a pleasurable exercise. Beyond the pleasure, it is also a great way to learn psychoanalysis in a way that integrates the basics with contemporary contributions. I highly recommend that you find a teacher who loves Freud and study with him or her, either within the Institute or outside it.

You say that the people you see in analysis are difficult. That is probably true, and for more than one reason. When the usual social façade is removed or becomes unimportant, the less attractive features of human nature tend to surface, and that is not always pretty. It echoes a saying attributed to Sullivan, that we are all more human than otherwise. But it is also due to other factors, mainly the shapes taken by contemporary psychopathology, which are often heavily colored by narcissistic and borderline features. Here you have my sympathy, though with important caveats. While it is true that this is often the presenting picture or initial understanding, bear in mind that these may be colored or skewed by theoretical predilections. I have frequently run into cases that were presented as narcissistic personalities, for instance, that turned out to be more hysteric and/or otherwise neurotic in terms of the actual underlying dynamics. Unlike medicine, we don't have the independently arrived at pathology findings to support our clinical impressions; hence, diagnosis is still largely an observational art subject to theoretical preferences. This is further complicated by the preference more often given to psychodynamics over diagnostic categorization. What is important to remember is that neurosis, as a human malady, has not disappeared from the face of the earth.

Having said that, there is another issue that has to do with what is ideally suitable for a candidate to enable him or her to learn psychoanalysis. The widening scope of psychoanalysis, together with the self-selection of those who elect to come to analysis and are ready to invest in it, have made it difficult to find suitable patients for analysis in terms of what was considered suitable in the past. As a result, I often meet candidates who do what I have come to call "heroic treatment" of a very difficult patient. While these therapies are often admirable, it is not always clear what the candidate has learned about what psychoanalysis is all about. It is a difficult issue that is also heavily burdened by political overtones, and it is best to take it up with one's supervisor. I can only wish you that at least some of the cases you will see in analysis will be of the more neurotic kind, so you may gain a more balanced view of analysis.

We come to your third difficulty, which has to do with the unpleasant, sometimes distasteful or anxiety-producing stuff these analysands project on you. You just raised what is perhaps the most fundamental and generally acknowledged feature of psychoanalysis: the transference. It does take time and effort, and most importantly your own analysis, to appreciate this aspect of analysis, perhaps better named analytic creation. As you well know, transference is ubiquitous and omnipresent in all of life. Yet it is the only place designed especially to allow it to take place unpunished, to gently foster its development, and to be able to work it toward freeing the person from his or her repetition compulsion—the only place you will find this in any real and deep sense is psychoanalysis.

It took me a long time to really understand this, but once you get it, it works like a charm. My initial difficulty had to do with my experience at the Austen Riggs Center I mentioned above. At Riggs every patient was seen four times a week in what we called "individual intensive psychoanalytically oriented psychotherapy." When I began to see patients in analysis in my training, it was at first difficult to understand the difference between this "psychoanalysis" and the "psychotherapy" I did at Riggs. I searched long for the answer and eventually came up with what for me is an important dimension that distinguishes between the two: It is a question of the *degree* to which both parties can feel free of the impact of external reality and focus on the inner world and psychic reality. At its best, analysis enables this much more than psychotherapy; yet it is always not an absolute but a matter of degree.

What is it then that enables you to work with the analysand's transference? The fact that you can offer yourself fully and uninhibitedly to the person you are treating, because what you offer him is your listening and understanding, your unwavering commitment to be there for the sessions, to create and maintain the analytic frame. It allows you to do all this and more because you grow to realize that the unpleasantness that comes your way—whether hate and aggression, resistance and stubborn stuckness, or debilitating adoration and demands for real intimacy—all have little to do with who you are as a real person. I know this is a much studied and debated subject, and the place of the analyst's real person is thought by many to play an active and even crucial role in what develops. Allow me to sidestep the learned writings and opinions of respectable colleagues and speak for myself. Of course, it is undeniable that we analysts, just like our patients, vary widely and deeply, and surely this affects what happens in the consulting room. Nevertheless, I believe that what every analyst (and for that matter, psychoanalytic psychotherapist) offers is a special part of his self (ego), a part that I think of as his or her professional, psychoanalytically trained part and the knowledge it has acquired—intellectual, emotional and experiential, even unconscious and reverie—and to offer it fully and without reservation. The other parts of the "real" person are present, of course, and will color the specificity of his professional self, but they must remain offstage, hiding in the wings. The only times they may come on stage is if something untoward happens to the main actor.

I realize this is a difficult one to take in. As I said, it has taken me a long time to understand. I share it with you now in the hope that it will somehow and somewhat ease the *transition* you must make: From experiencing and responding to people who treat you as their real object (pardon the psychoanalytic term), to whom you relate, as you should, as real objects who are entitled to project their transference concerns, feelings, and wishes on you. This transition is probably the most significant piece of learning you will accomplish.

This letter is becoming rather long, but I do have one last point I want to share with you. It too stems from my personal way and development; whether it suits you is something you will decide for yourself, based on your inclinations and preferences. I have in mind a side of psychoanalysis not often stressed, yet very influential in many ways: the politics of psychoanalysis. By politics I mean those activities, which take place outside the consulting room, in our public and social life, in which we also partake, as do our fellow human beings. It is an intricate, complex, and at times difficult undertaking, yet also very interesting and unquestionably influential on our professional existence and status. If we are, like all social endeavors, part of the marketplace, we must take it seriously, because the rules of the game in this marketplace are very different from the rules we adhere to in our practice. It involves such varying endeavors as being part of the university, influencing pertinent legislation, appearing in the media, etc. In an arena closer to home, it starts with our own institutions: the psychoanalytic society and institute we belong to, as well as our wider and more remote organizations, for example, our regional and global ones.

I realize fully that not every psychoanalyst sees this as an important aspect of his professional functioning, and some even regard it as countermanded to being a good analyst, one who spends all her time and effort in the consulting room.

I see it differently; I believe these aspects are not opposed or contradictory in any way. In fact, they may well enrich each other. I have done it myself—as chair of the Education Committee and president of our society, and as a four-term regional representative on the IPA Board and chair of several of its committees. So I do speak from experience. Psychoanalysis, as Freud saw it, is the special method for researching the human mind, the theory that derives from this method, and the treatment method based on this theory. But it is also a movement, which represents psychoanalysis to the world and to itself.

Whatever you may eventually choose to do, I wish you an enriching experience, one that will remain with you for life. I hope some of the ideas I shared with you will become part of this journey.

Good fortune!

34 Bent Rosenbaum
Copenhagen, Denmark

Dear Candidate,

You are standing before an entrance to a world of possibly creative and inspiring work—depending on you; your teachers and their modes of teaching; the group dynamics between candidates with whom you will be sharing your years of training; the inspirational moments of your analyst's interventions; and your supervisors' ability to balance between on one hand giving you insight into the trans-subjective basis of the transference-countertransference dynamics, derived from his/her own experience, and on the other facilitating your own creative thinking to grow in your efforts to meet and analyze the desire of your own analysands.

I welcome you very much for many reasons, and one of them is that progression within the psychoanalytic association needs serious young minds to re-read, re-think, and develop further our fundamental questions. You shall explore, in ways you have not done before, the dynamics of how minds meet, and in these meetings of minds surprises of unthought representations, intuitionistic expressions of unknown thoughts and integrative thinking, dynamics of anger, sadness, and anxiety—all these and more are mise-en-scène in ways that you may at first feel chaotic and confusing and later may experience as inspirational gifts enriching your life.

If you are entering your development and psychoanalytic formation within the Eitingon model, then you have probably already half-opened the door to this world by being in analysis for some time; tasted the difficulty of being open, honest, and direct in your listening to; and speaking the truth of yourself in the presence of another, your analyst. You have already sensed parts of yourself that you (consciously and pre-consciously) can hear more or less clearly, as well as the much larger parts of yourself that you cannot (and sometimes do not want to) hear and thus have not direct access to. The only access you have to these hidden, repressed and otherwise negated parts of yourself is through displacement of unconscious signifiers, and they will never find expressions in the right words or the right tone of voice when they are surfacing into consciousness and interfering in your daily work and social communications, your erotic life, and your artistic creativity in the transitional space between you and the other.

You are in the beginning of sensing how the subjects of the minds in the analytic setting are at the same time linked to and separate from each other, both dependent and independent, both mastering the other and being mastered by what comes from the other. You have had both good and troublesome moments of understanding the dynamics of your psyche by experiencing the different positions from which you and your analyst utter statements and words—the positions of the analyst (with evenly hovering attention) and the analysand (you, freely associating and not keeping back any "Einfall") meeting within a specific and very peculiar frame. And moreover, you have been touched by acknowledging how polysemous verbal and paraverbal language is in the exchange between conscious and unconscious layers of your speech.

Your *personal analysis*, enhancing your self-analysis, will continue many more years alongside with the soon coming addition of *theoretical seminars* (probably, and hopefully, beginning with an insight in the development of Freud's fruitful ideas, and their importance for establishing psychoanalysis as a clinical science with its own specificity) and the *supervision of cases* where you are placed in the position of the psychoanalyst. The concomitant existence of these three grounding activities prepares your listening capacities with special abilities in listening to the layers and orders of the chain of signifiers reaching your ears (including the third one), stemming from the unconscious of the analysand—the not-said, the not-heard, the not-yet-inscribed in the psyche which awaits moments of being created in new ways.

The dialectic between three areas of your psychoanalytic formation—your personal analysis, your reflections in the theoretical seminars, and your supervision experience—can be conceived as the Borromean knots, to borrow a model that Lacan uses to illustrate the relation between the Symbolic, The Imaginary, and the Real Order.

This model of knots shows the three dimensions bound together in such a way that if one of them is cut then all of them fall apart. You cannot have a psychoanalytic stance without all three of them. Elements as creativity, interest in playing with the meaning of speech, the not-knowing stance, capacity for listening for the harmonies and disharmonies of thoughts, and symbolic integration belong to each of these dimensions—although in a different manner.

You may feel that these statements about the three close-linked dimensions are common sense. However, when you are dwelling in one of them, you will experience how much work it takes to link and integrate the one with the two others. For instance, when you attend a seminar on Freud's "Three essays on sexuality," or "Drives and their vicissitudes" or other texts, then it takes a lot of work to relate the readings of the texts and the group discussions of them in your theoretical seminars to your personal experiences (expressed in your analysis) of erotic desire and binding drives to objects that you are deeply engaged with (music, dance, painting, specific activities, reading literature about specific topics—all of these related to your personal history), and furthermore to relate the readings of the theoretical texts to interventions that you feel concern your own analysand—interventions that you bring into supervision for comments from your supervisor.

I remember the transformation I experienced when I, in my formation as an analyst, began finding thoughtful threads connecting for instance the concept of "the breast as an object" with "the breast as lost object" and further with "subjective object to be found" transformed into "subjective object objectively perceived" (Winnicott), and further "awaiting the breast realizing the absence of the breast that might satisfy the waiting" (Bion). Not only could these seemingly different conceptualizations be linked in their abstract forms, but they also became present in the analytic space in the form of the calming and challenging couch being "the breast" and the thoughts of the analyst being the milk—sometimes being more nourishing and digestible than at other times. And with these links the concept of oral drive and orality became alive as "words, ideas or images being taken in, chewed on, bitten into pieces, tasted, swallowed, and easily or not-easily digested."

It is important when you reflect upon and bring yourself into the action of linking the three dimensions that this is done with the attempt to relate to the underlying question: "what is my desire to become an analyst?" This question is not one that you can answer at once or before you start your analytic training. It will pop up again and again during your formation and each time add different reflections to your answer.

Personally

It is exactly in the moments when you transform the idea of common sense of the relationship of the three dimensions into a deep interest in "how" they are connected and the multiple ways that can be done, that the formation to become an analyst may be satisfying and may continue in your life-long work as analyst, and thus certainly not ending with your graduation.

During my life as an analyst, I have more and more reflected upon what did drive and shape my "desire to become an analyst." I do not think I thought much about it in a direct manner when I started my training, but I am sure that it has influenced me: The double cultural background grounding my senses that meaning is grounded in divergent and convergent discourses; the early and deep interest in existential and political philosophy, giving the concept of the Unconscious a place in cultural and group discourse rather than in the single individual; the family gatherings in which chamber music and playing by ear had a central position thus teaching me that improvisation as well as precise and hard training is an art; having a director of the Royal theatre as an uncle and therefore having the understanding of theater texts, ways of performing with body and language, and background-foreground imaging, as part of my interest in the psychological dynamics; being deeply interested in Erich Fromm as an entrance to Freud and psychoanalysis; and a long-lasting interest in semiotics and structuralism, sharpening my listening for conscious and unconscious signifiers and signs as these emerge from the unconscious and are exchanged with their many communicative functions.

If I should summarize these experiences into an advice, then it would be: Psychoanalysis is not only a clinical science, it is also an art. Teach yourself to let your artistic background be reflected in your interventions. Let the hidden order of art make you feel how poetic and metaphorical use of language create new meanings that you may convey in your interventions and that may help the analysands create new links where attacks on linking have taken place.

Lastly, before you begin your training, it is important to be aware what the "personal analysis," "theory," and "supervision" do not mean. Personal analysis is *not* about learning introspection, theoretical seminars are *not* about building libraries of intellectual knowledge, and supervision experience is *not* about making you an expert in communication. These abilities—the belief that you can adequately see into yourself, know about yourself, and be an expert in communication—may just as well stand in the way of developing an analytic stance, in which the subject of yourself is positioned in the dimension of the Other, emerging without pre-given knowledge. Your teachers (discussants in theoretical seminars) and your supervisors may act as if they know this positioning in the Other. But remember: their affective thoughts and language are also produced by what they do not grasp.

The strength of psychoanalytic thinking will always be: The Unconscious can never be denied. Be open-minded to that basic idea, and make your mind ready for the reception of uncanny, not-understandable, un-familiar, chaotic, and anxiety provoking representations. They also harbor the aesthetics of beauty, harmony, and truth.

I send you best wishes for the future!

35 Fredric Perlman
New York, U.S.A.

Dear Candidate,

I am very pleased to have this opportunity to connect with you. In these few pages, I hope to share with you my enthusiasm for the work we do, offer you some spirited encouragement in confronting the challenges of training, and most of all, let you know how happy I am that you are joining our ranks.

I love being an analyst. I cannot imagine a calling more in keeping with my character or my sense of life. Growing up, I entertained lots of romantic notions about wildly different career ideas, and, for a time, actively pursued a career in theater. As an actor, I found that every character, no matter how noxious, tormented, or destructive, could be understood in terms of their life story, whether conveyed in the text or created by the actor. Some years later, working with troubled teens, I struggled to make sense of their very self-defeating, often antisocial behavior. I found that I could understand these kids, much as I came to understand characters in a play. Again, I found they made a kind of human sense to me once I could imagine their inner worlds and life stories. A social worker I knew during those years used to cite Harry Stack Sullivan's saying that "we are all much more simply human than otherwise." This rang true to me, and I found it moving. Some years later, in my own analysis, I discovered that my drive to understand others as well as myself was itself a product of my life story, a need that took shape in the childhood context of a complicated, sometimes tumultuous multigenerational family where passions often ran high, over my head but not without leaving their mark on my emotional life.

I love the fact that the essence of our calling is a human encounter designed solely for the purpose of understanding another person's life. We all need to feel understood, to be held in another's mind, in order to experience the feeling of safety and affirmation that make it possible to think about ourselves and the way we live. Let's face it: it is hard to be a person—hard for each of us in one way or another. We are not endowed by nature with an innately determined program for living. Each of us must fashion his or her own way of life. As analysts, we know that our efforts to do so are complicated by unconscious determinants and conflicts and by habits of childhood origin. As adults, many of us live with the oddities and self-defeating dysfunctions that we inherit from our childhoods, suffering the consequences of this inheritance, and holding ourselves to account as if we were to blame for our troubles. The shame and guilt that accompany this invalidation compounds the cost of our troubles.

The treatment we offer our patients is healing and restorative, a vital affirmation of authenticity and personhood in a world driven by the interests of production and consumption; of industry and commerce; and a culture industry that promotes whiter teeth, new shoes, and bigger cars as nutriments of happiness. These institutional interests are powerful. We encounter them not only in our personal lives, but in our professional lives as analysts: in the policies of insurance companies, the products of the pharmaceutical companies, and even in the educational curricula of mental health training programs. The institutional order promotes pills for the "chemical imbalances" it claims are the causes of human misery, or short-term treatment protocols with defined inputs, outcomes, and durations. Put simply, the culture mystifies and misleads, and when patients suffer, it offers fixes that may further their confusion and alienation. In this world, we psychoanalysts are outliers in our thinking and our practices, marginal to the mental health industry and to the larger culture that shapes it.

This is a difficult status to inhabit, but I encourage you to embrace it. Let it invigorate rather than dispirit you. Psychoanalysts are not agents of social adjustment, or symptomatic melioration, but healers of inner pain, midwives to selves emerging from confusion. We analysts are the only healers I know of whose core purpose is to understand and illuminate rather than to persuade: to help our patients make sense of themselves, to retrieve the lost stories behind their troubles, to restore their sense of coherence and self-worth, and over time, to promote their capacity and courage to create their own designs for living. Psychoanalysis is nothing if not a cure of the soul: a cure attained by curiosity not correctives, by thoughtful insights jointly ascertained, and by kindness conveyed in the currency of empathy, respect, and compassion.

In the same spirit, I want to encourage each of you to approach your training with the same respect for your own creativity and autonomy that you strive to bring to your patients. Your professional selves need to grow and develop in a fashion that is consistent with your own sensibilities and judgment. This takes years, perhaps a lifetime, for our ideas keep developing. I remember Martin Bergmann, on the occasion of his 85th birthday, commenting that he could not retire because, as he said, "I am really starting to get good at this!"

One of the most daunting obstacles to the development of a professional identity is the anxiety that analytic work entails. We bear a heavy responsibility to our patients. At the same time, an analyst is inevitably in uncharted waters as a treatment deepens. We are bound to find ourselves in states of confusion about the process and subject to doubts about our competence or our characters as we proceed. We need theory to ground ourselves, but there is no one single theory to rely on. The pathway to professional identity is much more of a maze than a highway.

I entered psychoanalytic training in 1981, at a time when psychoanalysis was already a pluralistic enterprise. Although some institutes in New York promoted a single school of analysis, the Postgraduate Center, where I trained, was a bustling center of diverse thought and practice. I entered training devoted to self-psychology, but, owing to circumstances at the institute, I entered analysis with a dyed-in-the-wool Freudian, and, of my two first-year supervisors, one was as an object relations analyst and the other an ego-psychologist. I found myself disagreeing with everyone—including myself! It soon became clear that I wasn't the only one with a problem. All of my classmates seemed to have similar anxieties—and similarly fixed ideas, often in accordance with the views of their training analysts or of admired supervisors. I remember thinking then, as I think now, that we were all driven by our anxieties toward totalistic identifications with one authoritative theory or another.

In my second year of training, following my refusal to continue in supervision with an oppressive and dominating supervisor, I entered supervision with a fellow named Alexander Wolf. Al was an independent thinker, an analyst whose clinical innovations included analysis in groups and whose central concern was always the promotion of free thought and individuality. He had been one of the candidates who, on the night of Horney's famous demotion in 1941, marched out of the New York Psychoanalytic Institute, along with Karen Horney and her other supporters, singing "Let My People Go." I will never forget my first formal supervisory meeting with Al.

Al began by telling me the story of his experience in supervision with Karen Horney. (Try to imagine Al speaking slowly, in a thick New York accent, pausing between phrases.)

> Every week I would go to supervision and I would tell Karen Horney everything that my patient told me. And I would listen very carefully to everything that Karen Horney said to me about the patient. And then I would tell the patient everything that Karen Horney had said to me. And then I would listen to everything my patient said, and then tell Karen Horney everything that my patient said, and then listen to everything that Karen Horney said, and then tell the patient everything that Karen Horney said. And it went on like this for week after week until I finally realized, "This is ridiculous. Why don't the two of them just get together and leave me out of it!"

With this hilarious narrative, delivered in the style of a Borscht Belt comic, Al introduced me to his core conviction about selfhood. "Your patient is always *your* patient," he emphasized, "not *my* patient. You will always know him better than I know him. And you will have to work with him *your* way, not *my* way." With some anxiety, I told him that, although I thought I had my own way before I started training, now I realized that I really didn't. I only had other people's ways. "Of course!" he replied. "You are just beginning. You have to find *your* way to be an analyst—just as you have to find *your* way to being a person."

Al's encouragement gave me the psychological space and support I needed to grow as an analyst. Like our patients, we each have to develop our own identities by consulting our experience and our sense of reality as we go along.

Of course, we can only learn one theory at a time, and perhaps it is necessary to adopt a single theory as a point of departure. But no theory ought to be held too tightly, clung to with absolute conviction or certainty. Certainty is appealing, but it is a set-up for more anxiety because no theory is ever complete. That's why psychoanalytic theory keeps expanding and proliferating.

It can be a struggle to form your own convictions in the face of multiple and competing "certainties" and pressures for conformity. Fritz Wittels, Martin Bergmann, and other analysts have cited the Biblical tale of Jacob's experience wrestling with an angel as an allegory to their own experiences of struggling to emancipate themselves from the authority of Freud. The Biblical tale, they write, affirms our freedom to disagree. In this context, I would urge you to tolerate anxiety, welcome doubt, and keep in mind that the surest path to an authentic selfhood lies neither in a definitive rejection nor a wholehearted adoption of any established theory, but in the exercise of your own faculties in search of the truth that makes the best sense to you.

36 Claudia Lucia Borensztejn
Buenos Aires, Argentina

Dear Candidate,

How are you? I have been thinking of you all these months since I received the invitation to write to you. I have been wondering if you are doing well. How do you feel? Have you found the good enough atmosphere you need to become a psychoanalyst? Perhaps you felt you did. Perhaps you have started your training and have already some experience in working, in reading Freud and the post-Freudians? Perhaps you have already been in supervision with some of your patients and also have started your own analysis recently or even some years ago. Still, the idea of having all these aspects together and at the same time for some years, namely, analysis, supervision, and seminars in a psychoanalytic institution belonging to the organization created by Freud with the purpose of keeping psychoanalysis alive, is a completely different experience.

I remember quite well my years as a candidate. The feeling of belonging to a special family of professionals gave me self-confidence. I was already working with patients and in a public institution, and simultaneously raising my children and building my own family. Psychoanalysis entered my everyday life. It was a way of living, it gave sense to the facts of life, it filled my desire for breathing truth and meaning. Reading and studying raised questions that were asked in seminars, but also came into my own analysis: Who am I? Did I have these symptoms? What kind of character am I? Is this a somatic expression, a sign of a conflict, and if so, what is this conflict about? Also, then with a patient: is this my problem or is it his? Why do I feel anxious before this patient rings the bell? Also, am I following the rules properly? Am I being a good enough psychoanalyst?

When I began my training, Argentina was still a place where analysts were in great demand. They had long waiting lists of future analysts. Some waited for years. I didn't want to linger that long. I was looking for an analysis for myself, not merely for the purpose of training. Consequently, when an analyst asked me if I had an urgent need to start adding that he wouldn't consider urgency, I thought this is not my analyst. I wanted to have a real analysis and not an "as if"—one just for the "purpose of training."

I think that we analysts have real problems to think about and work through when we decide to become analysts. It is not an intellectual matter; it is a very deep and emotional one. We get the feeling of confidence in the therapeutic power of psychoanalysis from the unique effect of being cured, whatever meaning we want to give to this word. If we do not have a clear idea of the effect that our own psychoanalytic therapy has had in our lives, in our minds, and in our relations, we won't be able to have the conviction of the power of the unconscious and its therapeutic possibilities through psychoanalysis.

When I speak with new candidates, I see the same enthusiasm I had when I started my own training. But there are differences in social and cultural parameters that are important and have to be considered. At the time of my training, once you were accepted to the seminars, after the analyst had confirmed that you were ready to start, an important door to a lot of clinical work was opened. In those years it was easy to treat patients in high frequency, not only for supervision but also for our normal practice. We young analysts had our practice full of patients who came four or five sessions a week, and three sessions were considered the minimum—with the exception of child analyses, which often started with two sessions per week. (I'm not talking about severely disturbed children who still accepted intense treatments, but about children, who suffered from phobias, enuresis, tics, learning disabilities, aggressive behavior, etc., hence neurotic symptoms; they often started to be treated with lower frequency, because children and parents had a heavy weekly agenda to follow.)

Then with the turn of the millennium and the technological acceleration of time, with intelligent mobile devices, the use of social networks, the offer of medication and short term therapies, which claimed to have curative effects, and also because of the economic decline and hardship of the middle class, people seeking analysis started demanding more for less. More results in less time. I believe this change in practice does not come from a resistance within the psychoanalyst, but from deep changes in our occidental way of living, which make many of us think that psychoanalysis is coming to an end. But I do not think this is the case. Rather I believe that our practice and clinical work is taking new shapes. This is equally true for our theory. There are new conceptions emerging from developments in theory that have enlarged our discipline to such a point that it is almost impossible to have a complete knowledge of it as a whole. We all have to choose which lines of thought will deepen our studies. Of course, Freud is indispensable, our point of departure, and we all should know at least the most important issues taken up by different Schools; then we'll see what is most useful to give ground and meaning to our practice, and what can be called the psychoanalytic reference for our own clinical practice.

At the beginning of your studies, each author gives you a particular point of view. But as time passes, these ideas will be integrated into your way of behaving when sitting with a patient; that way it becomes a part of your personality and of the psychoanalytic function of your personality, which makes you feel comfortable and natural when talking to a patient. Once you have internalized the psychoanalytic technique (and of course this is an interminable process), and once you have finished your regular course of seminars, you will have a set of unconscious theories to guide your work in a psychoanalytic direction.

I have found many differences in working with young students that have studied theory and have not yet had the experience of their personal analysis, students who train outside our institutions, in public services, or universities, or other non-I.P.A. institutions in my country and abroad. There is an intellectual way of getting in touch with theory that is not enough for the skills you need to help patients. You need to get in touch with all aspects of their personalities and talk with them on the level that allows for a move in a progressive sense thereby promoting mental and emotional growth. This is not a simple art to learn in a short time, because you need to be ready to transform yourself in the process. So when you read Freud and other writers, in order to make it a transformative reading, you have to get involved with them, discuss with them, and make it a complete body-mind-experience. Then when you work with a patient, you have to be ready to analyze your countertransference, to inquire about and discover blind spots in your listening and go through them with your analyst.

This is the most absorbing and mobilizing time in your psychoanalytic career. Times of passion, discussion, criticism, love, and hate for some, and times of illusion and disillusion, of hope and anxiety for others. You start to select the colleagues who will walk with you, work with you, write and exchange thoughts; you start to create your connections, your psychoanalytic family in your country and abroad, in the regional and international encounters.

You need to develop intuition as one important skill you will use when words are lacking in the conversation, when there is communication without articulation, when there are tears or silences. You will have to guess what a particular silence means, whether it speaks of the necessity of being alone with somebody, or expresses a negative transference, a resistance.

Also, while studying, you will have to write. Writing is very important, even if you are not interested in becoming a psychoanalytic writer—still you will need to write. You'll write down the sessions of patients you see for supervision, and surely you'll have to deliver some other written material. Many candidates have inhibitions to writing, but you will get help for that, and when you are able to do it, it will be immensely satisfying. The capacity to write is an important skill to develop, because it helps you clarify your thoughts and even discover thoughts that you didn't know you had. Right now, while writing this letter to you, I find myself creating something that would have remained unknown to me had I not been asked to write you. I talk to myself while talking to you. It is always like this: our voice is created through the special opportunity of a conversation. Writing is always a conversation with an imaginary reader, in this case with you, a candidate.

I hope that everything will go well with you and that you will have good professors. But do not expect the merely kind or classical teaching, or convenient lectures. No, your professors will encourage you to read and think, to ask questions and respond to them. Learning will go on forever. So, this is something to take as a personal quest, whatever the quality of teaching might be, sometimes excellent, sometimes lacking. You will always have to do the best of a bad job. This is a marvelous title, which brilliant English psychoanalyst Wilfred

Bion gave to one of his papers. Fact is that it also holds good for the work we have with patients. We have to learn how to get in touch with the most creative parts of their personality to help them deal with other parts that have been hurt or make them suffer as a whole. To be a psychoanalyst means that you will have to learn to bear suffering, to figure out what to do in each case, to decide what is relevant. For example, some days ago I commented on a patient who had a lot of problems. In my view his conflicts could be seen as a different kind of confusion. But there was one that had to do with a physical illness, that seemed to me necessary to focus on. The young analyst and the patient were trying to search for psychic explanations, and meanwhile his physical affliction was not getting the proper treatment because his medical examination had not produced clear enough results. This was for me the point of urgency. We need to clearly understand which are the points of urgency in the trajectory of a treatment as well as in each single session, because we are responsible for the persons who consult us; we need to give them the best opportunity one can think of for their particular problems.

When I was a candidate, we didn't have this idea of psychoanalysis as a treatment that has to be effective. We thought about it more as a timeless investigation of the unconscious. This is not the idea of our times now. Times are not good or bad, they just are, not more or less difficult, just different. And in these times when you are starting this passionate journey, I wish you the best of luck and happiness.

37 Jane Kite
Cambridge, U.S.A.

Dear Candidate,

I'll start with something that struck me when I first read it as very true of psychoanalytic training, which I'll return to at the end of my letter:

> I am reminded of something my father said…when he spoke of how we bring up our children. He said we supply them with a map of the Italian Lakes and send them to the North Pole. (Sandler, 1983, from a discussion with Anna Freud).[1]

I know I'm supposed to be writing you a letter many years removed from my own training—a kind of wise looking back—but the odd thing is, I still feel like I've just started. In real time I started 33 years ago at the San Francisco Psychoanalytic Institute; in my internal time I start afresh every morning. I go into my office with some mixture of anticipation, curiosity, and sometimes anxiety. What will today bring? What kind of analyst will I be?

This isn't to say that my psychoanalytic training in candidacy wasn't formative, but more on that in a moment. We all start training at unique historical moments in the field, and most memorable for me in starting psychoanalytic training was the fact that I could do it at all. My entry into full psychoanalytic training as a psychologist in 1987 had just been made possible by the fact that psychologists had won a class action lawsuit brought against the American Psychoanalytic Association for restraint of trade. The fact that non-MDs weren't permitted to fully train as clinical analysts in the US, and the amount of vitriol on both sides of this argument, had been protracted and demoralizing. More to the point for me was realizing that this was real discrimination, a "Keep Out" sign with no basis in reality. Having had to wait for 10 years beyond when I and hundreds of others were ready to start full clinical training made no sense then, and to this day remains a dark chapter in the history of American psychoanalysis. It's also a helpful reminder that the reflexive idealization of our field has never been warranted. Much later I read Freud's *The Question of Lay Analysis* (1926), which he wrote to express his opposition to the medicalization of psychoanalysis in order to gain legitimacy for the profession. A year later in a postscript to this essay he stated clearly that

"Psychoanalysis is a part of psychology; not of medical psychology in the old sense, not of the psychology of morbid processes, but simply of psychology" (Frued, 1926, p. 252). This experience was an early lesson for me in one of the ways that psychoanalysis can be misrepresented and/or misappropriated, and a premonition of the fact that we each create psychoanalysis anew in our own training and practice of it.

Once started, I was more than eager to dive in. The immediate mix of personal ("training") analysis, coursework, and supervision was an immersion unlike anything I'd ever encountered in a largely academic career, and I was hooked. I read voluminously, and began writing early in candidacy in an attempt to square what I was reading and hearing with my own experience—a form of kicking the tires I guess. I encourage all of you at the outset (and later, too) to read widely, and start writing early. Once you start writing, you'll find out what you're thinking. Writing a case report, for example, can yield a great deal about you and your analysand that may have escaped your notice in the work itself. This is one of the things I found remarkable in what could also seem like a drill; the many small flourishes of self-revelation.

In retrospect, however, the formal curriculum in 1987 seemed rote and lock step. There really was pretty much one way of "doing" analysis. Knowing what I know now, the largely drive theory/ego psychological approach to "classical" analysis in my institute was limited; the different schools—self-psychology, relational theory, object relations—were marginal in my didactic experience and definitely sequestered as "other." There was little by way of meaningful dialogue among them, and I began to have the experience of theory as stronghold, with values and unconscious prejudices of its own. How did a "classical" analyst work, and was it really that different from the work of a self-psychologist or a relational analyst, or a Kleinian? What was the expressed relationship of individual analysts to his or her own theories? At annual meetings of the American Psychoanalytic Association, each panel had to have a representative of each theoretical school, and there was little in the way of real exchange. The feeling was that each panelist would state his or her "position," maybe a discussant would attempt a synthesis, and that would be that. Why was nobody really talking with one another? Were there any real commonalities among analysts of different persuasions? Did an analyst pledge allegiance to a theory or use it creatively as a mode of inquiry?

It wasn't until after I graduated that what I consider to be my real psychoanalytic training began. My exposure to British Psychoanalysis, and Winnicott, Klein, Fairbairn, and Bion was a revelation. I began to travel and go to international conferences. Gradually it became clear that theoretical differences are less important than we imagine in conceptualizing the work of analysis. The psychoanalytic landscape had become iterative. I knew by that time that training wasn't as much a commitment to a particular curriculum as it was to a developmental process; I became more interested in analysts as serious and committed people than I was in the fine points of the theories they espoused. I became aware that for me what I was learning had more to do with who the analyst was and how he or she methodically developed a theory and a practice in his or her writing and teaching than it did with any *particular* theory. I admired consistency and conviction in thinking, as well as the kind of modesty evident in people like Winnicott. I shied away from stridency in theoretical skirmishes.

But I was also troubled by thinking about the analyst as a person. How *does* who we actually are inevitably shape our work as analysts? And what, by the way, was "technique"? Could it really be taught as something other than who we characteristically are? I knew that I had been interested in psychoanalysis ever since finding a book by Freud in our home library and being entertained by what he wrote about "the psychopathology of everyday life" (whatever that was). As an avid reader and riddled with as yet unformulated questions about why my life as a child was the way it was, and more specifically why my parents were the way they were, Freud appeared to be a keen observer. I know that it's really not as simple as all that, and that I probably had no idea as a 12-year-old what he was really talking about, but I knew that he was raising the right questions. I knew (or thought I knew) early on that the only way out of my particular misery would be something resembling psychoanalysis, and as soon as I could afford it as a young adult I committed myself to the process, long before analytic training was a real possibility. And once I did become a candidate, my orienting question (then and now) became "how does what is unconscious become conscious?" What do I know that I don't know that I know, and how do I get at it? I would say that this question is part of my character, and one that informs my work with every patient.

A crucial aspect of my development as an analyst has been writing. Often, we rely more on intuition than anything else in formulating ideas, and if we trust our own intuition in writing, we will often break new ground (or new ground for us). Early on as a candidate, using my own intuition and not really knowing what I was talking about, I wrote that we all "develop a technique that fits our character." Now I would put it more bluntly: character is technique. As Larry Friedman taught me early on, patients respond to a person, not to a theory.

I've realized with time that I am more interested here in questions of origin, why it was in some important way that we've *had* to become analysts, and these are the sorts of questions I would now ask you. Why did you want to become an analyst in the first place? It's time consuming, expensive, and often unclear. What are you getting into? What are you committing yourself to? Why this? You probably don't really know at the outset, but I urge you to keep thinking about your own motivation. It becomes clearer and more interesting, more generative, with time.

And then there's the central importance of your own analysis in this process. I firmly believe, based on experience, that in order to be deeply interested as an analyst in someone else's story, someone else has to have been deeply interested in you. Some of us have had parents who were interested in us, and others haven't. For those of us who haven't, in particular, the analyst's interest is crucial. And by "deeply interested" I don't mean just liking; I mean being interested in raising the wreck – getting to the bottom of it. This is the job description of being an analyst. It is a form of commitment unlike any other. It is a process that is never complete, but having some idea that it's possible, and how to do it, is essential. Your own experience of analysis is crucial in becoming an analyst yourself, with supervision as a close second. It has been said that every supervision is the chance for another analysis. The presence of the supervisor as a third term in your work with patients and often in your own analysis is vital. The combination of analysis and supervision offers (or should offer) infinite ways of refracting your own experience of being a person and an analyst, something that just doesn't happen in "real life." If you read the psychoanalytic literature carefully, you'll find that the trajectory of any one analyst's writing—in addition to its subject—maps the course of that analyst's personal development. It is also helpful to go back into analysis with another as needed. You are never done, and there is always more to learn. I've always found this point to be uniquely reassuring. I think it's safe to say that my interest in psychoanalysis could be described as a love affair. It has to start with an "other," but with luck it will continue privately for the rest of your life.

That said, the thing that has probably troubled me the most during candidacy and since has nothing to do with theory, or how we were taught, or analyzed. Actually, it's what we *weren't* taught, something that perhaps couldn't be taught, something necessarily unformulated about how we behave as people/analysts. What I have in mind here is something we euphemistically refer to in the breach as "boundary violations;" essentially, the analyst's misuse of patients. I think that we generally come into the field taking ethics for granted, assuming that psychoanalysis is basically an ethical practice and that we are basically ethical people. At the very least, we will do no harm. At this point in my experience and my career I think I can safely say that psychoanalysis isn't *inherently* anything. It's what we make it and make of it. It is a particular method of inquiry, one which involves two people alone in a room together "just talking" for years at a time. It has taken me many years post-training to understand what should be self-evident: our own ethics as people are entirely personal and largely unconscious, engraved in our minds by our own early experiences. How have we been mistreated or misused, understood or misunderstood? Unearthing these deeply buried feelings is the essential piece of our own analyses. On the other hand, what is deeply unknown in us will sometimes emerge when we least expect it, often in action in the analytic work we do. We may proactively recognize this as countertransference, or we may go on to enact it before we "know" what we're doing. Enactments in the form of sexual boundary violations in particular are devastating, and no different unconsciously from actual incest. Historically, psychoanalysis has treated these episodes as extra-analytic and real, something to be adjudicated and dispensed with. Even as these instances of analytic malfeasance are now taken seriously, and discussed somewhat more openly, they can simultaneously sour, demoralize, and confuse entire generations in training. I urge you to examine idealizations in yourselves and in others, to keep talking with colleagues, and to turn *toward* analysis rather than away from it when you are disappointed and demoralized. Don't confuse the actions of a few with the potential psychoanalysis holds as a method of inquiry, a theory of mind, and the best method we have of ameliorating psychic suffering.

I realize that in writing this letter I have pivoted from a love affair with psychoanalysis to the potential it also holds for severe disappointment and disillusionment. Both are true. The success, if we can call it that, of your career as an analyst will depend on the use you can make of it, first as a person and then as a professional, in sickness and in health. You will have to interrogate it, both as a theory and as a practice, but you don't have to do it on your own. You will have teachers, colleagues, and students with you, depending on you. I hope that you will never turn back, even if you find yourself at the North Pole; *especially* if you find yourself at the North Pole. At the time when Freud told Anna that children were given a map of the Italian Lakes and then sent to the North Pole, the Italian Lakes were a well-known European vacation venue and the North Pole an unknown destination for intrepid adventurers. I believe that this image was intended. As analysts we are all explorers of our own unknowns, and the maps we are given early in our training will inevitably morph into something that maps us in ways we could never have imagined. Analysis is an impossible profession, yes, but also incomparably rewarding. I wish for you the staying power to use it and practice it fully.

Note

1 Sandler, J. (1983). *Discussions with Anna Freud on "The Ego and the Mechanisms of Defense: The Ego and the Id at Puberty."* IJP 64:401-406.

38 Gabriela Goldstein
Buenos Aires, Argentina

Dear Candidate,

Why do you want to become a psychoanalyst? Perhaps you don't know that you already know that psychoanalysis is a universe of knowledge, of questions, and passionate work. It does not hold the answers for all, but on the contrary, it poses questions and listens to the subjectivity, as you may probably already be doing, while listening to yourself when thinking about training as a psychoanalyst. During this process, you will learn from your professors, from your supervisors, from your own "training analyst," but, above all, from your patients, and about human nature. And you will come to realize the explicative power of the psychoanalytic discovery.

Dear candidate: you have chosen to begin training for a passionate task, unfinishable and "impossible" (like educating and governing, as Freud said): to psychoanalyze. I love psychoanalysis, and that is why I chose this profession and this institution for my training: the Asociación Psicoanalítica Argentina (A.P.A.). In the A.P.A. one breathes psychoanalysis in an atmosphere that is at the same time one of freedom and commitment. The Freudian psychoanalytical imprint dialogues with post-Freudian authors, such as Klein, Winnicott, and Lacan among others, navigating toward contemporary schools of thought, within a framework of creativity.

Let me tell you about my path. I wanted to become a psychoanalyst ever since I have memory. But I also liked art. That is why, because of one of those twists in life, I decided to study Architecture (and later on I would discover how much architecture, art, and psychoanalysis have in common). I finished my studies, worked as an architect and learned many things: I learned how to transform an idea into a Work, and what we call creativity. But the need of reaching toward psychoanalysis persisted. That is why I decided to study psychology to start my training since the 1990s; the A.P.A. allows one to become a psychoanalyst with a medical or psychology degree. Being already in analysis with a training analyst of this society, I applied for the interviews to begin my training. Not everyone would get through in this round of interviews. I do remember very well when I was told that I could begin my training. I was so happy. What I will never forget is the moment in which, we, the new candidates, were greeted by the Director of the Institute. I thought: "I am in the A.P.A. It is here." *Here* is where I felt an indescribable emotion—Fulfillment.

Soon after, we were welcomed by the president of the "organization of candidates." They invited me to be part of one of the candidate committees in the A.P.A. I was not sure about starting right away taking part in these activities, so I consulted a friend and senior analyst: "Of course, don't doubt it!" he said. "During your training, you will make friends for life." And that is how it was and how it still is. Throughout my life, I made many friends, but the fraternity and friendship with my colleagues during my time among the "candidates" and taking the "seminars" was something special. When I had the opportunity of being the vice-president of I.P.S.O. (the I.P.A. candidates' organization), something similar took place. I think I was lucky, but I am sure that you will also share this experience. My best friends in the wide psychoanalytic world are the colleagues with whom I shared those training years, in A.P.A., I.P.S.O., and I.P.A.

Dear candidate: I would tell you to enjoy, to get in touch, to interchange ideas with your fellow trainees in your society and around the world; these relationships will last for life. As well as psychoanalysis.

I want to tell you about my Institution: the training, within the Freudian fundamental pillars, consists of a *pluralist* educational program that allows you to study other frames of references, such as the "Argentinean school": the A.P.A. founders and pioneers that made important contributions to psychoanalysis in Argentina and Latin America, like Garma, Rascovsky, Racker, Langer, Bleger, and the Barangers. The so-called "golden age" of psychoanalysis was also a time of innovative revolutions in culture and society in Argentina. These were exceptional times, the 1950s and 1960s.

I did my training in other, more recent, times. These were stimulating times as well. Today, times have changed. The contemporary world has other dimensions, other complexities, other struggles, and other debates going on.

How do I imagine you?

A future analyst of the psychoanalytic world of today.

Will you be willing to face the challenges of today's psychoanalytic work? Are you perhaps thinking about new technologies, in diversities, in "gender," in autism, perhaps in clinical severe depression? Will you enter the dialogue between the fundamental concepts of psychoanalysis and the great cultural changes of our time, without losing the specificity of our field and "clinical thinking"?

I consider the psychoanalytic training through the "tripod" as a "full immersion" in psychoanalysis that enables one to make of the transmission of psychoanalysis, a psychoanalytic experience of your own; to become involved in the ethics of our task in our contemporary world; and to navigate the uneasy waters of our clinical experience, the anxieties of our patients, and our own. It is the way to continue the research of the "psyche" (soul), while studying and getting to understand the effects of the change in the subjectivity of each epoch.

I think that each time has its own style. Don't you think? Which will be your style? Not every time is the same, we know that. Neither Freud's time in Vienna nor the "golden times" of Argentinean psychoanalysis. Psychoanalysis has spread into many different spheres of life and culture. Here, in Buenos Aires, many people are in "therapy" or do psychotherapy. Is this perhaps the reason why Buenos Aires remains an incognita regarding the "psychoanalytic phenomena"? The actual multiplication of "schools of psychoanalysis" that offer education in psychoanalysis can be disconcerting. I can imagine. The spreading of the idea of short therapies or of fast solutions are among the challenges psychoanalysis has to face today.

I think that the best psychotherapist is a trained psychoanalyst. Because those who train to be a psychoanalyst will go through the experience of their own analysis, will attend seminars, and have supervision, *simultaneously*. An effect takes place, which I understand as one of *de-alienation* and *subjectivation*.

How do you imagine me?

Today, I am a professor of seminars at the Institute and a training analyst. I am also a supervisor. And beyond all the resistances, I see an increasing interest in psychoanalysis. Because the discovery of that which is produced by psychoanalysis, as a dimension of *thinking,* is revolutionary. We are always surprised—I understand this is the Unconscious in act—by the effect of psychoanalysis and its efficacy.

Keeping our analytic hearing open is a challenge. The repression and the "formulas" are easy solutions that avoid the anxiety and the work with the unknown, the strangeness, the Otherness in our work and in life.

Dear candidate, the effect of transmission of psychoanalysis and training is, because of all of these aspects, a unique experience. What circulates in this shared experience, combined, and permanently traversed by the limits of what we don't know and cannot solve, produces a subjectivizing effect that settles within oneself a potential of transformation that never abandons us, named psychoanalysis. Your path is open.

39 Eva Schmid-Gloor
Zurich, Switzerland

Dear Candidate,

I want to write you the letter I would have liked to receive at the time of my training in the early 1980s, when I was looking for answers to so many questions, some of which may be similar to the ones you struggle with today.

When I look back at the start of my training, I remember above all a feeling of confusion. At that time a split had shaken the psychoanalytical community in Zürich, and my start in training was marked by deep uncertainty about where my path should lead me. On the one side there were my politically left-leaning colleagues, a kind of older "sibling generation," holding the cultural theory of a non-institutional psychoanalysis in high esteem and refusing to accept the I.P.A. requirements of evaluation before being admitted as a member of the Swiss Psychoanalytic Society. In the spirit of 1968, I sympathized with this attitude of rebellion. On the other side there was the "parent generation" of the Zürich group, a small remaining team, that maintained the Freud Institute as a training center of the Swiss Psychoanalytic Society and offered a classical clinical-theoretical education in the sense of the I.P.A.

For a beginner like me, the situation was confusing, and I could not expect any guidance or support, because whomever I consulted at that time was representing one of the two parties and was therefore biased. I finally decided for classical clinical-theoretical training with the parent generation, which was recognized by the I.P.A. At that time, I couldn't fully appreciate what belonging to the I.P.A., as opposed to non-institutionalized psychoanalysis, would mean for my later professional life. Today I am very happy that I have chosen this path, because it has given me privileged access to a community that facilitates professional exchange with analysts from all over the world in various committees on the occasion of meetings and conferences, and thus an incredible expansion of my horizon considering my experience in clinical and organizational work. Had I remained in the exclusively local group, these opportunities would never have come my way.

Although these circumstances were specific for Zürich at the time of my training, I wanted to tell you about them, because I think that time and again, we experience in our institutes and societies movements that can lead to splits.

In the course of my long professional career, which has taken me to many places in Europe and around the world, I have seen traces and effects of such splitting processes in psychoanalytic communities, which have a decisive influence on both the development of certain groups and on differences in theory formation.

What I want to tell you, dear candidate, is this: Be careful when you get into situations in your training that require a choice between one of two or even more sides—when you are urged to be a comrade-in-arms of a certain party that advocates certain theoretical positions or beliefs! If you find yourself under such pressure, you should realize that you are in a psychoanalytic culture that has lost its ethics. If you have teachers who are convinced that they know everything better than everybody else and who want you to side with them, then you should feel alarmed and look out for help.

Psychoanalytic trainers should have an ethical position that requires a fundamentally open attitude toward different ways of thinking. Even if they are convinced that their theoretical orientation is the only helpful one, they should at least not openly advocate this and thus step in the way of your finding your own psychoanalytic position. Teachers should respect that over time—as you become more proficient in theory and technique—you will choose and settle with what you find most helpful for your clinical work. Today a vibrant psychoanalytic culture hopefully includes representatives of different schools of thinking who are willing to discuss and explore with each other why this or that concept might fit one clinical situation better than another. Although this ethical ideal is now widespread, situations may still arise in which candidates are abused by training analysts as desired companions.

Recalling the beginning of my psychoanalytic training in Zürich, I would like to tell you about another concern that bothered me at that time. Confronted with the immense body of theoretical psychoanalytical literature, I felt a great confusion. It seemed absolutely impossible to ever comprehend it in depth. In seminars there were some candidates who seemed already well versed in one theory or another and who would shine with cleverly formulated contributions. They impressed me, but I did not understand a word of what they said. Psychoanalytic theory seemed like a jungle of concepts, and I wished for nothing more than a guide, a tutor, who would have supported me in my attempts to find some orientation. I attended many seminars—each on specific topics and areas—and gradually I was able to build some knowledge. However, what I missed was a kind of large map of the geography of psychoanalytic theories, a map that would have traced how and where the individual schools of thought have developed apart from or even against each other, and how they were still interrelated with each other.

Do I have such an overview today? By and large yes, but there are still some blanks on my personal psychoanalytical map. As an experienced clinician, I can live with this fact quite well. My personal analysis has reduced my desire "to have an overview of everything" to a realistic proportion. Now I have a useful theoretical "toolkit" at my disposal, which supports me in all kinds of clinical problems and situations. And if I feel blocked and I can't get any further with a certain patient, I exchange ideas with colleagues and they in turn contribute ideas from their "toolkit," so that I can find new, often surprising ways to work with my patients.

That much I can offer you: Don't be discouraged when you realize how infinitely large our theoretical corpus is. During your training you will hopefully get a first idea of the wide range of different theoretical approaches to psychoanalysis. Feel free to choose what makes sense to you, what you find useful in your daily clinical work. It will be a good start.

When we, as training analysts, conduct admission interviews with potential future candidates for psychoanalytic training, we want to find out whether our interlocutors have the potential to develop an access to their unconscious through personal analysis and psychoanalytic training. In other words, we listen for their "capacity for introspection," their potential openness to the unknown, the formless. And a few years later, at the end of their training, when we have to decide whether we can admit them as members of our psychoanalytical society and the I.P.A., we evaluate the candidates' psychoanalytical competence: we listen to their clinical material to determine not only their psychoanalytic position and identity, but also their sensitivity, mobility, and receptiveness in working with their patients. Is our future colleague able to revise, if necessary, opinions once formed, rethink theoretical positions if they miss the patient, and remain open to accept what initially elicited some internal resistance? Can the candidate tolerate the feeling of failure and hear when his patient tells him that he is barking up the wrong tree? In other words: is there a stable enough inner space that allows for continuous working through processes with regard to idiosyncratic defenses and ideological proclivities and dead ends?

It is exactly this kind of consideration, dear candidate, that I would like to recommend to you if you are concerned about your psychoanalytic teachers and the psychoanalytic culture in which you study. It will help you find your way. As mentioned above, a good psychoanalytical climate consists of representatives of different schools discussing openly with each other and being prepared to rethink their own positions, just as we should be prepared in our clinical work to constantly rethink and, if necessary, question our ideas and positions.

In 2018 at the European Psychoanalytical Federation's Forum on Education, training analysts spoke about current learning goals in psychoanalytical training. I particularly noted one demand: good trainers and lecturers should support future analysts in developing their own path in the acquisition of psychoanalytic knowledge. They should help candidates orient themselves within the broad and diverse theoretical environment in such a way that they are ultimately able to develop their own style and do not uncritically bow to a particular school of thought. In 2019, a survey by the Psychoanalytic Education Committee of the I.P.A. also revealed that current psychoanalytic training places put great emphasis on the seminar's function to help students develop their own analytical identity by giving them plenty of room for their own understanding of the clinical and theoretical material.

After having addressed the qualities of our current psychoanalytic training, I would like to briefly remind you how much the conditions under which psychoanalysts learn nowadays have changed since the early years. Imagine, dear candidate, that in 1927, when the first theoretical psychoanalytic course started at the Berlin Institute, our colleagues were delighted that, in their view, the psychoanalytic theory finally had reached a form that would allow teaching trainees an exact and unified theory in a two-year course. The learning goal was: "… to convey the established foundations of the psychoanalytic principles of experience and the system of concepts in a clear, homogenous form, which corresponds to the current state of our science, but as little rigid as possible thus enabling further development" (Alexander, 1930, p. 58).

This brief review is to give you an idea of the different world we are living in today, 100 years later, when we are engaged in psychoanalytic training—whether as a student or as a teacher.

I wish for you that you find your own way and meet interesting, lively, and cosmopolitan colleagues who will support you!

40 Adriana Prengler
Seattle, U.S.A.

Dear Candidate,

I want to take this opportunity to encourage you in your work and wish you success in carrying on with Freud's legacy. As a candidate you are a part of the future of psychoanalysis and a part of its present, as well.

I have certainly wondered, and perhaps you have also wondered, why you are called a "candidate." The word "candidate" suggests that you are in training and under consideration to do something in the near future. But the work of analysis is already a part of the process of being trained to become a psychoanalyst. And beyond all that, you are already a mental health professional, learning psychoanalytic theory and technique, offering your ideas, your creativity, and your experience. So, to a certain extent you're not really a "candidate" as you are already DOING the work and FULFILLING the role.

So, why are you called "candidate," if you are already exposed to all these aspects of the work from the moment you began the training as a psychoanalyst? In some countries, especially in Latin America, where I trained, candidates are called "analysts in training." And that's how I like to think of you.

Your training is not a career choice like any other. Psychoanalysis is not only your profession, it also a way of life—a way of relating to others and engaging with the world. It is a way of thinking that does not end at the end of the training, but rather continues for the rest of your life. It is like learning another language and having it open doors to new lands, peoples, and cultures. Learning psychoanalysis is moving away from the usual way of perceiving the world and others. It means abandoning forever the world of concrete thinking and discovering a world of meaning in metaphoric and symbolic interpretations. To think psychoanalytically is to develop the ability to read between lines, listen with the third ear, and dance in between the manifest and the latent. Psychoanalytic training is an education for understanding life experiences in a new and different way, discovering meaning below the surface.

Your training, based on the three pillars of psychoanalytic education—seminars, supervision, and personal analysis—is a journey that, once begun, never ends. It is an expedition through your own unconscious and a process of identification with a way of life built on the idea that words, acts, symptoms, dreams, and fantasies have unconscious meanings that, when understood, offer insight into our lives. And once we are able to read between the lines and reveal what is hidden by the defenses, we can never go back to seeing things in the same literal way ever again.

Becoming a psychoanalyst involves a process of maturation and personal reflection, leading to the discovery of one's own unconscious. Your personal analysis and your psychoanalytic work with your patients lead you to look within.

Your training is more than the acquisition of information. It is an initiation into a new way of seeing things. But be careful not to stay too long in an unending process, thinking that you are never quite ready for graduation, as if you were an eternal child, never quite mature enough. You are already a professional. You will be welcomed as a member, and then you will continue learning and growing throughout the rest of your life.

Being an analyst in training, and subsequently being a psychoanalyst, also implies taking an active role in your professional community: a local, regional, and international community. It implies not only going through your personal analysis, attending your seminars, your supervisions, and having a high frequency clinical practice, but also playing an active role in your institute, being part of a work group, fulfilling a commitment with your institute, your local society, or your regional or international associations. You belong to local, regional, and international organizations with thinkers and clinicians, from all around the world. Everyone has a supportive role to play, working together while respecting and enjoying our differences, which naturally support the growth of our theoretical and clinical work.

As a member of the I.P.A., you will belong to a group of almost 13,000 members in about 65 countries, speaking multiple languages, in different cultural contexts. You will be able to participate in conferences, exchange ideas, and discuss clinical work with other analysts from all around the world. Some of those analysts will become your trusted friends and colleagues for many years to come. You will see them in I.P.A. congresses, conferences, and meetings, and they will become a part of your professional and personal worlds.

Although your intention was to become a psychoanalyst, the training itself invites you to become a professional contributor writing papers about your ideas, presenting your clinical casework, conducting research, and collaborating with international colleagues. You chose to be a clinician, but as a psychoanalyst you are also invited to be a contributor to advance theory and technique, to write papers and books, to expand the reach of psychoanalysis, and to apply it to contemporary issues beyond the consulting room.

While in training, there is so much happening in your clinical work. I would have loved to have been told, from the first day of my training, that a part of being a psychoanalyst is being a writer. If I had known that, I would have written much more, describing in detail clinical situations that were fascinating to me and that reliably occur during one's training. Without encouragement to write from the beginning, those experiences are often forgotten even though, at the time, we think we will never forget them.

It will be much easier to be a "psychoanalytic writer" if you start from the first day describing your adventures with your patients! Let go of the fear of expressing your thoughts about your work in the office, your mistakes, the impasses, the "good" and "bad" interpretations, the startling observations, your fantasies and countertransferential feelings. Look at it all as an adventure and write about it.

We build our analytical identity based on our chosen theoretical preferences, transferences, identifications, ideals, history, culture, social groups, desires, losses, yearnings, clinical experiences, and training experiences. We assume the legacy of our professors, analysts, and supervisors, based on what they taught us to do, and also what they taught us NOT to do while they were doing it themselves. All these are parts of your amalgamated training, sculpted by time.

Dear candidate, you are the future of psychoanalysis and a part of its present, as well. You may belong to I.P.S.O., your international association, and as soon as you graduate, you will join the I.P.A. There are many benefits of belonging to an international association like ours. You have the possibility of enriching yourself through the interchange of ideas with analysts from other countries and cultures different from your own. This diversity will enrich you and stimulate your development and creativity.

Being part of the I.P.A. means belonging to a world organization. In this time of international upheaval, when mass migrations are taking place, you may soon discover the need to emigrate yourself or you might be presented with the opportunity of welcoming emigrating analysts to your institute and/or society. Will you let the emigrating analysts from far off lands threaten you, or will you see how their differences can enrich you and widen your horizons?

I have been long interested in the way experienced analysts welcome candidates into the profession and pass the torch to them. How does this transmission occur? How should it occur? Whenever I think about it, I am always reminded of "The Maestro," Dr. Mauricio Goldenberg—the pioneer psychiatrist of mental health training in Argentina and teacher of several generations of psychoanalysts, including Horacio Etchegoyen. Dr. Goldenberg's influence was significant in psychiatric training throughout Latin America and in Europe, as well. At the time of the Dirty War in Argentina, he left Buenos Aires and went into exile in Caracas, Venezuela. I was living in Caracas at the time, and as soon as I graduated as a psychologist, I pursued a postgraduate degree in Clinical Psychology at a psychiatric hospital in Caracas where Mauricio Goldenberg was a well-recognized and highly esteemed professor. Unfortunately, I was the only student to apply for the first year of that program, so the program could not even get formally started. Dr. Goldenberg saw the situation and offered to allow me to attend his seminars with the group that was already in its second year. I joined with shyness and with the feeling of being an intruding beginner in an already constituted group of graduate students. In the first session, in the middle of the class, someone brought a tray with small disposable plastic cups of steaming hot Venezuelan coffee for everyone, but also on the tray, was one fine thin porcelain cup for the Master. Mauricio took his porcelain cup, the only one on the tray, poured some coffee into it, and handed it to me, while he chose for himself one of the disposable plastic cups. This simple act produced in me a strong effect.

It was the gesture of a wise and generous teacher granting a place to the young student, generously inviting her to exist in that space, with a right to be, to receive the teachings, and to contribute. This was a powerful and positive experience of the professional relationship between the generations, which, among other things, aroused in me a fervent desire to learn, and identify myself with the bearer of that knowledge and that generosity. I wanted to become his heir and transmitter of that same attitude toward the next generation.

In the transmission of psychoanalysis, language occupies a fundamental place, but no less important are those transmissions beyond words. Fundamental is the experience of being heard in the analysis itself, and there is also the confidence of being able to share your ideas without being the victim of dogmatic points of view on the part of your teachers and supervisors. When fully listened to, we have the opportunity to discover our own difficult truths. And the experience itself fosters our ability to listen to others.

Respect for the other, the granting of a place, openness and tolerance for differences in thinking are all part of the transmission of psychoanalysis. Dear candidate, I hope you have the good fortune to have encountered analysts who know how to enjoy and take pride in the success of their students, have offered you encouragement, and welcomed your creativity, your thoughts, and the free expression of your ideas, even if those ideas diverge from the model offered by your teachers. I hope you have the enriching experience of encountering generous teachers, who encourage you to think for yourself, without perceiving you as a challenging opponent threatening to put their position at risk. In any case, with time and experience, you will take their place, and we need you to be prepared for that, by learning theory and technique, being willing to make mistakes, admit your errors, think about them, and carry on.

Even when we work in the privacy of our offices, we are not working in total solitude. We descend professionally from our teachers, we transmit what we have received to our students, and they, in turn, will pass it on to the next generation. So, as you prepare to begin your career as a psychoanalyst, dear candidate, let me present to you, metaphorically, a small porcelain cup.

41 Rachel Blass
Jerusalem, Israel

Dear Candidate,

I am thinking of your choice to become an analyst, to undergo the training you are now in, with requirements that are strenuous in so many ways, practical and emotional. I imagine that there may be different reasons for this choice. I know that for some candidates it involves educational and professional aims and ambitions. For others, therapeutic considerations are central, guided by the notion that analysis is an additional kind of treatment that can be most efficacious with certain kinds of patients. In this letter I would like to share with you another central motivation, one that has influenced my choice as well as my understanding of what it is to be an analyst. My hope is that this may influence your understanding as well and may highlight, arouse, or bring to the fore latent motivations in you, which can in turn be a source of support and encouragement in the course of your training. What I have in mind may be referred to as an "ethical motivation," a motivation that is intimately tied to what I consider to be an analytic identity.

What I mean here is that while psychoanalysis offers an understanding of the person that falls into the field of psychology, and a practice that could be considered a form of therapy, the unique nature of the psychological understanding and therapeutic practice that it offers also shapes a profound ethical vision. We can and should, in my view, be motivated by this vision.

I consider this vision to be one regarding the power of truth and of love. It proposes that failure to know oneself, one's inner truths, is what lies at the foundation of psychic disorder, and analytic cure is to allow the patient to come to know these previously unknown, unconscious, truths. Coming to know truth in this context is not simply an intellectual matter, but rather involves the integration of parts of ourselves; it means a lived experience of these parts. And it is also a motivated act, as is the failure to come to know. That is, we, in a sense "choose" to know and "choose" to deny and, in this sense, we are also responsible for our psychic suffering and the suffering we cause others as a result. In other words, what I'm emphasizing here is that psychoanalysis provides the person with a way to know and be oneself—to choose to live truthfully, to take responsibility for who one is and what one does. This is an ethical aim, and to become an analyst is to embrace it. Therapeutic relief through analysis, in this context, is only a derivative of striving toward this analytic aim—one of its important benefits. That is, to be an analyst, as I see it, is not to seek the best ways toward symptom relief but to be part of a search for the deepest integration of the patient's unconscious mind, of the truths with which at bottom he struggles.

And what is this struggle? What needs to be denied? Here we see another essential aspect of psychoanalysis' ethical vision. While there are many sources of pain and suffering in life—actual losses, deprivations and injustices, and environmental deficits of various kinds—ultimately, psychoanalysis' concern is not with difficult reality per se, the normal distresses associated with life. It is concerned rather with the patient's inner world, his inner phantasies and meanings that distort reality and make life unnecessarily difficult, as may be seen in the depression, sense of emptiness, anxiety, obsessions, and problematic relationships of various kinds with which our patients present.

At the heart of this inner world, these inner phantasies, is a struggle between love and hate; between the love of our objects and the hate of them—hate because of inevitable frustrations, the existence of the third, envy, etc. The hatred of loved objects (or the love of hated ones), our phantasies of the destruction of those we love, are unbearably painful, and so we conceal from ourselves the hate or the love or the conflict or the feelings that the conflict arouses and especially guilt. We modify the world to fit our needs and desires. We deny reality. In a sense, we destroy it as it is, the bad as well as the goodness that it contains in order to serve our own self interests. These ideas regarding what underlies our psychic well-being and disorder find different forms of expression in Freud's theories—for example, in his Oedipus complex, his theories of narcissism and sexuality, the life and death instincts—and in their elaboration in Klein and her thinking on the depressive position, reparation, and envy.

This struggle with our love stands in the way of it finding full expression. And thus, the integration that psychoanalysis facilitates, the truth that it allows for, also frees the person to better see the other and to better love him. Psychoanalysis frees the person to love.

The *process* of analysis is also one of love. In its course, the patient, in part driven by a love of life and of reality, is willing to suffer the pain that comes with the recognition of truth. He is willing to come in touch with his inner world with all the feelings of guilt, loss, and limitation that this entails, so that his objects can be truly recognized and valued, and reparation for harm done to them can begin. In turn, the analyst treats the patient with a certain kind of love as well—an analytic one. In maintaining this analytic attitude, he suffers the patient's inner world, is subject to the patient's projections, and faces the unbridled forces of his unconscious. Inclinations to defend or to submit to such projections and drives, to become the good or bad objects the patient wishes to find in the analyst, are restrained for the patient's good. The analyst remains attuned to reality and especially to the patient's difficult inner reality out of love of truth and the desire to help the patient to integrate and live his own truth, through coming to know it. To become an analyst, as I understand it, is to embrace this ethical view of the person and to actively participate in furthering it.

I hope that reflecting on this view of what becoming an analyst means will help you along your path—in the course of your training and afterwards as well. It may draw your attention to the foundational ethical ideas that underlie the numerous psychoanalytic theories and techniques that you will have to learn about. This may allow for a richer and more unified and therefore meaningful view of many of these theories and techniques as well as a better understanding of how and why they differ from nonanalytic ones. It may also allow for a better grasp of competing approaches within the contemporary analytic field. While usually not acknowledged as such, often underlying the differences are competing ethical visions, and this requires you to make an ethical choice. The question is not which approach is better proven or more efficacious in general, but rather which is better in the light of our view of what it means to be well and how we conceive of our role as analyst in this regard. Being a supportive encouraging figure may at times be helpful to a patient, may even bring about symptom relief, but it does not serve the ethical vision to which I am committed as an analyst, and I would therefore find it wrong to do so as an analyst. But there are today (as in the past too) other visions of what the person can and should attain through analysis. Some are less concerned with the inner world, more concerned with environmental/developmental deficits and the analyst's responsibility to fill them. For an analyst who embraces such a vision, supportive comments may be deemed necessary and the right thing to do. Recognizing that these are competing ethical visions makes clear the kind of choice you are faced with between approaches. The eclectic option, so popular in some analytic circles today, is not really tenable when dealing with ethical visions, and just waters down and ultimately distorts what truly divides them.

I think that recognition of the ethical vision of psychoanalysis also helps clarify the value of becoming an analyst to those who are already practicing psychoanalytic therapy. I would think that many psychoanalytic psychotherapists, especially those supervised by psychoanalysts, are guided by an analytic ethical vision. To the extent that they are, they may, in a sense, already be regarded as analysts. However, if one ascribes to the ethical vision of psychoanalysis as I understand it, such therapists are not working in a context that allows them to fully express their analytic identity. The couch and the frequency play a crucial role in the process of encountering the powerful unconscious struggles going on in our patients minds and meaningfully integrating denied parts of them. It is in the analytic setting that this analytic vision of the person and the analytic relationship is best realized. Analytic training lets adherents of analysis become analysts most fully.

One would hope in this context that your psychoanalytic institute and society also plays a role. That is, that the support of the ethical vision of psychoanalysis that these provide will also help you better be an analyst. It is, indeed, hard to work alone. But such support is not always forthcoming. Instead, your institutions may adopt a more pragmatic view of analysis as a practice justified by its general efficacy for certain patients or encourage eclecticism or visions of analysis that are less uniquely analytic in nature. In this case you may find it especially difficult and lonely to hold on to the analytic ethical vision, to practice from within it. And in this case, it may be comforting to keep in mind that this ethical vision is a powerful one and is still today maintained by many analysts throughout the world. It is, I think, important that you seek them out—find them in analytic conferences in your country or abroad, in clinical seminars, in contemporary analytic journals, and discussion groups. That is, I recommend to you not only to recognize the profound ethical vision of psychoanalysis that Freud brought forth, but to join the movement he created to support it.

I wish you all the best on your analytic path.

42 Donald Campbell
London, England

Dear Candidate,

Congratulations on being accepted for a psychoanalytic training.

Because I don't know you, anything I write in this letter that strikes you in a personal way will depend upon your response to the personal in me that I will try to convey to you. So, think of reading this letter a bit (and only a bit) like listening to a patient and listening to yourself at the same time. Only you can be more selfish. In fact, I hope something I write will reverberate in you in a way that you can use to deepen your experience of your analytic training and practice.

So, here goes.

I became a patient before I was a candidate. For some people it's the other way around, at least consciously.

I don't know anything about your background or how you came to be a candidate, but I found that how I became a candidate influenced my training and how I practice psychoanalysis. If I tell you a bit about how I became a candidate, I think you will see what I mean.

I was 25 and living in Washington, D.C., when I had to admit that, after graduate study and several different jobs, I didn't know what I wanted to be when I grew up. More importantly, I realized that I wasn't able to answer that question myself. I needed help. A friend recommended that I go to a psychoanalyst. So, I did—with some trepidation. The first and most formidable step in becoming a psychoanalyst is becoming a patient.

As you probably know by now, becoming a patient is not as easy as it sounds. Psychoanalysis is a painful process that is based on an unusual relationship. By the time I inquired about an analysis for myself, it was a last resort. Even so, I resisted the process of being a patient; lying on the couch, facing shame, guilt, uncertainty and doubt while trying to trust someone I didn't know, couldn't see, and who didn't relate to me like a normal person. Someone who did nothing to relieve awkward situations, who limited their contact with me to 50 minutes, and then recommended that I see him five times a week. And I haven't even mentioned paying a lot of money for all this, which was another source of resistance and resentment.

I know some patients approach psychoanalysis with a stereotypic medical model in which the patient is usually encouraged to accept the doctor's diagnosis and carry out their treatment recommendations. In contrast, as an analytic patient I learned that my analyst would not only fail to answer my questions but would interpret my resistance to exploring my own questions.

I can personally confirm Freud's view of psychoanalysis as the analysis of resistance. It took me a while to overcome, with my analyst's help, my resistance to becoming a patient. But when I did, well never entirely, the experience of psychoanalysis confirmed something about how I wanted to relate to myself and others at a very fundamental level. This experience confirmed my conviction that I wanted to become a psychoanalyst. However, for me that also wasn't as easy as it sounds.

At that time, the late 1960s in the United States, the American Psychoanalytic Association did not accept for training applicants who were not medically qualified, which was my situation. However, I had heard about the child psychotherapy training at what is now called the Anna Freud Centre in London, which was a four-year training including three years that were full time, required a five times weekly training analysis, and five times a week analysis of an under-five-year-old, a latency child, and an adolescent. In an interesting twist, the Anna Freud Centre required a post-graduate degree, but did not accept medically qualified applicants. I took the quickest post-graduate route possible, a two-year full-time course to get a Masters in Social Work. Two years after my initial inquiry about training, I applied to the Anna Freud Centre and was accepted much to my relief and excitement. I mention this to illustrate my desire to train to become an analyst. As I write this now, I can see how much effort, time, and money was involved in my application, but at the time it did not really feel like a sacrifice or a hardship. I felt I had found psychoanalysis and it would enable me to become who I was meant to be, whatever shape that would take.

Some of my friends did not share my enthusiasm for training to become an analyst. Hopefully attitudes have changed, but in 1969, some of my friends denigrated my decision with remarks like: "Oh, really? Isn't that passé? I didn't realize people still did that. A friend of mine just came back from a weekend marathon group. They locked her in a room with a group of people, and they started having a go at each other. Have you tried primal scream therapy?" Another typical mocking response went something like this: "Opps! I'd better be careful what I say. I suppose you can read my mind." Or, a more sarcastic reply along the lines of: "You must have really sorted yourself out, become a contented, confident person."

While becoming a *patient* is the first step to becoming a psychoanalyst, even when you become a psychoanalyst you never stop being a patient because you only learn more about what you don't know. Like being a patient, we analysts will be engaged in our self-analysis throughout our careers because our patients and, indeed, we ourselves keep us wondering, questioning, trying to understand, and second-guessing ourselves. Being a psychoanalyst is not as easy as it sounds.

We analysts tend to be skeptical of early insights and easy answers because we are struck by the power of the unconscious to dominate our consciousness without our knowing it. Much of the unhappiness and pain in our lives arises from a failure of our conscious selves to come to terms with fears and anxieties that are rooted in our unconscious. The problem with the unconscious is that it is unconscious, and it is unconscious because it is a threat to our conscious selves. And, because the unconscious is so dangerous, we erect defenses against it and resist attempts to uncover it. That's why we only have access to it when it breaks through in our dreams, mistakes, slips of the tongue, thoughts that catch us by surprise, and states of reverie. Understanding these manifestations of the unconscious takes time.

In the British Psychoanalytical Society, where I trained, we believe that taking time means being in a training analysis five times a week and seeing your training cases five times a week for as long as it takes. You may wonder why we insist on five times a week training analysis and five times a week analytic treatment of two training cases when almost every other psychoanalytic institute has reduced the frequency of training analysis to four or three times a week. It is because we need all the help we can get to understand our unconscious and the patient's impact on us. More help is better than less help.

I have found that working analytically with a patient is difficult. It is hard work. I am often mentally and emotionally exhausted. Most sessions fill me with doubt and uncertainty. And I make mistakes. That's why I also need all the help I can get from my colleagues, including those who do not think and work as I do. There is diversity in every psychoanalytic society because they are made up of groups who represent different traditions or emphasize different aspects of the same tradition. In the British Society our diversity is represented by the existence of three groups representing the Contemporary Freudian, Independent, and Kleinian traditions. I have the impression that the healthy psychoanalytic societies are those that *support and contain diversity*. However, fewer societies actively encourage *plurality*, that is, consciously attempt to *understand* the other. I think we lose an opportunity to get help for ourselves if we do not try to understand and learn from those who represent ways of thinking and working that are different from our own. During our training the reading and discussion in seminars should expose us to difference, which will be familiar to us as we learn about ourselves and our patients, as we discover our own foreignness, and the unaccepted other in ourselves and our patients.

One of the ways we have built in the encouragement of plurality in the British Society is that the Society pays for each candidate to have ten consultations on their first training case, after the first year, with a training analyst who is not from their own tradition. These consultations provide the candidate with an opportunity to learn first-hand about how an analyst from a different tradition works, and, in the process, to develop a deeper perspective on how the candidate works. Learning by exposure to difference facilitates the process of becoming one's own analyst. In my case, I arrived at the British Society having trained in the Contemporary Freudian tradition at the Anna Freud Centre, both my supervisors of my adult analytic training cases at the British Psychoanalytic Society were Independents, and after I qualified, I was supervised by Kleinian analysts. Whichever analytic tradition you identify with should provide you with a solid developmental base and theory of technique. For me, my Contemporary Freudian tradition gave me the confidence to: (1) second guess myself, learn from mistakes, and tolerate doubt, and (2) learn from the other traditions in the British Society in order to build my own theoretical models and technique. Whichever tradition you come from it helps to know that your analysis changed your life—that's what sustains your psychoanalytic identity. For me a psychoanalytic identity is strangely solid *and* evolving, like having a firm footing, but never arriving. In fact, one of the requirements of annual accreditation in the British Society is membership in a group of analytic colleagues that meets monthly to take turns presenting clinical session material. It is hoped that these Continuing Professional Development groups will reflect the diversity of traditions in the British Society.

From my perspective of more than 50 years of practice in London, I would like to leave you with four thoughts as you start out on your own analytic adventure. Firstly, you may recall that I mentioned that I had a rather checkered career before I became a candidate. If that is true of you, too, don't be embarrassed or dismiss your background—embrace it. In fact, having a life outside the consulting room is not only another source of insight, but it keeps us humble. Secondly, you can make a decent living as a psychoanalyst, but you are unlikely to get rich. I hope you are able to resist the temptation to reduce the frequency of your patient's sessions in order to charge him or her higher fees. Thirdly, you are joining a profession where you will learn primarily from experience. That means that the longer you practice, the better you get. You will become less anxious, more confident, and wiser. And, finally, there is always the intangible reward of knowing that you relieved suffering and helped some patients live a more rewarding life.

Best wishes for your training and beyond.

43 P.S.

I imagine you will respond to these letters in different ways, and ultimately your responses are the conclusion to this book. If you have been stimulated to reflect upon your candidacy and the profession you are entering, this for me is the best result of these letters. I hope it leads to some interesting discussions among local candidate groups and throughout the candidate world. I also hope that those involved in the education of our future colleagues will find wisdom in these pages to think about our methods of teaching.

Briefly, also, I want to thank the contributors to this book whose enthusiasm for the project was central to its creation. I think you can tell that these analysts have thought deeply about our profession and worked hard to bring their thoughts to you.

Best wishes for your future.
Fred Busch
March 2020

References

Alexander, F. (1930). Der theoretische Lehrgang. In Rado, S., Fenichel, O. and Müller-Braunschweig, C. (Eds.), *Zehn Jahre Psychoanalytisches Institut*, pp. 54–58. Vienna: Internationaler Psychoanalytischer Verlag.

Assoun, P.-L. (1995). L'Amour au Premier Regard: Spectroscopie du 'Coup de Foudre'. *Dans Le regard et la voix, Tome 2, Figures*, pp. 45–61. Anthropos.

Bird, B. (1972). Notes on Transference: Universal Phenomenon and Hardest Part of Analysis. *J. Am. Psychoanal Assoc.*, 20:267–301.

Boesky, D. (2015). Action and the Analyst's Responsibility: Commentary on Greenberg. *J. Amer. Psychoanal. Assoc.*, 63:65–83.

Busch, F. (2013). *Creating a Psychoanalytic Mind*. London: Routledge.

Busch, F. (2019). *Troubling Problems of Knowledge in Psychoanalytic Institutes*. Int. J. Controversial Issues, 2:3–26.

Celenza, A., & Gabbard, G. (2003). Analysts Who Commit Sexual Boundary Violations: A Lost Cause? *J. Am. Psychoanal. Assoc.*, 51:617–636.

De Urtubey, L. (1985). Fondamentale Métapsychologie, Inevitable Polyglottisme. *Rev. Franç. Psychoanal.*, 49:1497–1521.

Dewald, P. A. (1973). *Psychotherapy: A Dynamic Approach*. Oxford: Blackwell Scientific Publications.

Fraiberg, S., Adelson, E., & Shapiro, V. (1972). Ghosts in the Nursery: A Psychoanalytic Approach to the Problems of Impaired Infant-Mother Relationships. *J. Amer. Acad. Child Psychiatry*, 14(3):387–421.

Freud, S. (1908). Creative Writers and Day-Dreaming. S. E., Vol. 9, pp. 141–154. London: Hogarth Press.

Freud, S. (1914). Remembering, Repeating and Working-Through. S. E., Vol. 12, pp. 145–156. London: Hogarth Press.

Freud, S. (1915). Observations on Transference-Love. S. E., Vol. 12, pp. 159–171. London: Hogarth Press.

Freud, S. (1920). Beyond the Pleasure Principle. S. E., Vol. 18, pp. 1–64. London: Hogarth Press.

Freud, S. (1926). The Question of Lay-Analysis: Conversations with an Impartial Person. S. E., Vol. 20, pp. 183–250. London: Hogarth Press.

Green, A. (1986). *On Private Madness*. London: Hogarth and Institute of Psycho-Analysis.

References

Hartmann, H. (1959). Psychoanalysis as a Scientific Theory. In Hook S. (Ed.), *Psychoanalysis, Scientific Method and Philosophy*, pp. 3–37. New York: New York Univ. Press.

Joseph, B. (1985). Transference: The Total Situation. *Int. J. Psychoanal.*, 66:447–454.

Kappelle, W. (1996). How Useful is Selection? *Int. J. Psychoanal.*, 77:1213–1232.

Kohut, H. (1968). The Evaluation of Applicants for Psychoanalytic Training. *Int. J. Psychoanal.* 49(4):548–554.

Laplanche, J. (1999). *Entre Seduction et Inspiration: L'Homme*. Quadrige: Presses universitaires de France.

Loewald, H. W. (1980 [1960]). On the Therapeutic Action of Psychoanalysis. In *Papers on Psychoanalysis*, pp. 221–256. New Haven, CT: Yale University Press.

Loewald, H. W. (2000 [1988]). *Transference and Love*. In *The Essential Loewald: Collected Papers and Monographs*, pp. 549–563. Hagerstown, MD: University Publishing.

Macalpine, I. (1950). The Development of Transference. *Psychoanal. Quart.*, 19:501–539.

Pick, I. B. (1985). Working through in the Countertransference. *Int. J. Psychoanal.*, 66:157–166.

Roussillon, R. (2008). L'Objet « Médium Malléable » et la Réflexivité. In *Le Transitionnel, Le Sexuel et la Réflexivité*, pp. 37–50. Paris: Dunod.

Roud, R. (Ed.) (1980). Jean Renoir to 1939. *Cinema: A Critical Dictionary, Volume Two*, pp. 835–845. New York, NY: Viking.

Sharpe, E. F. (1930). The Technique of Psycho-Analysis. *Int. J. Psychoanal.*, 11:251–277.

Strachey, J. (1934). The Nature of the Therapeutic Action of Psychoanalysis. *Int. J. Psychoanal.*, 15:127–159.

Winnicott, D. W. (1968). *The Use of an Object and Relating through Identifications*. In *Playing and Reality*, pp. 115–127. London: Tavistock (1971).

Winnicott, D. W. (1969). The Use of an Object. *Int. J. Psychoanal.*, 50:711–716.

Index

age of bewilderment 27
American Psychoanalytic Association (A.Psa.A.) 41, 61, 67, 78, 85, 99, 100, 115, 138, 159; medical degree prerequisite 159
The Analysis of the Self (Kohut) 115
analysis *vs.* dynamic psychotherapy 86
analysts. *see* psychoanalysts
analytic couples, problems with 70–1
analytic function *vs.* psychotherapist function 88
analytic patient, construction of 28, 36
analytic relationship 55
analytic training. *see* psychoanalytic training
analytic voice 62
analytical sessions, not flawless 11
the analyzed and unanalyzed 47
Anna Freud Centre 159
anonymity, neutrality, abstinence triad 86
Antigone syndrome 44
A.Pde.B.A. *see* Buenos Aires Psychoanalytic Association (A.Pde.B.A.)
A.Psa.A. *see* American Psychoanalytic Association (A.Psa.A.)
Argentinean school 144
Asociación Psicoanalítica Argentina (A.P.A.) 143
Asociación Psicoanalítica de Madrid 84–5
Assman, Jan 74
associations, progression within 126
Assoun, Paul-Laurent 73
Austen Riggs Center 121

Baltimore-Washington Institute 84
Bayona, Ines 104–7
Beckett, Samuel 9
Berlin Institute 149

bio-psychosocial model 15
Blass, Heribert 50–3
Blass, Rachel 154–7
Bleger, José 111
Bolognini, Stefano 35–7
Borensztejn, Claudia Lucia 134–7
Boston Psychoanalytic Society and Institute (B.P.S.I.) 41
Brenner, Charles 23
British Psychoanalytic Society 54
British Psychoanalytical Society 160
Bronstein, Abbot 80–3
Buenos Aires Psychoanalytic Association (A.Pde.B.A.) 112, 113
Busch, Fred 162

Campbell, Donald 158–61
Canadian Psychoanalytic Society 5
candidates: analysts in training 114, 150; bonds formed 112; clinically inclined 9; institutional rigidity, opposing of 116; intuition, use of 140; jack of all trades 101–2; language difficulties 63; origin of 12–3; political beings, as 12; relationships between 41; theoretically inclined 9; unconscious, belief in 102, 103, 129
Canetti, Elias 31
case reports, writing of 60–1
Cassorla, Roosevelt 11–4
character is technique 140
citizens first 19, 21
class makeup, importance of 2
classical analysis, and personality disorders 86
classical clinical-theoretical training 146
clinical work: personal analysis 69; problem in 69; self-analysis by analysand 87; soul, and the 7

colleagues: commonness 121; cyber-communication with 85; dialogue between 43, 44, 147–8; encouragement of 2, 147–8, 160; feedback from 65; fraternity of 144; international exchanges 63–4; parent generation 146; sibling generation, older 146; support of 75, 134
committee work 61
community work 45
complementary training 45
concrete thinking, abandonment of 150
Contemporary Freudian tradition 161
the couch and psychoanalytical identity 105
countertransference, managing 23
"Creative Writers and Day-Dreaming" (Freud) 117
creative writing 12

da Rocha Barros, Elias 54–7
da Rocha Barros, Elizabeth 54–7
de-alienation 145
democracy 19
Diamond, Michael 6–10
digital world *vs.* internal world 27–8
disappointments 10
discourse and transformation into clinical material 55–7
disillusionment: colleagues, encouragement of 2; disruptive chairman 3–4; sexual assaults 3–4
diverse teachings 2
diversification of affiliation 116
dogmatic thinking, reduction of 13–4
dynamic psychotherapy *vs.* analysis 86

Eitingon, Max 107
Eitingon Model 20, 85, 91, 126; pillars of 50–1
Eizirik, Cláudio Laks 19–22
El día que Nietzsche lloró (the day Nietzsche cry) (Yalon) 106
elderly patients 21
elitism in meetings 92
Erlich, H. Shmuel 121–5
Etchegoyen, Horacio 152
ethical motivation 154–7
ethical visions 154–7; competing 156
ethics 4
European Psychoanalytical Federation (E.P.F.) 53

European Psychoanalytical Federation's Forum on Education 148
extra-analytic life 64–5, 124, 161

Fainstein, Abel Mario 43–5
family support 82
F.E.P.A.L. *see* Latin American Psychoanalytical Federation (F.E.P.A.L.)
Fraiberg, Selma 118
free thought and individuality 132
French Model 51, 89
Freud-bashing 38
Freud Institute 146
Freudian Group of Tehran 101
Freudian orthodoxy 115
friends support 82
Furlong, Allannah 73–5

Garma, Angel 44
Gaskill amendment 81
Ghosts in the Nursery (Fraiberg) 118
golden age of psychoanalysis 144
Goldenberg, Mauricio 152
Goldstein, Gabriela 143–5
Golinelli, Paola 70–2
Green, André 55
Greenberg, Jay 46–9
group psychology 90
groups: bonds formed 112; identification with 30; parents 68; pressure to conform 74–5; study 61; writing 61
Guyomard, Patrick 44

Hebrew University of Jerusalem 122
Hinze, Eike 63–5
Homayounpour, Gohar 101–3
Horney, Karen 132
hostile patients 23
human beings first 21

idealizations 8, 141–2
identifications 8
identifications, imaginary 44
impossible profession 6, 37, 64, 106, 122, 142
inner phantasies 155
Instincts and their Vicissitudes (Freud) 97
institutional-external reality 89
institutions: administrative time 40; Antigone syndrome 44; democratization of 11; foreignness, boundaries set by 30; generational struggle 40; idealization of

90; non-institutions 99–100; participation in 20, 78; personal analyst, choice of 32–3; political and social influences on 20; rigidity of 115–6; selection of 32; social and political influence on 20
interdisciplinary dialogue 45
internal world vs. digital world 27–8
international experience 30; foreignness set by language 30; otherness 30–1
International Psychoanalytic Association (I.P.A.) 3, 13, 20, 39–40, 43, 51, 63, 65, 78, 89, 100, 105, 112, 144, 146, 151; benefits of membership 152
International Psychoanalytic Studies Organization (I.P.S.O.) 13, 20, 144, 152
intuition 26
intuition, development of 136
IPA. see International Psychoanalytic Association (I.P.A.)
I.P.A. congresses 67
I.P.S.O. see International Psychoanalytic Studies Organization (I.P.S.O.)
Israel Psychoanalytic Institute 121

Jacobs, Daniel 58–62
Jacobs, Theodore 23–6
Jefferson Medical College of Philadelphia 84

Kant, Immanuel 50
Kernberg, Otto F. 32–4, 79
Kite, Jane 138–42
Klein, Melanie 81
Kohut, Heinz 115
Kravitz, Henry 5

Langs, Robert 2
language difficulties 63, 85–6
Latin American Psychoanalytical Federation (F.E.P.A.L.) 43, 45
lay analysis 99, 115
Leaving today: The Freuds in Exile 1938 (Freud) 107
Leonoff, Arthur 1–5
Leuzinger-Bohlebe, Marianne 53
listening, active 16–7
Livingston, Angela 106
Loewald, Hans 24, 118–9
Lohser, Beate 106
López, Benito 113
love and hate, patients struggle with 155
love relationships 21

Malcolm, Janet 106
Marcus, Eric 15–8
Marion, Paola 27–31
marketing 68
mass psychology 44
meetings: elitism in 92; for networking 67–8
Meltzer, Donald 113
mentors, emulation of 78
metaphoric interpretations 150
metapsychological polyglottism 87
Mill, John Stuart 7
Mis claves para Ser feliz, (My clues to be happy) Sigmund Freud (Moreno) 106
Moore, Marianne 60
Moreno, Sebastian Dozo 106
Moses and Monotheism (Freud) 107
Moss, Donald 108–10

narcissism 9
native self, trusting in 71
Nazism 19
neurobiology of the mind 33
New York Psychoanalytic Institute (N.Y.P.S.I.) 99–100, 115, 132
Newton, Peter M. 106
non-institutional psychoanalysis 146
N.Y.P.S.I. see New York Psychoanalytic Institute (N.Y.P.S.I.)

object malleable 73
Observations on Transference-Love (Freud) 118
otherness 30–1; privilege of migration 31; test of the foreign 31
An Outline of Psychoanalysis (Freud) 7, 38

Paniagua, Cecilio 84–7
parent generation 146
parent groups 68
Paris Psychoanalytical Society (S.P.P.) 88, 89
patience 8, 45, 82; analytic learning process, with 6; oneself, with 6; patients, with 6
patient as a person 1
patient care 15
patients: and analyst, splitting of 55; and analyst as fused dyad 55; anxieties of 144; attitude towards 23; broad spectrum of 33–4; construction of 28, 36; difficulty of 122–3; elderly 21; emotionally connect with 68; future

view of 24; hate and love struggle with 155; as honored guests 24; hostile 23; listening to 7; love and hate struggle with 155; lower fees 82, 161; marketing for 68; misuse of 141; plain English, use of 68; present view of 24; recruiting, difficulty in 36, 67–8, 90, 123; regressive 21; seeing on their terms 29; self-analysis, and 59; as teachers 24
Perlman, Fredric 130–3
personal analysis 2–3, 4, 6–7, 13, 16, 20, 44, 69, 82, 88, 111, 126, 127, 145; Eitingon Model 51; French model 51
personal analysis not introspection 129
personal biases 48
personal educational process 51
personality disorders and classical analysis 86
piece workers 4–5
Pinsky, Ellen 117–20
Prengler, Adriana 150–3
The Price of Monotheism (Assman) 74
professional identity, development of 131
psyche, research of 144
psychic-internal reality 89
psychoanalysis: analysis of resistance 159; analytic attitude 54–5; analytic relationship 55; application of 17–8; as art 53; art and clinical science 128; authoritarian governments, and 14, 19, 113; blind faith, and 8, 19, 21; changes in 20, 27–8; classical literature 24–5; clinical science and art 128; colleague support in 83; connotative scientific theory 53; cultural changes, and 144; cure for the soul 131; dedication to 86; democratic regimes, and 19; ethical vision, shaping of 154–7; flexibility of 94; future of 21–2; golden age of 46–7, 144; human condition, and the 4; humanities, relation to 33, 119–20; invisible walls 108–9; lay analysis 99; limited vision of 35; love, freedom to 155; metaphoric interpretations 150; observational art, an 123; painful process 158; patients, broad spectrum of 33–4; patient's inner world, and 155; personal journey 88; pluralistic 20; politics of 124–5; preservation of 117; process as love 155; reality, *vs.* 28–30; rigidity of thought 64; rules 94; scientific nature of 53; semantic science, as a 85; separation form personal life 18; sexual boundary violations 141; short therapies 145; significant others, and 18; Skype, and 92–3; slow magic, as 110; specificity of, understanding 54; standards, change of 93–4; symbolic interpretations 150; talking cure 118; 3 pillars of 105; transference, negative 123–4; transmission of 153; understanding another person's life 130–1; uniqueness of, understanding 54; way of life 134, 150
Psychoanalysis: Burgeoning and Beleaguered (Richards) 115
Psychoanalysis: The Impossible Profession (Malcolm) 106
psychoanalysts: the arts, and 21; authoritarian governments 113; bear suffering, learn to 137; becoming one, on 101; citizens first 19, 21; depression, and 97; desire to be 128–9; diversification of affiliation 116; family, and 21; finding your way 132–3; formation of 88; intuition, and 26; love relationships, and 21; medical degree prerequisite 138, 159; mindset 95–6, 100; otherness in work and life 145; otherness *vs.* conformity 75; as outliers 131; and patient, splitting of 55; and patient as fused dyad 55; patient first 158–61; as a person 140; personal analysis, and 141; personal development 117; personal equation of 74; personal journey 89; position of 55; pragmatic rewards 49; public life 124; referral mailing lists 102; selection of 86; social life 124; supervision, and 141; support of 75; test for qualification 119, 120; writing as development 140; writing papers 151–2
psychoanalysts in training 114, 150
psychoanalyst's mind 21
psychoanalytic ancestors, adherence to 48–9
psychoanalytic communities: discussions, open 148; diversity in 160; involvement in 151; loss of ethics 147; splitting processes in 147
psychoanalytic competence, development of 52
psychoanalytic encounter 50
psychoanalytic group 65
psychoanalytic literature 117–20;

comprehension, difficulty in 122, 147–8; transformative reading 136
psychoanalytic plague 14
psychoanalytic technique, internalization of 135
psychoanalytic theories: competing approaches 156; conflicting theories 23–4; developments in 135; disagreement with 25–6; exclusive identification with 29; immeasurable single parent 29; integration of 102; openness to 54; personal 33; plurality of 43, 47, 51–2, 114; psychoanalytic ancestors 48
psychoanalytic training 51; anxieties in 52–3; authenticity 61–2; authoritarian attitudes 92–3; bear suffering, learn to 137; case reports, writing of 60–1; change, challenges of 91–4; change, resisting 92; clinical work, and 151; committee work 61; conformity in 68–9; continuous 105; the couch 105; creative personality 137; de-alienation 145; emotional costs 66; emotionally demanding 15; ethical approach 52; exercise in uncertainty 58; extra-analytic life 64–5; financial costs 66, 67; financially difficult 15; formation 88; Freud, importance of 88–9, 97, 103, 135; generational differences 92; in-person vs. technology mediated 91–2; medical degree prerequisite 111, 138, 143, 159; the need to pursue 121–2; negative transference 59; not knowing, and 58; pluralistic 114, 160–1; pluralistic program 144; post-graduation learning 139–40; problem in 68–9; reading 33, 82, 139; self-confronting 15; shame 58–9; social circle 64; standards, changes to 40; struggles expected 81; study groups 61; subjectivation 145; supervisors 77; techniques, learning of 71–2, 140; technological acceleration of time 135; technology mediated vs. in-person 91–2; temporal costs 66–7; theoretical inconsistencies 64; 3 pillars of 127–8, 139, 145, 150–1; time, your own 104–7; time intensive 15; transformative reading 136; uncertainty in 58, 146; unconscious, belief in 102, 103; value of 59–60; writing 82, 139; writing, importance of 136; writing groups 61; writing mentors 60; yourself, be true to 108–10
psychoanalytic writing: importance of 136; papers 151–2; problems with 12
psychoanalytical identity 104–7, 147, 152, 154
psychotherapist function vs. analytic function 88
public life 124

"The Question of Lay Analysis" (Freud) 120, 138–9

references 163–4
referral mailing lists 102
regressions, challenges of 8
regressive patients 21
relationships, importance of 18
Remembering, Repeating and Working-Through (Freud) 118
remote training 91–2
Renoir, Jean 118
Richards, Arnold 115–6
Richardson, Arlene Kramer 99–100
Rosenbaum, Bent 126–9
Roud, Richard 120
The Rules of the Game (Renoir) 118, 120

Salome, Her Life and Work (Livingston) 106
San Francisco Psychoanalytic Institute 81, 138
Schmid-Gloor, Eva 146–9
Schmidt-Hellerau, Cordelia 38–42
self-analysis 127
self-identity 106–7
self-knowledge 154–5
Self-Psychology 2
seminars 86–7, 145; elitism in 92
sensibility is cultivated 54
Sharpe, Ella Freeman 119–20
Sheppard Pratt Hospital 80
short therapies 145
sibling generation, older 146
Skype 92–3
social life 64–5, 124, 161
social media 68
social psychological field 33
societies, participation in 20
solitary life 65
Sor, Darío 113
soul, research of 144
Sparer, Ellen 88–90

S.P.P. *see* Paris Psychoanalytical Society (S.P.P.)
S.P.S. *see* Swiss Psychoanalytic Society (S.P.S.)
Stalinism 19
Stimmel, Barbara 76–9
student/teacher relations 77
study groups 61
subjectivation 145
Sugarman, Alan 66–9
supervisors 16, 77, 145; analytic method 20; candidate's evaluation 148; evaluations 113; free thought and individuality 132; French Model 90; learning from 77–8; oppressive 132; personal analysis, and 141; selection of 33, 86; shortage of 101; trust in 53
support: colleagues, from 75, 134; family, from 82; friends, from 82
Swales, Peter 2
Swiss Psychoanalytic Society (S.P.S.) 39, 146
symbolic interpretations 150

talking cure 118
teacher-student relationships 152–3
The Man with the Beautiful Voice: And More Stories from the Other Side of the Couch (Rubin) 106

time, technological acceleration of 135
time demands 66–7
Transference and Love (Loewald) 118–9
transference onto theories 29
transferences challenges of negative 8
treatment is human to human 16

unconscious, belief in the 82, 102, 103, 129
unconscious, power of the 159–60
Ungar, Virginia 111–4
Unorthodox Freud: The View from the Couch (Lohser and Newton) 106
Uruguayan Model 51

websites 68
William Alanson White Institute 47
Winberg, Maj-Britt 95–8
Wolf, Alexander 132
Wolfe, Harriet 91–4
writing: creative 12; groups 61; importance of 136; mentors 60; papers 151–2

Yalon, Irvin D. 106

Züricher Freud-Institute 39